Cass R. Sunstein

D1563736

The Cost-Benefit State

The Future of Regulatory Protection

 Section of Administrative Law and Regulatory Practice

Cover design by Diane Kaz

The materials contained herein represent the opinions of the authors and editors and should not be construed to be the action of either the American Bar Association or the Section of Administrative Law and Regulatory Practice unless adopted pursuant to the bylaws of the Association.

Nothing contained in this book is to be considered as the rendering of legal advice for specific cases, and readers are responsible for obtaining such advice from their own legal counsel. This book and any forms and agreements herein are intended for educational and informational purposes only.

Library of Congress Cataloging-in-Publication Data

The cost-benefit state: the future of regulatory protection / by Cass R. Sunstein.
        p. cm.
    Includes bibliographical references and index.
    ISBN 1-59031-054-3
        1. Air—Pollution—Law and legislation—United States—Compliance costs. 2. Air—Pollution—Law and legislation—United States—Cost-effectiveness. 3. Law—United States—Compliance costs. 4. Law—United States—Cost effectiveness. 5. Cost-effectiveness. I. Title.

KF3812 .S86 2002
344.73'046342—dc21   2002016394

Discounts are available for books ordered in bulk. Special consideration is given to state bars, CLE programs, and other bar-related organizations. Inquire at Book Publishing, ABA Publishing, American Bar Association, 750 North Lake Shore Drive, Chicago, Illinois 60611.

www.ababooks.org

"Courts should be reluctant to apply the literal terms of a statute to mandate pointless expenditures of effort. . . . Unless Congress has been extraordinarily rigid, there is likely a basis for an implication of de minimis authority to provide exemption when the burdens of regulation yield a gain of trivial or no value."[1]

"It seems bizarre that a statute intended to improve human health would . . . lock the agency into looking at only one half of a substance's health effects in determining the maximum level of that substance."[2]

"It is only where there is 'clear congressional intent to preclude consideration of cost' that we find agencies barred from considering costs."[3]

"In order better to achieve regulatory goals—for example, to allocate resources so that they save more lives or produce a cleaner environment—regulators must often take account of all of a proposed regulation's adverse effects, at least where those effects clearly threaten serious and disproportionate public harm. Hence, I believe that, other things being equal, we should read silences or ambiguities in the language of regulatory statutes as permitting, not forbidding, this type of rational regulation."[4]

"The rule-implicit valuation of a life is high—about $4 million—but not so astronomical, certainly by regulatory standards, as to call the rationality of the rule seriously into question, especially when we consider that neither Hepatis B nor AIDS is a disease of old people. These diseases are no respecters of youth; they cut off people in their working years, and thus in their prime, and it is natural to set a high value on the lost years."[5]

---

1. Alabama Power Co. v. Costle, 636 F.2d 323, 360-61 (D.C. Cir. 1979).
2. American Trucking Ass'n v. EPA, 173 F.3d 1027, 1052 (D.C. Cir. 1999).
3. Michigan v. EPA, 213 F.3d 663, 678 (D.C. Cir. 2000).
4. Whitman v. American Trucking Ass'ns, 531 U.S. 457, 475 (2001) (Breyer, J., concurring in part and concurring in the judgment).
5. American Dental Ass'n v. Martin, 984 F.2d 823, 827 (7th Cir. 1993).

CONTENTS

INTRODUCTION

Gradually, and in fits and starts, American government is becoming a cost-benefit state. By this I mean that government regulation is increasingly assessed by asking whether the benefits of regulation justify the costs of regulation.

The cost-benefit state remains in its initial stages. It continues to encounter strong resistance. But it is unquestionably emerging. For over 20 years, American presidents have required agencies to perform cost-benefit analysis (CBA) of major rules. In a number of ways, Congress has shown considerable interest in CBA, not least in the Safe Drinking Water Act, one of the most highly publicized of all federal pollution statutes. For their part, courts have adopted a series of "cost-benefit default rules," allowing agencies to consider costs, to consider the substitute risks introduced by regulation, and to exempt trivial risks from governmental control. One of my major goals here is to trace these rules and to suggest their implications for the future of regulatory law.

The rise of the cost-benefit state is creating a number of intriguing and novel challenges for policy analysts, for all branches of government, and for the law in general. The challenges are likely to intensify in the next decades. If a statute allows agencies to balance lives against costs, how will the balancing occur? What are the legal limitations on the agencies' choice of how to balance costs and benefits? How can lives and health be turned into monetary equivalents? What is the value of life? How should an agency handle a small risk of catastrophe, from terrorism, nuclear power, natural causes, or some other source? How, if at all, should future generations be counted? What does it mean to say that agencies can exempt trivial risks from regulation? How do we know that a risk counts as "trivial"? How can it be legitimate for courts to allow agencies to make such exemptions? I hope to make some progress on such questions here.

Systems Rather Than Snapshots

To appreciate what the cost-benefit state is all about, it is important to see that social problems never exist in isolation. Risks are part of systems. For that reason, any effort to solve a single problem will have a range of consequences, some of them likely unintended.

If the Federal Aviation Administration (FAA) increases security at airports to make flying safer, it will also make flying less convenient and more expensive, and thus lead some people to drive instead.[1] Flying is much safer than driving, and hence the FAA's measures might increase the number of lives lost on balance. The point certainly applies in the midst of fear about terrorism; if the FCC and the airlines provide enhanced protection against the risk of terrorism, and thus lead people to use cars, more people might end up dying. If noise levels are reduced at the Grand Canyon so that people can enjoy the area in peace and quiet, air tourism there will have to be dramatically reduced, so that fewer people can enjoy the area at all.[2] If the Environmental Protection Agency requires aggressive corrosion control technologies to reduce lead in water, it might thereby produce increases in other contaminants, because the very technologies that reduce lead can contribute to water pollution.[3] If the Occupational Safety and Health Administration increases regulation of benzene, a carcinogenic substance, it might lead companies to use an unsafe or perhaps a less safe substitute; it might also decrease wages of affected workers, and decrease the number of jobs in the relevant industry. People who have less money, and who are unemployed, tend to live shorter lives—and hence occupational regulation might, under certain circumstances, sacrifice more lives than it saves.[4] Of course, the unintended consequences of risk regulation might be desirable rather than undesirable—as, for example, where regulation spurs new pollution control technologies.

Now consider the following cases:

The Clean Air Act requires the Environmental Protection Agency (EPA) to issue standards controlling any substance that "contributes significantly" to pollution problems in certain areas. EPA issues regulations governing relevant pollutants, but without considering the costs of compliance. Industries challenge the regulations on the ground that cost is a statutorily relevant factor.[5]

The National Highway Traffic Safety Administration (NHTSA) is asked to promote fuel economy in automobiles "to the extent feasible." NHTSA issues fuel economy standards that are admittedly feasible, in the sense that no one doubts that they are technologically and economically possible. But the Coalition for Automobile Safety, a public interest organization, contends that the effect of the standards will be to lead manufacturers to produce smaller and more dangerous cars. The Coalition contends that NHTSA acted unlawfully in failing to take this effect into account.[6]

The EPA has decided to regulate arsenic under the Safe Drinking Water Act. It chose a maximum level of 10 parts per billion (ppb). In so doing, it concluded that the annual monetized costs ($210 million) significantly exceed the annual monetized benefits ($150 million). At the same time, it concluded that the nonmonetized benefits—in terms of health gains that cannot yet be quantified—

justify the 10 ppb standard. A coalition of water companies challenges the standard on the ground that the nonmonetized benefits cannot possibly make up for the $60 million shortfall.

A federal statute requires the Occupational Safety and Health Administration to regulate toxic substances "to the extent feasible."[7] OSHA interprets this language to require it to consider whether the regulation is technologically feasible and whether it is "practicable," economically speaking, for the industry to comply. OSHA imposes a regulation that is admittedly "feasible" under this test; but the statute cannot pass a cost-benefit test, because the benefits are low and the costs are high. Insisting that costs should be compared with benefits, industries subject to the regulation complain that it is unlawful.[8]

In which of these cases has the agency acted unlawfully? The question is important, in the first instance, to regulatory agencies themselves, which have to decide how much to regulate, and why, and which have to think carefully about the constraints of the law.[9] Here agencies are the principal architects of what is unmistakably a form of common law. But courts will undoubtedly play an important role,[10] and it is in the interaction between agencies and judges that binding law will emerge. I hope to cast light on that interaction here.[11]

First Generation, Second Generation

There is a still more general point in the background. We are slowly nearing the conclusion, in all branches of government, of a "first generation" debate over whether CBA is desirable.[12] That debate appears to be terminating with a general victory for its proponents, in the form of a presumption in favor of their view (signaled above all, perhaps, by President Clinton's substantial endorsement of cost-benefit balancing via Executive Order[13]).

The "second generation" debates raise difficult questions about how (not whether) to engage in CBA—how to value life and health, how to deal with the interests of future generations, how to generate rules of thumb to simplify complex inquiries, how to ensure that agencies do what they are supposed to do, how and when to diverge from the conclusion recommended by CBA, how to determine the roles of agencies and courts in contested cases. I attempt to make a contribution to these "second generation" debates here. That contribution is intended, above all, to explore how government might save both lives and money—the latter not because it is important in itself (it isn't), but because money can be used to help promote many valuable things, including greater safety, better health, and longer lives.

Notes

1. *See* Robert W. Hahn, *The Economics of Airline Safety*, 20 HARV. L. & PUB. POLICY 791 (1997).

2. Grand Canyon Air Tour Coalition v. FAA, 154 F.3d 455 (D.C. Cir. 1998).

3. American Water Works v. EPA, 40 F.3d 1266, 1271 (D.C. Cir. 1994).

4. *See* Robert Hahn et al., *Do Federal Regulations Reduce Mortality?* (Washington, D.C.: American Enterprise Institute, 2000); *Symposium, Risk-Risk Analysis*, 8 J RISK AND UNCERTAINTY 5 (1994).

5. *Cf.* Michigan v. EPA, 213 F.3d 663, 678 (D.C. Cir. 2000) (finding cost a permissible factor for the agency to consider under a similar statute); Lead Industries v. EPA, 647 F.2d 1130 (D.C. Cir. 1980) (finding cost an irrelevant factor under provisions governing national ambient air quality standards).

6. *See* Competitive Enterprise Institute v. NHTSA, 956 F.2d 321 (D.C. Cir. 1992).

7. 29 U.S.C. 655(b)(5).

8. ATMI v. Donovan, 452 U.S. 490 (1981).

9. Hence, for example, different agencies have come up with different dollar figures by which to value statistical lives; this is a central part of agency-made common law of CBA. See the table in Matthew Adler & Eric Posner, *Implementing CBA When Preferences Are Distorted*, 29 J. LEGAL STUD. 1105, 1146 (2000). There are also striking variations in agency selection of discount rate, that is, the treatment of costs and benefits (such as lives saved) in the future. See Comment, *Judicial Review of Discount Rates Used in Regulatory CBA*, 65 U. CHI. L. REV. 1333, 1364-69 (1998) (documenting variations ranging from 2% to 10%). These issues are treated below.

10. *See, e.g.*, Corrosion Proof Fittings v. EPA, 947 F.2d 1201 (5th Cir. 1991) (striking down agency regulation of asbestos under statute calling for cost-benefit balancing).

11. It is important to see that many federal agencies do not comply with the apparent requirements of cost-benefit balancing in existing executive orders. Robert Hahn has shown that compliance is episodic and that a great deal needs to be done to systematize the process. *See* Robert W. Hahn et al., *Empirical Analysis: Assessing Regulatory Impact Analysis: The Failure of Agencies to Comply With Executive Order 12866*, 23 HARV J.L. & PUB. POL. 859 (2000). Here as elsewhere, there is a large difference between law on the books and law in the world. I do not attempt here to address the important issue of how to ensure compliance with principles that call for attention to costs and benefits. But judicial review of agency action can serve as a partial corrective at least, ensuring that in the egregious cases, agency action will be held invalid for failure to comply with the principles. This point is discussed at several places below.

12. For discussion, see *Symposium*, 29 J. LEGAL STUD. 837 (2000); Lisa Heinzerling, *Regulatory Costs of Mythic Proportions*, 106 YALE L.J. 1981 (1998).

13. *See* Executive Order 12866, 58 Fed. Reg. 51735 (1993).

PART I
OVERVIEW

FROM 1970S ENVIRONMENTALISM TO THE COST-BENEFIT STATE? 1

Introduction

The rise of interest in cost-benefit balancing signals a dramatic shift from the initial stages of national risk regulation. Those stages were undergirded by what might be called "1970s environmentalism." In the 1970s, the national government placed a high premium on immediate responses to long-neglected problems; emphasized the existence of problems rather than their magnitude; and often based its judgments on moral indignation directed at the behavior of those who created pollution and other risks to safety and health.[1]

   Important aspects of 1970s environmentalism can be found in many places. Consider, for example, the apparently cost-blind national ambient air-quality provisions of the Clean Air Act[2] and statutory provisions requiring that standards be set by reference to the "the best available technology" without a balancing of costs against benefits.[3] For more recent illustrations, consider the public demand that airports and train stations must be made "safe" in the aftermath of the terrorist attacks in New York City on September 11, 2001.

The Record

No one should deny that 1970s environmentalism has done an enormous amount of good, helping to produce dramatic improvements in many domains. These include the increased safety of cars and consumer products, and above all the context of air pollution, since ambient air quality has improved for all major pollutants.[4] Indeed, 1970s environmentalism appears, by most accounts, to survive cost-benefit balancing, producing aggregate benefits in the trillions of dollars, well in excess of the aggregate costs.[5] The Environmental Protection Agency's (EPA's) own estimates suggest that as a result of the Clean Air Act, there were no less than 184,000 fewer premature deaths among people 30 years of age or older in 1990—and also that there were 39,000 fewer cases of congestive heart failure, 89,000 fewer cases of hospital admissions for respiratory problems, 674,000 fewer cases of chronic bronchitis, and 850,000 fewer asthma attacks.[6] It is worth pausing over these extraordinary numbers, for each of them reflects a significant improvement in the real lives of real people, not least through substantially lengthened lives. EPA finds annual costs of air pollution control at $32 billion—hardly a trivial number, but less than 4 percent of the annual benefits of $1.1 trillion.[7] To be sure, the EPA's own numbers show what reasonable observers see as an implausibly high ratio. But significant adjustments to correct for possible errors by EPA still reveal that the benefits of air pollution controls are far higher than the costs.[8]

More generally, the Office of Management and the Budget (OMB) has, for the last several years, engaged in a detailed accounting of the costs and benefits of regulation.[9] In general, the reports show benefits in excess of costs. While the government's own numbers should be discounted—agency accounts may well be self-serving—at least they provide a place to start.[10] In its 2000 report, OMB finds total regulatory benefits ranging from $254 billion to $1.8 trillion, with total costs ranging from $146 billion to $229 billion, for net benefits ranging from $25 billion to $1.65 trillion.[11] A more disaggregated picture is also encouraging. In the transportation sector, the benefits range from $84 billion to $110 billion, with the costs from $15 billion to $18 billion, for net benefits of $66 billion to $95 billion.[12] There is considerable uncertainty about environmental benefits and costs, producing a range from $73 billion to over $1.5 trillion in net benefits.[13] For most government action, however, the benefits seem to exceed the costs.[14] As especially good examples, consider the regulations, all from recent years, displayed in Exhibit 1-1.

But even though the overall picture is no cause for alarm, a closer look at federal regulatory policy shows a wide range of problems. Perhaps foremost is exceptionally poor priority setting, with substantial resources sometimes going to small problems and with little attention to some serious problems.[15] Among experts, the problem of security at airports has long counted as a neglected problem; many others could be mentioned. There are also unnecessarily high costs, with no less than $400 billion being attributable to compliance costs each year,[16] including $130 billion on environmental protection alone.[17]

OMB's own report shows some disturbing numbers: For the next 15 years, the Occupational Safety and Health Administration's (OSHA's) methylene chloride regulation will have annual costs of $100 million and

Exhibit 1-1 Good Cost-Benefit Ratios

Regulation	Net benefits in millions of dollars			
	2000	2005	2010	2015
Head impact protection	310-370	1,210-1,510	1,210-1,510	1,210-1,510
Conservation reserve program	$1,100	$1,100	$1,100	$1,100
Restriction on sale and distribution of tobacco	9,020-9820	9,020-9820	9,020-10,220	9,020-9820
Acid rain controls	260-1900	260-1900	260-1900	260-1900
Energy conservation standards for refrigerators	330	330-360	510-580	440-500
New surface-water treatment	50-1,200	50-1,200	50-1,200	50-1,200
Emission standards for new highway heavy-duty engines	0	110-1200	110-1200	110-1200
Disposal of PCBs	136-736	136-736	136-736	136-736
Particulates standard	0	0	12,000-113,000	-20,000-86,000

annual benefits of $40 million;[18] a regulation calling for roadway worker protection has benefits of $30 million, but equivalent costs; the cost-benefit ratio for airbag depowering regulation seems bad, though there is uncertainty in the data,[19] EPA's regulation for financial assurance for municipal solid-waste landfills has monetized benefits of $0 but costs of $100 million, and this is expected for the next 15 years.[20] By way of general illustration, consider the data, drawn from recent regulations, in Exhibit 1-2.[21]

These figures, drawn from regulations in a single year, show a less than coherent pattern of regulation, especially when Table 1 is combined with Table 2. According to one study, better allocations of health expenditures could save 60,000 additional lives each year at no additional cost— and such allocations could maintain the current level of lives saved with

Exhibit 1-2: Questionable Cost-Benefit Ratios

Regulation	Net benefits in millions of dollars			
	2000	2005	2010	2015
Exposure to methylene chloride	-60	-60	-60	-60
Roadway worker protection	0	0	0	0
Financial assurance for municipal solid-waste landfills	-100	-100	-100	-100
Pulp and paper effluent guidelines	-150 to 0	-150 to 0	-150 to 0	-240 to 0
Ozone standards	0	-235 to 240	-840 to 1190	-9,200 to -1000
Child restraint system	-40 to 40	-40 to 40	-40 to 40	-40 to 40
Vessel response plans	-220	-220	-220	-220
Nitrogen oxide emission from new fossil fuel–fired steam-generating units	-57 to 29	-57 to 29	-57 to 29	-57 to 29

$31 billion in annual savings.[22] The point has been dramatized by repeated demonstrations that some regulations create significant substitute risks,[23] and that with cheaper, more effective tools, regulation could achieve its basic goals while saving billions of dollars.[24]

The Basic Case for Cost-Benefit Balancing

In these circumstances, the most attractive parts of the movement for cost-benefit analysis (CBA) have been rooted not in especially controversial judgments about what government ought to be doing, but instead in a more mundane search for pragmatic instruments designed to reduce the three central problems: poor priority setting, excessively costly tools, and inattention to the unfortunate side effects of regulation. By drawing attention to costs and benefits, it should be possible to spur the most obviously desirable regulations, to deter the most obviously undesirable ones, to encourage a broader view of consequences, and to promote a search for least-cost methods of achieving regulatory goals.[25]

Indeed, the Office of Information and Regulatory Affairs (OIRA) has often used CBA in just this way, issuing "return letters" for regulations that seem to cost much but do little, and now issuing "prompt letters" to encourage agencies to issue regulations that promise to improve health or safety while not costing a great deal.[26] Thus CBA is not only an obstacle to unjustified regulation but a spur to government as well, showing that it should attend to neglected problems. To make the point more concrete, consider the initial prompt letters issued by OIRA in 2001. The first of those letters, to the Food and Drug Administration (FDA), involved mandatory disclosure of trans-fatty acids in the Nutrition Facts panel of food. Drawing attention to evidence that trans-fatty acids contribute to coronary heart disease, the letter noted that a disclosure rule seemed to be supported by the FDA's preliminary analysis, which estimated that, 10 years after the effective date, the rule would prevent 7,600 to 17,100 cases of coronary heart disease and avert 2,500 to 5,600 deaths per year. Over a 20-year period, the FDA estimated the benefits of such a rule would range from $25 billion to $59 billion, while the costs would be $400 million to $850 million. The prompt letter strongly encouraged the FDA to issue a disclosure rule or to explain its failure to do so.

The other prompt letter, involving automatic external defibrillators (AEDs), was sent to the Occupational Safety and Health Administration, with a firm request that the agency "consider whether promotion of AEDs should be elevated to a priority." The letter referred to an editorial in the *New England Journal of Medicine*, noting that only 2 percent to 5 percent of the 225,000 persons who have sudden and unexpected cardiac arrest each year outside a hospital are successfully resuscitated compared to the 17 percent to 38 percent success rates found with AEDs. The prompt letter observed that "some preliminary cost-effectiveness calculations" showed that "AEDs in the workplace might prove to be a very cost-effective intervention." Indeed, AEDs, now mandated on air carriers by the Department of Transportation, are estimated to save nine lives per year at the comparatively low price of $2.4 million in annual costs. The prompt letter suggested that OSHA should consider following the Department of Transportation's lead.

These prompt letters are an important and illuminating development. For far too long, the idea of cost-benefit analysis has been wrongly associated with dogmatic opposition to regulation as such. To be sure, an exploration of costs and benefits often shows that regulation cannot be justified. This remains one of the most important functions of cost-benefit analysis. But cost-benefit analysis often can show, and has shown, that government action is worthwhile—and indeed that government should do more. The government's analytical capacities should be used not only to constrain agency action that is inadequately justified, but also to point out areas in which regulation can do more good than harm.

If cost-benefit balancing is supported on these highly pragmatic grounds, the central question is whether that form of balancing actually produces what can be taken as policy improvements by people with diverse views about appropriate policy. On these counts, we lack full information. But the record of CBA, at least within the EPA, is generally encouraging.[27] Assessments of costs and benefits have, for example, helped produce more stringent and rapid regulation of lead in gasoline; promoted more stringent regulation of lead in drinking water; led to stronger controls on air pollution at the Grand Canyon and the Navajo Generating Station; and produced a reformulated gasoline rule that promotes stronger controls on air pollutants.[28] In these areas, CBA, far from being only a check on regulation, has indeed spurred governmental attention to serious problems.

CBA has also led to regulations that accomplish statutory goals at lower cost, and that do not devote limited private and public resources to areas where they are unlikely to do much good. With respect to asbestos, for example, an analysis of benefits and costs led the EPA to tie the phase-down schedules to the costs of substitutes, and also to exempt certain products from a flat ban.[29] With respect to lead in gasoline and control of chlorofluorocarbons (CFCs) (destructive of the ozone layer), CBA helped promote the use of economic incentives rather than command-and-control regulation;[30] economic incentives are much cheaper and can make more stringent regulation possible in the first place. For regulation of sludge, protection of farmworkers, water pollution regulation for the Great Lakes, and controls on organic chemicals, CBA helped regulators produce modifications that significantly reduced costs.[31] For modern government, one of the most serious problems appears to be not agency use of CBA, but frequent noncompliance with executive branch requirements that agencies engage in such analysis.[32]

Of course, CBA is hardly uncontroversial.[33] Some people will be inadequately informed, and hence be unwilling to pay for benefits that would make their lives better.[34] Rather than private willingness to pay, perhaps regulatory agencies should seek public judgments, as these are expressed in public arenas.[35] Society should not be taken as some maximizing machine, in which aggregate output is all that matters. In any case, we ought to care about who bears the costs and who receives the benefits. Sometimes a regulation producing $5 million in benefits but $6 million in costs will be worthwhile if those who bear the costs (perhaps representing dollar losses alone?) are wealthy and can do so easily, and if those who receive the benefits (perhaps representing lives and illnesses averted?) are especially needy. Insofar as both costs and benefits are being measured by the economic criterion of "private willingness to pay," there are many problems. Poor people often have little ability and hence little willingness to pay. Fortunately, agencies typically use a uniform number per life saved. The use of a uniform number reflects a judgment that the lives of poor people should not count for less than those of wealthy people.

In my view, the strongest arguments for cost-benefit balancing are based not only on neoclassical economics, but also on an understanding of human cognition, on democratic considerations, and on an assessment of the real-world record of such balancing.[36] I will investigate these issues in detail in due course, but let me offer a brief overview here. Ordinary people have difficulty in calculating probabilities. We tend to rely on rules of thumb, or heuristics, that can lead to systematic errors.[37] In particular, we often rely on experiences in which a risk turned out to be significant; a risk that is cognitively "available" is likely to receive special attention. The problem with the use of the "availability heuristic" is that it can lead us to err, exaggerating some risks and downplaying others. When people understate the risks associated with poor diet and lack of exercise and overstate the risks associated with pesticides and air travel, it is often because the availability heuristic leads them astray. Because CBA gives people a more accurate sense of the level of risks, it is a natural corrective here.

There is another problem. People often have intense, highly emotional reactions to particular incidents, and as a result, they can fail to think much about the *probability* that the underlying risks will come to fruition.[38] When people think about the "worst case," they might not consider the fact that there is an infinitesimal chance that the worst case will actually occur. Cost-benefit balancing should help government resist demands for regulation that are rooted in a kind of hysteria. In addition, people have a hard time understanding the systemic consequences of one-shot regulatory interventions.[39] Unless they are asked to seek a full accounting, they are likely to focus on small parts of problems, producing inadequate or even counterproductive solutions.[40] CBA is a way of producing that full accounting. Studies show as well that people tend to be "intuitive toxicologists," making a number of errors about toxic substances, such as, for example, how likely it is that those exposed to a carcinogen will get cancer.[41] Cost-benefit balancing helps to ensure that these errors are not translated into regulatory policy.

With respect to democracy, the case for CBA is strengthened by the fact that interest groups are often able to use these cognitive problems strategically, thus fending off desirable regulation or pressing for regulation when the argument on its behalf is fragile.[42] Here CBA, taken as an input into decisions, can protect democratic processes by exposing an account of consequences to public view. With respect to pragmatic considerations, a review of the record suggests that cost-benefit balancing can lead to improvements, simply because such balancing leads to more stringent regulation of serious problems, less costly ways of achieving regulatory

goals, and a reduction in expenditures for problems that are, by any account, relatively minor.[43]

None of these points suggests that CBA is a panacea for the problems
that I have identified. Everything depends on questions of implementation.
If regulators will use CBA in an unhelpful or biased way, the argument for
CBA is greatly weakened. I have referred to the government's encouraging
use of both "return letters" and "prompt letters," but all this is merely a
start. There are also hard questions about appropriate valuation. Sometimes respect for rights, or concerns about irreversibility, justify a rejection
of cost-benefit balancing.[44] The central point is that CBA can be seen not as
opposition to some abstraction called "regulation," and not as an endorsement of the economic approach to valuation, but as a real-world instrument, designed to ensure that the consequences of regulation are placed
before relevant officials and the public as a whole, and to focus attention
on neglected problems, while at the same time ensuring that limited resources will be devoted to areas where they will do the most good. So
understood, CBA promises to attract support from a wide range of people
with diverse perspectives on contested issues—a promise realized in the
apparently growing bipartisan consensus on some form of cost-benefit balancing in many domains of regulatory policy.[45]

Post-1980 Developments

All this has been highly abstract; let me turn now to actual practice. Since
1980, all three branches of government have shown increased interest in
cost-benefit balancing. Within the executive branch, the interest has been
longstanding.[46] But the decisive step came within a month of President
Reagan's inauguration in 1981, with the formal creation of a mechanism
for OMB review of major regulations.

The most important of the new innovations, contained in Executive
Order 12291, were: (1) a set of substantive principles for all agencies to
follow, "to the extent permitted by law," including a commitment to CBA;
(2) a requirement that a regulatory impact analysis, including CBA, accompany all "major" rules; and (3) a formal mechanism for OMB over-
sight, with a general understanding that the agency had some (undefined)
substantive control. President Reagan considered subjecting the independent agencies to the new order but ultimately declined to do so, partly
because of concerns about legal authority but mostly because of fears of an
adverse congressional reaction. The independent agencies were asked to
comply voluntarily with Executive Order 12291; all of them declined. A
small office within OMB, the Office of Information and Regulatory Affairs (OIRA), became an influential part of the executive branch, with the
authority to move regulation in new directions or even stop it in its tracks.
President Reagan also created a Presidential Task Force on Regulatory Re-

lief, evidently designed to scale back costly or otherwise undesirable regulations.

Executive Order 12291 proved extremely controversial. Nonetheless, President Reagan expanded on the basic idea four years later with Executive Order 12498. That order established a requirement that agencies submit "annual regulatory plans" to OMB for review. The result was an annual publication, the *Regulatory Program of the United States*, which contained a discussion of all proposed actions that might be either costly or controversial. Executive Order 12498 served to increase the authority of agency heads over their staffs by exposing proposals to top-level review at an early stage. But it also increased the authority of OMB by giving it supervisory power over plans and by making it hard for agencies to proceed without OMB preclearance. None of this meant that regulations would be carefully scrutinized to ensure that the benefits exceeded the costs. In practice, OMB's role was only intermittent, and there was no general effort to ensure that the executive branch would engage in sensible priority setting or ensure that private and public resources would be devoted to areas where they would do the most good. But at least a mechanism was put in place that would, in principle, allow OMB to reject initiatives that promised to cost much and to do little.

Under President George Bush, the principal innovation (not going far beyond President Reagan's Task Force on Regulatory Relief) was the Council on Competitiveness, chaired by the vice president. The council engaged in occasional review of agency rules, operating as a kind of supervisor of OMB. It also set out a number of principles and proposals for regulatory reform. In essence, however, the Bush Administration followed the basic approach of its predecessor, continuing with OMB review under the two Reagan executive orders.

The election of President Clinton raised a number of questions about whether cost-benefit balancing would continue to have a role within the executive branch. Many environmentalists have been (and continue to be) skeptical of the idea, and environmentalists were expected to have a significant influence in the Clinton Administration. But in a significant and dramatic step, President Clinton endorsed the essential features of the Reagan-Bush orders in his Executive Order 12866. The crucial point about Clinton's order is that it accepted the basic commitments of the two Reagan-Bush orders by requiring agencies to assess both costs and benefits and to proceed only when the latter exceeded the former. At the same time, President Clinton offered several changes to the Reagan-Bush processes. First, he attempted to diminish public concerns about interest-group power over regulation by providing a process to resolve conflicts and by creating new procedures designed to ensure greater openness. Second, his order drew agency attention not only to costs and benefits but also to (1) "equity," (2) "distributive impacts," and (3) qualititative as well as quantitative factors.

Third, the Clinton order changed the Reagan requirement that benefits "outweigh" costs to a requirement that benefits "justify" costs. These changes are best understood as an effort to "soften" the cost-benefit requirement so that agencies could make adjustments in the decision process and abandon the outcome of a strict cost-benefit assessment where this seemed sensible.

These are noteworthy shifts. But the formal text of the governing Executive Order is less important than the actual practice that it inspires. Under President Clinton, OMB made little attempt to ensure that the benefits of regulation actually justified its costs. The major activity in the Clinton Administration came through the various "reinventing government" initiatives, which were, to be sure, an effort to ensure more effectiveness and lower cost in the regulatory process. This is not the place for a full overview of those initiatives. But it is fair to say that they produced a number of significant improvements—and that they fell far short of a large-scale shift of the regulatory process toward serious problems and away from small ones. For those interested in higher benefits and lower costs, an enormous amount remains to be accomplished.

What about Congress? In dealing with the role of benefits and costs, federal statutes tend to fall in the categories listed below. I order the statutes roughly in accordance with their treatment of cost-benefit balancing, beginning with those that most flatly reject it and ending with those that unambiguously embrace it.

Flat Bans on Consideration of Costs

Some statutes, exemplifying 1970s environmentalism, appear to forbid any consideration of cost. Perhaps the most famous example is the Delaney Clause, now partly repealed, which for a long period flatly and generally prohibited food additives that "induce cancer in man or animal."[47] (The clause now exempts pesticide residues on processed foods but still applies to food additives in general.) In the face of that apparently rigid language, the government eventually sought to permit additives that, while carcinogenic, created only the most minuscule risk of cancer—lower, in fact, than the risk from eating one peanut with the FDA-permitted level of aflatoxins every 250 days, and much lower risk than from spending about 17 hours every year in Denver (with its high elevation and radiation levels) rather than the District of Columbia.[48] Nonetheless, the Delaney Clause was taken to forbid any form of balancing. [49]

A still more important example comes from the most fundamental provisions of the Clean Air Act, governing national ambient air-quality standards.[50] For a long time, the national ambient air-quality standards set under that act have been understood to be based on "public health" alone.[51] The EPA's judgment is to be grounded only in benefits; the cost of compliance is irrelevant.

Significant Risk Requirements

An alternative formulation is to require the agency to address only "significant" or "unacceptable" risks. In this view, risks that do not reach a certain level need not and perhaps may not be addressed. This is the prevailing interpretation of the Occupational Safety and Health Act under both the toxic substance provisions and the more general provisions.[52] A requirement of a "significant risk" falls short of cost-benefit analysis in the sense that it is entirely *benefits-based*; costs are irrelevant as such. Once benefits fall below a certain threshold, regulation is not required and in fact is banned.[53] Once benefits rise above that threshold, regulation is permissible, even if the benefits seem low in comparison to the costs. But a "significant risk" statute is very different from absolutism, because it gives the agency the power, and even imposes on it the obligation, to exempt hazards that do not rise to a certain magnitude. This is a substantial limitation on regulation that promises to accomplish little.

Substitute Risks and Health-Health Trade-offs

Some statutes require agencies to consider whether a regulation controlling one risk would, in so doing, create a substitute risk. If so, agencies are permitted to decline to regulate, or to regulate to a different point. This is clear statutory recognition of *health-health trade-offs*, which arise when there are health concerns about both more and less regulation.[54] Consider, for example, the possibility that fuel economy standards for new cars will lead manufacturers to produce smaller and more hazardous vehicles, causing a number of deaths in the process. Surely the government should be permitted to take this possibility into account in deciding on fuel economy standards.

Many statutory "consideration" requirements[55] have an unambiguous feature of this sort—for example, by requiring agencies entrusted with reducing air pollution problems to take into account "non-air-quality health and environmental impact and energy requirements."[56] Here is an explicit recognition that the EPA is allowed to consider the danger that a regulation that decreases air pollution will also create water pollution or some other environmental problem.[57] The reformulated gasoline program takes this basic form,[58] as does the provision governing emissions standards for new vehicles, which authorizes the EPA to examine "safety factors" as well as cost and energy issues.[59] Thus the EPA is instructed to ask whether a program designed to reduce air pollution might thereby make cars more dangerous; if so, EPA should reconsider the program.

The Toxic Substances Control Act similarly requires the EPA to consider substitute risks.[60] Under the fuel regulation program of the Clean Air Act, the EPA administrator is not allowed to prohibit a fuel or fuel additive unless "he finds, and published such finding, that in his judgment such prohibition will not cause the use of any other fuel or fuel additive which will produce emissions which will endanger the public health or welfare to the same or greater degree than" the prohibited item.[61]

Feasibility Requirements

Some statutes require agencies to regulate "to the extent feasible" or "achievable."[62] These expressions are far from transparent. But as generally understood, such statutes put the focus not on benefits but solely on costs, and on costs in a particular way: They forbid an agency from regulating to a point that is neither (a) technically feasible, because the relevant control technology does not exist, nor (b) economically feasible, because the industry cannot bear the cost without significant or massive business failures.[63] The line between (a) and (b), usually treated as crisp and simple, is hardly that; whether a requirement is technically feasible will usually depend on the level of resources devoted to it. In practice, (a) and (b) therefore overlap, with (a) serving as a separate category only on those occasions when, even with massive use of existing resources, the technology cannot be brought into existence. Noteworthy here is the fact that while a significant risk requirement is entirely benefits-based, a feasibility requirement looks exclusively at the cost side of the equation. Such a requirement is a "block" of excessively expensive regulation.

"Consideration" Requirements

Many statutes ask agencies to "take into consideration" various factors, including cost, in addition to the principal factor to which the statute draws the agency's attention (such as clean air or water). The most common formulation, now standard in federal law, asks the agency to produce the "maximum degree of reduction" that is "achievable" after "taking into consideration [1] the cost of achieving such emission reduction, and [2] any [a] non-air-quality health and environmental impacts and [b] energy requirements."[64] The basic idea here is that the agency is supposed to qualify the pursuit of the "maximum" achievable reduction by asking (a) whether the cost is excessive, (b) whether energy requirements would be adversely affected, and (c) whether the "maximum" requirement might create health and environmental harms by, for example, increasing water pollution though reducing air pollution.

Cost-Benefit Requirements

Several statutes ask agencies to balance costs against benefits, mostly through a prohibition on "unreasonable risks," alongside a definition of "unreasonable" that refers to both costs and benefits. Prominent examples are the Toxic Substances Control Act[65] and the Federal Insecticide, Fungicide, and Rodenticide Act.[66] Here the agency is required to calculate both costs and benefits and to compare them against each other. If the costs exceed the benefits, regulation is unacceptable. More recently, cost-benefit analysis is mandated by the Safe Drinking Water Act amendments.[67] Under the act, EPA is authorized to back away from the maximum feasible level if the benefits of the stricter standard "would not justify the costs of complying with the level."[68] While Congress has thus far resisted efforts to impose a cost-benefit "supermandate" calling for a general decision rule based on cost-benefit balancing,[69] Congress has enacted legislation requiring assessment and public disclosure of costs and benefits of major regulations.[70] OMB itself has been required to produce annual accounting of costs and benefits.[71]

In the abstract, the distinctions among these kinds of provisions should be clear enough. A statute that calls for consideration of substitute risks does not require cost-benefit balancing, because it is more narrowly concerned to ensure that risks (generally to health) do not increase on balance. Under a statute calling for health-health trade-offs, it is irrelevant that costs as such exceed benefits. A statute that requires that regulations be "feasible" is ordinarily taken to entail no comparison between costs and benefits, but a cost-focused inquiry into what industry is able to do—whereas a statute that regulates "significant risks" is ordinarily taken to entail no comparison between costs and benefits, but a benefit-centered inquiry into the magnitude of the risk to be addressed.

It is important to underline the point that several statutes expressly require agencies to compare costs against benefits before issuing regulations. For years, moreover, Congress has been considering more aggressive "supermandates" cutting across all existing legislation in order to require all agencies to balance costs against benefits. Some of the proposed mandates would be more substantive: They would make cost-benefit balancing the basis of decision. An enactment of this kind would be extremely dramatic. It would alter the full universe of provisions described above, converting them all into cost-benefit provisions. To date, however, no such legislation has been enacted. Thus Congress has restricted itself to more particular procedural requirements, asking for an accounting of costs and benefits to ensure that the public has relevant information.

The Unfunded Mandates Reform Act takes some modest steps in the direction of statutory cost-benefit requirements for all regulations. In cases in which a federal mandate "may result" in an aggregate expenditure of $100 million or more, that act requires the government to provide "a qualititative and quantitative assessment of the anticipated costs and benefits of the Federal mandate," alongside an estimate of its "future compliance costs" and of its "effect on the national economy, such as the effect on productivity, economic growth, full employment, creation of productive jobs, and international competitiveness of United States goods and services." But this assessment seems to be only procedural. It does not seem to have affected the judgments of regulatory agencies, and indeed it lacks any legal authority at all.

Notes

1. *See* Bruce Ackerman and Richard B. Stewart, *Reforming Environmental Law*, 13 COLUM. J. ENV. L. 171 (1988).
2. 42 U.S.C. 7409(b).
3. *See, e.g.,* 33 U.S.C. 1311(b)(1)AA), 42 U.S.C. 7411(a)(1), 7412(d)(2), 7475(a)(4), 7502(c)(1).
4. *See Economic Analyses at EPA* 455-56 (Richard Morgenstern ed. 1998); Paul Portnoy, *Air Pollution Policy, in* PUBLIC POLICIES FOR ENVIRONMENTAL PROTECTION 77, 101-105 (Paul Portnoy and Robert Stavins eds. 2000).
5. *Id.*
6. Portnoy, *supra* note 4, at 102-03.
7. *Id.* at 109.
8. *Id.* at 113 (showing a benefit-cost ratio of 3 to 1).
9. *Available at* http://www.whitehouse.gov/omb/inforeg/index.html.
10. For a good but dated overview, see Robert Hahn, *What Do the Government's Own Numbers Tell Us?, in* RISKS, COSTS, AND LIVES SAVED (Robert Hahn ed. 1995). More recent outside evaluations can be found at the web site of the American Enterprise Institute–Brookings Joint Center for Regulatory Studies, http://www.aei.brookings.org.
11. *Id.; see* 2000 report, charts, table 4.
12. *Id.*
13. *See id.*
14. *See id.*, table 5.
15. This is the theme of STEPHEN BREYER, BREAKING THE VICIOUS CIRCLE (Cambridge: Harvard University Press, 1995).
16. Thomas Hopkins, *The Costs of Federal Regulation*, 2 J. REG. AND SOC. COSTS 5, 25 table 2 (1992).
17. Paul Portney & Robert Stavins, *Regulatory Review of Environmental Policy*, 8 J. RISK AND UNCERTAINTY 111, 119 n.1 (1995).
18. *Id.*, table 12.
19. *Id.*
20. *Id.*
21. *Id.*
22. Tammy Tengs et al., *Five Hundred Life-Saving Interventions and Their Cost-Effectiveness*, 15 RISK ANALYSIS 369 (1995).
23. *See* JOHN GRAHAM & JONATHAN WIENER, RISK VS. RISK (Cambridge: Harvard University Press, 1995).
24. *See, e.g.,* A. DENNY ELLERMAN ET AL., MARKETS IN CLEAN AIR (Cambridge: Cambridge University Press, 2000); Robert Stavins, *Market-Based Environmental Policies, in* PUBLIC POLICIES FOR ENVIRONMENTAL PROTECTION, *supra*, at 31, 35-55.
25. For many examples, *see* ECONOMIC ANALYSIS AT EPA (Richard Morgenstern ed. 1996).
26. *See* http://www.whitehouse.gov/omb/inforeg/regpol.html.
27. *See* ECONOMIC ANALYSIS AT EPA, *supra* note 25.
28. *See id.* at 458.
29. *Id.* at 458.
30. *Id.* at 49-86, 131-69.

31. *Id.* at 458.

32. *See* Hahn, *supra* note 10.

33. For a general challenge to quantification, *see* Lisa Heinzerling, *Regulatory Costs of Mythic Proportions*, 106 YALE L.J. 1981 (1998).

34. *See* Mathew Adler & Eric Posner, *Rethinking Cost-Benefit Analysis*, 109 YALE L.J. 165 (1999).

35. Many of these points are pressed in ELIZABETH ANDERSON, VALUE IN ETHICS AND ECONOMICS (Cambridge: Harvard University Press, 1993).

36. I attempt to develop this point in Cass R. Sunstein, *Cognition and Cost-Benefit Analysis*, 29 J. LEGAL STUD. 1059 (2000). In the same vein, *see* Allan Gibbard, *Risk and Value*, in VALUES AT RISK 94-112 (Douglas MacLean ed. 1986).

37. Amos Tversky & Daniel Kahneman, *Judgment under Uncertainty: Heuristics and Biases, in* JUDGMENT UNDER UNCERTAINTY: HEURISTICS AND BIASES 3, 11 (Daniel Kahneman, Paul Slovic, and Amos Tversky eds. 1982); Roger Noll & James Krier, *Some Implications of Cognitive Psychology for Risk Regulation*, 19 J. LEGAL STUD. 747 (1990).

38. *See* Cass R. Sunstein, *The Laws of Fear*, HARV. L. REV. (forthcoming 2001); GEORGE LOEWENSTEIN ET AL., RISK AS FEELINGS (forthcoming 2001).

39. *See* DIETRICH DORNER, THE LOGIC OF FAILURE (1994).

40. *Id.*

41. *See* PAUL SLOVIC, THE PERCEPTION OF RISK (2000).

42. *See* Timur Kuran & Cass R. Sunstein, *Availability Cascades and Risk Regulation*, 51 STAN. L. REV. 683 (1999).

43. *See* ECONOMIC ANALYSIS AT EPA, *supra* note 25 at 455-76.

44. TVA v. Hill, 437 U.S. 153 (1978).

45. *See* Executive Order 12866, 58 Fed. Reg. 51,735 (1993).

46. *See* CASS R. SUNSTEIN, RISK AND REASON ch. 1 (Cambridge: Cambridge University Press, forthcoming 2001).

47. 21 U.S.C. 376(b)(5)(B).

48. Public Citizen v. Young, 831 F.2d 1108 (D.C. Cir. 1987).

49. *Id.*

50. 42 U.S.C. 7409(b).

51. Lead Industries v. EPA, 647 F.2d 1130 (D.C. Cir. 1980). The Supreme Court accepted this view in *Whitman v. American Trucking Ass'ns*, 531 U.S. 457 (2001). *See also* Union Electric Co. v. EPA, 427 U.S. 246 (1976) (holding that EPA may not consider economic and technological feasibility when approving or disapproving a state implementation plan).

52. Industrial Union Dept., AFL-CIO v. API, 448 U.S. 607 (1980); International Union, UAW v. OSHA, 37 F.3d 605 (D.C. Cir. 1994).

53. American Trucking Ass'n v. EPA, 175 F.3d 1027 (D.C. Cir. 1999), appears to endorse this view for regulation of air pollutants on the theory that an interpretation that would allow the EPA to pick any point it chooses would violate the nondelegation doctrine.

54. *See* JOHN GRAHAM & JONATHAN WIENER, RISK VS. RISK (Cambridge: Harvard University Press, 1995).

55. 42 U.S.C. 7429(a)(2) (OSHA); 42 U.S.C. 300g-1(b)(4)(B) (Safe Drinking Water Act).

56. 42 U.S.C. 7411(a)(1).

57. *See* American Petroleum Inst. v. EPA, 52 F.2d 1113 (D.C. Cir. 1995) (recognizing this point but also holding that EPA had unlawfully elevated these "consideration" factors).

58.   42 U.S.C. 7545(k)(1).

59.   42 U.S.C. 7521(a)(3)(A).

60.   Corrosion Proof Fittings v. EPA, 947 F.2d 1201 (5th Cir. 1991).

61.   42 U.S.C. 7545 (c)(2)(c).

62.   *See, e.g.,* 29 U.S.C. 655(b)(5) ("feasible"); 42 U.S.C. 7521 (A)(3)(A) ("will be available"); 42 U.S.C. 7412(d)(2) ("achievable"); 42 U.S.C. 6411(a)(1) ("has been adequately demonstrated").

63.   American Textile Manufacturers v. Donovan, 452 U.S. 490, 508-09 (1976); AFL-CIO v. OSHA, 965 F.2d 962, 980 (11th Cir. 1992); National Lime Association v. EPA, 23 F.3d 625 (D.C. Cir. 2000).

64.   42 U.S.C. 7429 (a)(2) (OSHA); 42 U.S.C. 300g-1(b)(4)(B) (Safe Drinking Water Act); 42 U.S.C. 7411 (a)(1) (new source performance standards under Clean Air Act); 42 U.S.C. 7412(d)(2) (hazardous air pollutants under Clean Air Act); 42 U.S.C. 7521 (a)(3)(A) (emissions standards under Clean Air Act).

65.   15 U.S.C. 2605 (a).

66.   7 U.S.C. 136a(a).

67.   42 U.S.C. 300g-1(b)(3).

68.   42 U.S.C. 300g-1(b)(6).

69.   *See* Cass R. Sunstein, *Congress, Constitutional Moments, and the Cost-Benefit State*, 48 STAN. L. REV. 247 (1996).

70.   5 U.S.C. 1532, 1535.

71.   *See, e.g.,* section 625 of the Treasury and General Government Appropriations Act, 1998, PL 105-61; section 638(a) of the 1999 Omnibus Consolidated and Emergency Supplemental Appropriations Act.

IS COST-BENEFIT ANALYSIS FOR EVERYONE? 2

Introduction

Sometimes an initiative in law and policy receives near-universal support on the ground that all will be helped and none will be hurt—or at least that most will be helped and few will be hurt, and those who are hurt lack a reasonable ground for complaint.

This happened in the 1970s and 1980s, when consensus developed around an extremely controversial idea—that the airlines, trucking, and railroad industries should be deregulated. For the most part, deregulation has been a spectacular success, producing lower costs and better performance for consumers, while at the same time increasing jobs and raising wages. Something similar happened in the 1990s, when support grew for the formerly controversial concept that, in many domains, regulation via economic incentives, such as emissions-trading systems, should replace regulation via national command-and-control. Here, too, the evidence has been exceptionally encouraging.[1]

Might the same thing happen for cost-benefit analysis (CBA)? In a sense, it already has. As we have seen, Presidents Reagan, Bush, and Clinton have all issued executive orders requiring agencies to pay close attention to the costs and benefits of regulation. It is highly likely that future American presidents, regardless of party, will continue on this path. We have also seen Congress show great interest in requiring accounts of the costs and benefits of regulation, as evidenced by new legislation.[2] Part II explores a quiet revolution within the federal judiciary: Federal courts have also moved in the direction of questioning regulatory absolutism of any kind, and of both permitting and requiring agencies to engage in careful balancing of both sides of the ledger.

Nonetheless, it would be premature to say that CBA has received the kind of social consensus now commanded by economic incentives and deregulation of airlines, trucking, and railroads. I believe that CBA should command such a consensus, at least as a presumption, and that the presumption in favor of CBA should operate regardless of political commitments. In short, a suitably devised system of CBA is for everyone—committed environmentalists and those who think of environmentalism as a form of hysteria, people who believe that markets generally succeed and those who believe that markets frequently fail, people who think that workers deserve much more protection and those who think that worker-protection programs have gone much too far. Recall in this connection that it was CBA that helped legitimate one of the largest environmental programs in American history—the complete phaseout of lead in gasoline—and also the phaseout of chlorofluorocarbons (CFCs), which was imposed when the Council of Economic Advisors, under President Reagan, concluded that in light of the likelihood of numerous additional skin cancers and cataracts, severe, even draconian regulatory steps would be a complete bargain.

The Basics of CBA

What does a cost-benefit state do? And what does CBA involve? First and foremost, a government committed to CBA will attempt to analyze the consequences of regulations, on both the cost and benefit side. Such an analysis will include quantitative and qualitative accounts of expected effects, including, for example, a statement of the expected lives saved, curable cancers prevented, asthma attacks averted, and much more (see Appendix A for an example). Where science does not permit specific predictions, government should produce ranges, as, for example, in a statement that the regulation will save between 100 and 240 lives per year (see Appendix A). Whenever possible, expected benefits should be translated into monetary equivalents, not because a life is really worth, say, $6 million, but to permit sensible comparisons and priorities.

Some Qualifications

These ideas should be limited to regulations of a certain magnitude, such as those that impose costs of at least $50 million per year. Many regulations do not impose substantial costs, and for routine or low-cost measures a formal analysis should not be required (and it has not been under the relevant executive orders). The central point is that the extent of the requisite analysis should depend on the magnitude of the regulation—and that a formal analysis should be required for all regulations imposing costs beyond some identified point.

Quantification will be difficult or even impossible in some cases. For arsenic in drinking water, government cannot really come up with specific numbers to link exposure levels to deaths and illnesses. At this stage, science is able to produce only ranges of anticipated benefits, which are not precise but are nonetheless highly illuminating.[3] For regulations protecting airport security in the face of terrorist threats, quantification of the benefits is at best a guess. We do not know the magnitude of the risks, and a full-scale cost-benefit analysis would be silly. But even here, an effort to be as specific as possible about costs and anticipated efficacy is likely to help us to promote airport security in the most reasonable manner.

Substantive Requirements

Thus far I have been discussing CBA as a *procedural* requirement—as a requirement that information be compiled and disclosed. But the cost-benefit state imposes a substantive requirement as well. In order to proceed, an agency should be required to conclude, in ordinary circumstances, that the benefits justify the costs, and to explain why. If, for example, a regulation is expected to save 80 lives, each valued at $6 million, and if it would cost $200 million, it is fully justified. But if a regulation is expected to save four lives and cost $400 million, an agency should ordinarily be barred from issuing it. If an agency seeks to proceed even though the benefits do not justify the costs, it should have to explain itself—by saying, for example, that those at risk are young children, and that because they cannot protect themselves, and because a number of years of life are involved, unusual steps should be taken.

At this point, it might be possible to question whether a large amount of money (say, $400 million) would really be too much to spend to save a small number of lives (say, two). Who is to say that $400 million is too much? The best answer is heavily pragmatic. Each of us has limited resources, and we do not spend all of our budget on statistically low risks. We spent a certain amount, and not more, to protect against the risks associated with poor diet, motor vehicle accidents, fires, floods, and much more. In allocating our resources, we set priorities, partly to use resources to prevent the more serious safety problems and partly to use them on other things we care about, such as education, recreation, food, and entertainment. The same is true for governments, which cannot sensibly spend huge amounts on small hazards. If an agency requires a $400 million expenditure to save two lives, it will be expending resources that might well be spent on other matters, including the saving of more lives. Indeed, evidence suggests that high expenditures—of perhaps $15 million or more—will cause the loss of a statistical life, and hence that regulations with high costs and low benefits may cause more deaths than they prevent.[4] When governments ban high expenditures for low benefits, it is not because they are indifferent to the loss of even a single life, but because they want to ensure that limited resources are used where they will do the most good.

The point applies in every domain. If government refuses to regulate extremely low concentrations of arsenic in drinking water, it is probably because it believes that the health gains would be low and that the costs (in the form of higher water bills) would be significant. If government takes some steps but not others to increase security at airports, it is probably because it believes that the rejected steps would not really promote safety but might well impose real costs in the form of greater inconvenience, higher ticket prices, or both. It is not as if people are, with respect to some risk, either "safe" or "unsafe." The real questions are whether and how to reduce the risks to which they are now subject. Cost-benefit analysis is a tool for ensuring good answers to those questions.

None of this suggests that the government should be rigidly bound by the "bottom line." Cost-benefit analysis ought not to place agencies in an arithmetic straightjacket. The benefits should ordinarily be required to exceed the costs, but regulators might reasonably decide that the numbers are not decisive if, for example, children are mostly at risk, or if the relevant hazard is faced mostly by poor people, or if the hazard at issue is involuntarily incurred or extremely difficult to control. I do not mean to offer a detailed policy program here, or to specify the grounds on which agencies might be allowed to proceed when the costs seem high and the benefits relatively low.[5] The basic ideas are simple: Agencies should be required to investigate both costs and benefits, to show that benefits justify costs in most circumstances, and to offer a reasonable explanation for any decision to proceed when costs exceed benefits. As we shall see, these requirements should help to overcome problems that we all face in thinking about risks, while at the same time reducing interest-group power and promoting accountability in government.

The argument for CBA is clarified and strengthened by comparing it with some alternatives. Consider three popular ideas that tend to compete with CBA: pollution prevention, the precautionary principle, and sustainable development.

Pollution Prevention

The notion of pollution prevention is designed to ensure that regulators prevent pollution before it enters the system and do not settle for "end of the pipe" controls imposed on polluting technologies.[6] As examples of pollution prevention, consider the phaseout of lead in gasolines, the use of solar power (as opposed to nuclear power and fossil fuels, which produce many air pollution problems), and the substitution of electric cars for cars powered by gasoline. Advocates of pollution prevention tend to think that this is by far the most effective way to deal with pollution problems, partly because it promises larger and more dramatic pollution reductions, and partly because it does not rely on after-the-fact technological "fixes."

Often pollution prevention makes a great deal of sense. The elimination of lead from gasoline was a story of successful pollution prevention. But sometimes pollution prevention makes no sense at all. Consider some examples. The best way to prevent automobile pollution would be to eliminate the internal combustion engines that power most trucks and cars. The best way to prevent pollution from current power sources would be to stop relying on fossil fuels, now used by utility power plants. Should the EPA be told to ban the internal combustion engine and coal combustion? If this would be a ludicrous conclusion—as I think it would be—it is because in any view, the costs of the ban would dwarf the benefits.

When it is convincing, the case for pollution prevention rests, at bottom, on some form of cost-benefit balancing. Where the balance does not support regulation, pollution prevention is probably a mistake. Sometimes projections of the future will involve a degree of guesswork and speculation. But when this is so, good CBA calls for a range of possibilities. What is not justified is to "prevent" pollution without an inquiry into the consequences, good and bad, of prevention.

The Precautionary Principle

All over the world, there is increasing interest in a simple idea for the regulation of risk: In the case of doubt, follow *the precautionary principle*.[7] Avoid steps that will create a risk of harm. Until safety is established, be cautious. In a catchphrase: Better safe than sorry. In ordinary life, pleas of this kind seem quite sensible. People buy smoke alarms and insurance. Shouldn't the same approach be followed by regulators as well?

There is some important truth in the precautionary principle. The truth rests in the acknowledgment that a small probability (say, 1 in 100,000) of a serious harm (say, 100,000 deaths) deserves extremely serious attention. The fact that a danger is unlikely, even very unlikely, is hardly a decisive point against regulatory controls. In the context of airplane safety, and general protection against terrorist attacks and other catastrophes, we do a great deal to protect ourselves against low-probability risks. But dangers are often on both sides of the equation. Consider the case of genetic modification of food. A failure to allow genetic modification might well result in many deaths and a small probability of many more. This is because genetic modification of food might help provide nutritious, low-cost food to millions of people, and because there is a chance that genetically modified food will actually save millions of lives each year.

Something similar can be said about nuclear power. To be sure, a ban on nuclear power might seem fully justified by the precautionary principle; nuclear power carries a small risk of catastrophe. But the very failure to use nuclear power will also create a small risk of catastrophe, because the energy sources that will be used instead of nuclear power also carry risks—including the risks of catastrophe associated with global warming. Or consider that problem itself. It might well seem that the precautionary principle justifies significant steps to protect against the risks associated with global warming. But those very steps will likely carry risks, including potentially catastrophic ones. If we dramatically increase the costs of energy, there is a small probability of many serious problems, including significant increases in unemployment and poverty. I do not mean to say that global warming should be disregarded; on the contrary, I believe that significant steps should be taken to reduce the risk. I simply wish to illustrate that in many cases the precautionary principle is paralyzing: It stands as an obstacle to regulation and nonregulation, and to everything in between.

A competent cost-benefit analysis takes good account of the precautionary principle by incorporating low-probability risks of significant harms. CBA subsumes this risk, as it does all others, into the overall assessment. Of course, nothing in CBA precludes a policymaker from concluding that a 1 in 10,000 risk of 100,000 deaths is worse, or less bad, than a 1 in 1,000 risk of 10,000 deaths. This is a political judgment, not a technical one to be decided by mechanical use of the numbers.

Sustainable Development

The notion of sustainable development has had an extraordinary influence in international environmental debates, so much so that it now serves as a kind of symbol for any serious commitment to environmental protection. But the notion is highly ambiguous. What kind of development counts as sustainable? What counts as unsustainable? In a standard formulation, the idea of sustainable development is said to refer to "development that occurs on a scale that does not exceed the carrying capacity of the biosphere."[8]

To the extent that endorsement of sustainable development will guarantee that future generations will not lack clean air and water, everyone should support sustainable development. Any minimally sensible policy will ensure decent lives and options for future generations. No sane person is opposed to that. Indeed, cost-benefit analysis itself calls for sustainable development, because a competent analyst incorporates the interests of members of future generations. But outside of the easy cases for environmental protection, the real question is not whether development is sustainable or unsustainable; it involves what level of resources to commit to environmental protection. Often there is no simple line to divide the sustainable from the unsustainable. If certain regulatory steps would increase sustainability but cause a great deal of suffering and misery simply by virtue of their expense, a sensible administrator will take that point into account. And if the sensible administrator is thinking in this way, he or she is balancing the various considerations, very much the way that cost-benefit analysis does. In the international context, the administrator might even ask for financial help from wealthier countries, help that is probably required from the standpoint of justice.

Because cost-benefit balancing requires consideration of the interests of future generations, the goal of sustainable development is in no conflict with that form of balancing. Indeed, cost-benefit analysis strongly supports the idea that sustainability is a desirable goal. It also helps give content to the hard question, which is how much should be done to improve environmental quality in poor as well as wealthy nations.

Pollution prevention can be an excellent idea, but it would sometimes lead to disaster, not least because it would increase serious risks. Sometimes it is better to be safe than sorry, and here the precautionary principle makes sense. People do, and should, buy insurance. But sometimes the precautionary principle leads to paralysis, and in any case some precautions are simply not worthwhile. Everyone should support sustainable development, and it is important to ensure that policies are sustainable rather than the opposite. But in poor nations as well as rich ones, regulators need much better guidance than that.

Of Economics, Cognitive Psychology, and Democracy

Many of the most popular defenses of CBA come from neoclassical economics.[9] For economists, goods should be measured in accordance with private "willingness to pay." The idea is not as strange as it might seem. Each of us must make choices about how much to spend for additional increments of safety—by, for example, buying smoke alarms or especially strong locks, or taking certain jobs. Everyone is, as a practical matter, willing to pay a certain amount—no more and no less—to increase the current level of safety; each of us will demand a certain amount to be subject to an additional level of risk. Studies suggest, for example, that the value of a statistical life, measured in terms of private willingness to pay, is between $3 million and $8 million.[10] If a regulation will save 20 lives per year, it will produce between $60 million and $160 million in benefits. It follows that we can assess the value of proposed regulations by comparing their aggregated costs to their aggregated benefits, thus measured. Suppose that the regulation would also produce $40 million in other benefits, because of the morbidity and aesthetic gains that it would generate. If the same regulation would cost $200 million, it would fail CBA.

But there are some problems with using private willingness to pay as the basis for assessing regulatory benefits. Some of these problems are internal to the economic framework; some amount to a rejection of that framework. The strongest arguments for CBA seem to rest not with neoclassical economics but with common sense, informed by behavioral economics and cognitive psychology.[11] The basic idea here is that it is exceedingly difficult to choose the appropriate level of regulation without looking at both the benefit and cost sides. Without some kind of accounting, ordinary thinking is likely to go wrong in such a way as to lead individuals, and governments, to favor policies that do less good than they might, or even more harm than good. Recall, for example, the finding that if we reallocated current spending to devote our resources to the most serious problems rather than the less serious ones, we could save over 60,000 more lives each year, and without spending a single penny more.[12]

Pitfalls of Risk Evaluation

Why do ordinary people make mistakes about risks?[13] The most obvious difficulty is that most of us, most of the time, are inadequately informed. But there are more interesting points in the background. I have noted that in thinking about risk, people tend to rely on heuristic devices, or mental shortcuts, that often work well in daily life but also lead to systematic errors. For example, we tend to think that an event is more probable if an example is cognitively "available," in the sense that it comes easily to mind. It is for this reason that a highly publicized problem can produce a kind of rush to judgment (and regulation); it is also for this reason that people tend to think that more deaths are due to accidents than diseases, whereas the opposite is true.

Consider two examples. In the aftermath of the hazardous waste problem at Love Canal in the early 1970s, many people came to believe that abandoned hazardous waste dumps are among the most serious of environmental problems and that a great deal should be done to clean them up. As a matter of fact, abandoned hazardous waste dumps can be a serious health hazard, but they cannot possibly be ranked among the most pressing environmental issues. In the aftermath of the terrorist attacks on New York City on September 11, 2001, many people came to believe that air travel was unsafe, and indeed that America in general was unsafe. As a matter of fact, airport security had been a neglected issue; but people were far more fearful than the facts warranted, and their fear grew out of the fact that they were well aware of a single, exceptionally vivid incident. In short, the terrorist attacks were universally "available." To say the least, it is hard to do a cost-benefit analysis of antiterrorist measures. But in ordinary circumstances, an effort to quantify the risks, and the costs of reducing risks, should correct mistakes that come from our inevitable use of mental shortcuts.

The problem is compounded by social influences, through which information can be spread rapidly. If many people are starting to think that genetic modification of food is dangerous, others may well be led to agree, not because they have reliable information, but because without that information they tend to accept the views of others. This is perfectly rational at the individual level, but it can lead to grave public errors. These often take the form of "availability cascades," sometimes involving mass panics over small risks, with a strong call for governmental response.[14] Precisely because it draws attention to the actual risk, and to the costs of addressing it, CBA can serve as a corrective here, ensuring that a governmental response will occur only if public fear is rooted in reality.

In addition, people may fail to see that health risks are on many sides of the problem, and that some regulations designed to protect health and safety can actually compromise them. For example, fuel economy standards, designed to promote environmental goals and energy independence, can lead to smaller, less safe cars, and thus more injuries and deaths. We have seen that regulation of nuclear power plants, designed to increase safety, might create health risks if it increases people's use of fossil fuels, which create a range of environmental and health risks, including those from global warming. "Health-health trade-offs"—and the introduction of substitute risks as a result of regulation—are omnipresent, and analysis of those trade-offs is important in its own right and a significant step in the direction of CBA, which puts the adverse health effects of regulation on the public viewscreen.

There is a more general issue. Sometimes people are alert to the dangers at issue but fail to see the problems, economic and otherwise, with eliminating or reducing those dangers. CBA has the advantage of putting both sides of the picture before the public and relevant officials. And if people's emotions are getting in the way—as they sometimes do in the domain of risk, especially when a bad outcome would be catastrophic but its probability is tiny—CBA can have a salutary "cooling effect." Of course, sometimes CBA will show that public concern is warranted, or even that it needs to be far more intense. In these various ways CBA is admirably well suited to overcoming cognitive problems faced by ordinary people in thinking about risks.

CBA's Democratic Properties

At the same time, CBA might well have significant democratic advantages, reducing interest-group control and promoting public attention to what is really at stake in a way that increases both accountability and transparency. Well-organized private groups very often exploit the cognitive mechanisms just described by pushing regulation, or nonregulation, in their preferred directions. And all too often, citizens and their representatives do not attend to the serious questions at stake, or the actual consequences of competing approaches. CBA can improve the process and substance of decisions by allowing people to evaluate agency decisions in an informed way, not clouded by evasions of the central issues. There is a strong *democratic* case for CBA, one that does not depend on controversial claims from neoclassical economics.

The point is strengthened if we pay attention to the extraordinary power of well-organized groups in the world of risk regulation. Often purportedly public-interest measures are really a bow in the direction of self-interested agents. Among the most infamous examples is the effort of eastern coal producers, in the late 1970s, to ensure that the Clean Air Act did not prove a disadvantage to them, even though western coal is much cleaner.[15] The relevant provisions of the act amounted to a multimillion-dollar bailout for producers of dirty coal. A careful effort to compare the environmental benefits with the economic costs would have been a great help here. At a minimum, it would have ensured greater transparency, showing that the approach selected by the EPA both cost more and cleaned the air less than easily imaginable alternatives.

Or consider the endless fights over fuel additives. Among the most serious air pollutants are benzene and its aromatic siblings, which contribute to ozone, particulates, and carbon dioxide. Which fuels would be most helpful in reducing those pollution sources? Interest groups, rather than analysis, have played a key role here, ensuring that fuel additives receive governmental endorsement if a powerful organization likes them (as in the case of the farm lobby's support of ethanol). Cost-benefit analysis would not eliminate the problem, but it could be a big help, because it would draw attention to the right questions. As a final example, consider the possibility that the EPA's ozone rule (discussed below), not easily supported on health grounds, reflects the lobbying power of Northeast energy sources, which are seeking to reduce competition from energy sources in the Midwest. When the public is not likely to benefit, and when interest groups have been at work, cost-benefit analysis can provide greater clarity and perhaps a motivation to do better.

A final point involves congressional fragmentation. As it currently stands, the national legislature is in a poor position to ensure that regulation makes overall sense and engages in sensible priority setting. Often an initiative owes its origin to the fact that a single committee, led by one or more powerful officials, is able to insist on it, and the technical issues are simply too complex for others to resist. For example, agricultural issues have a great deal to do with environmental problems; a sensible approach to farming, one that was integrated with environmental policy, could do a great deal to help with global warming, protection of wetlands, and off-road emissions of important air pollutants. But the committee structure ensures that the environmental dimensions of agriculture will be distorted or neglected. Cost-benefit analysis can help to cut through these problems by ensuring that all dimensions of the situation are put before public officials. In the long run, we need institutional solutions to the problem of congressional fragmentation so that problems are seen as a whole. Cost-benefit analysis is not, by itself, an institutional solution. But it is an indispensable tool for producing sensible overviews, and perhaps an appreciation of that fact could even help motivate Congress to move toward more substantial reforms of its own procedures. Stranger things have certainly happened.

The proof of these claims depends on what people actually do with CBA. There can be no assurance that interest groups will not be misuse the process. Nevertheless, CBA has a great deal of promise in helping to counteract some of the worst pathologies in modern regulation.

Notes

1. *See* A. DENNY ELLERMAN ET AL., MARKETS IN CLEAN AIR (Cambridge Univ. Press 2000).
2. *See* U.S.C. 1411, 1532, 1535.
3. *See* Cass R. Sunstein, *The Arithmetic of Arsenic*, GEORGETOWN L.J. (forthcoming 2002).
4. *See* ROBERT HAHN ET AL., DO FEDERAL REGULATIONS REDUCE MORTALITY? (American Enterprise Institute, 2000).
5. *See* CASS R. SUNSTEIN, RISK AND REASON, ch. 1 (Cambridge Univ. Press, forthcoming 2001) for more details on this point.
6. *See* BARRY COMMONER, MAKING PEACE WITH THE PLANET (1990).
7. PROTECTING PUBLIC HEALTH & THE ENVIRONMENT: IMPLEMENTING THE PRECAUTIONARY PRINCIPLE, Carolyn Raffensberger & Joel Tickner eds. (Island Press 1999).
8. *See* ROBERT PERCIVAL ET AL., ENVIRONMENTAL REGULATION: LAW, SCIENCE, AND POLICY 1182 (Little, Brown & Co. 2000).
9. Economists have, however, raised serious questions about CBA. For an overview and attempted response, see Mathew Adler & Eric Posner, *Rethinking Cost-Benefit Analysis*, 109 YALE L.J. 17 (1999).
10. *See* W. KIP VISCUSI, FATAL TRADEOFFS (Oxford Univ. Press 1992).
11. *See* CASS R. SUNSTEIN, RISK AND REASON (Cambridge Univ. Press 2001).
12. *See* Tammy Tengs & John Graham, *The Opportunity Costs of Haphazard Social Investments in Life Saving, in* RISKS, COSTS, AND LIVES SAVED 167, 172 (Robert Hahn ed. 1996).
13. I develop the argument in this section in Sunstein, *supra* note 5.
14. *See* Timur Kuran & Cass R. Sunstein, *Availability Cascades and Risk Regulation,* 51 STAN L. REV. 683 (1999).
15. *See* BRUCE ACKERMAN & WILLIAM HASSLER, CLEAN COAL/DIRTY AIR (1983).

PART 2
A QUIET REVOLUTION:
COST-BENEFIT DEFAULT RULES

I now turn to an important but largely unnoticed aspect of regulatory law: a series of judge-made cost-benefit default rules. These rules are making a large difference to federal regulatory policy. They amount to a quiet revolution. They authorize federal administrative agencies to do a great deal.

Let us begin with the legal background. Everyone agrees that if Congress has been genuinely clear, the legal issue is at an end. But statutory terms are frequently ambiguous. In addition, a problem of interpretation might be created by general language that seems not to reflect anything like congressional consideration of the specific point at issue. In the face of statutory uncertainty, federal cases can be found to support for each of the following principles. The law is more developed for some of the principles than for others, but each is an identifiable part of contemporary public law.

- Unless Congress has clearly said otherwise, agencies will be permitted to make de minimis exceptions to statutory requirements by exempting small risks from regulatory controls.[1]
- Unless Congress has clearly said otherwise, agencies will be permitted to balance the health risks created by regulation against the health benefits created by regulation.[2]
- Unless Congress has clearly said otherwise, agencies will be permitted to take costs into account in issuing regulations. In its current form, this principle means that where statutes are ambiguous, agencies will have the authority to consider costs as well as benefits.[3]
- Unless Congress has clearly said otherwise, agencies will be permitted to decline to regulate past the point where regulation would be economically or technologically feasible.[4]
- Unless Congress has clearly said otherwise, agencies will be expected to balance costs against benefits in issuing regulations.[5]

Now let us explore some details.

Notes

1. *See, e.g.,* Committee on Sensible Transportation, Inc. v. Dole, 826 F.2d 60 (D.C. Cir. 1987).

2. This principle appears to underlie American Trucking Ass'ns v. EPA, 175 F.3d 1027 (1999).

3. State of Michigan v. EPA, 213 F.3d 663, 678 (D.C. Cir. 2000).
4. *See* NRDC v. EPA, 824 F.2d 1146 (D.C. Cir. 1987).
5. Competitive Enterprise Institute v. NHTSA, 956 F.2d 321 (D.C. Cir. 1992).

DE MINIMIS EXCEPTIONS AND SUBSTITUTE RISKS 3

The most modest default rules allow agencies to exempt trivial risks from regulation while permitting them to take account of the new or "substitute" risks introduced by regulation. These are modest rules because they fall far short of calling for full-fledged cost-benefit analysis. But they are nonetheless exceptionally important, allowing agencies to move regulatory policy in more sensible directions. My goal in this chapter is to understand the nature of the emerging doctrine. In subsequent chapters, I will attempt to defend it and to untangle some ambiguities.

Exempting Trivial Risks: The Basic Idea

In a series of cases, courts of appeals have developed a principle authorizing agencies to make "de minimis exceptions" to regulatory requirements. The initial case was *Monsanto Co. v. Kennedy.*[1] There the agency banned acrylonitrile on the ground that it counts as a "food additive," migrating in small amounts from bottles into the drinks contained within. The FDA concluded that the ban was justified on safety grounds, a conclusion that the court found inadequately justified. But what is most important in the case is the general language with which the court remanded the case to the FDA. The court stressed that the agency had discretion to exclude a chemical from the statutory definition of food additives if "the level of migration into food . . . is so negligible as to present no public health or safety concerns."[2] Here the court appears to be stating a principle for the future, one that gives agencies a general authority to decline to regulate trivial risks.

A related case presented the question whether the EPA was permitted to make categorical exemptions under the Prevention of Significant Deterioration program of the Clean Air Act.[3] Here the court spoke in more ambitious terms, showing considerable enthusiasm for de minimis exemptions. It stated:

> [c]ategorical exemptions may be permissible as an exercise of agency power, inherent in most statutory schemes, to overlook circumstances that in context may fairly be considered de minimis. It is commonplace, of course, that the law does not concern itself with trifling matters, and this principle has often found application in the administrative context. Courts should be reluctant to apply the literal terms of a statute to mandate pointless expenditures.[4]

In fact the court expressly connected this principle with the idea that the court should "look beyond the words to the purpose of the act" to avoid "absurd or futile results."[5] Thus the court concluded, in its broadest statement on the point, that "most regulatory statutes, including the Clean Air Act, permit" de minimis exemptions upon an adequate factual showing.[6]

In the same vein, consider *Sierra Club v. Department of Transportation.*[7] At issue there was a statutory requirement that the Secretary of Transportation refuse to approve the "use" of significant public park land unless "the program or project includes all possible planning to minimize the harm to the park … resulting from the use."[8] The statutory question was whether limited commercial jet landings in an airport in the Grand Teton National Park should qualify as a "use," in the face of a reasonable agency finding that the increase in flights would not result in a "significant" change in noise. The court found that the term "use" should be understood to authorize de minimis exceptions.[9] There are many decisions to the same effect.[10]

Here, then, are a number of explicit opinions recognizing agency authority to exempt de minimis risks from regulatory controls. The authority operates as a clear statement principle, no less but also no more: Where Congress has unambiguously banned such exceptions, agencies are bound, and may not create de minimis exemptions even in compelling circumstances.[11]

The OSHA Variation: Requiring Exemptions

A noteworthy variation on the basic idea of permitting de minimis exceptions can be found in the plurality opinion in *Industrial Union Department, AFL-CIO v. API*, known as the Benzene Case.[12] What the plurality said represents a variation on the basic idea for two reasons. First, the plurality *forbids* the agency to regulate trivial risks; it goes well beyond permitting the agency to create exemptions. Second, the plurality's substantive standard is phrased not in terms of de minimis exceptions to regulation, but of limiting regulation to significant risks, and hence prohibiting regulation of risks not shown to be significant. The second difference might or might not be important, because it is not clear whether risks that do not qualify as "significant" should be treated as de minimis, though this does appear to be what the plurality had in mind.

The central issue in the case was whether OSHA had to show a "significant risk" in order to regulate a toxic substance (benzene). In arguing that it did not, the government pointed to the central statutory provision, which said (and says) that in promulgating the relevant standards, the secretary "shall set the standard which most adequately assures, to the extent feasible, on the basis of the best available evidence, that no employee will suffer material impairment of health or functional capacity, even if such employee has regular exposure to the hazard dealt with by such standard for the period of his working life"[13] (emphasis added). The statute's general definition of occupational safety and health standards said (and says) that these are standards "reasonably necessary or appropriate to provide safe or healthful places of employment."[14]

A straightforward interpretation of the statutory terms, urged by four justices on the Supreme Court, would seem to suggest that no significant risk need be shown.[15] The key statutory language is the "no employee will suffer" phrase, which indicates that even if a toxic substance places only one or a few workers in jeopardy, the agency must act to provide protection. Whatever the meaning of the obscure general definitional clause ("reasonably necessary or appropriate"), the more specific provision, dealing with toxic substances, would appear to trump any contrary indications in the more general one. Nonetheless, a plurality of the Court rejected OSHA's argument to this effect and hence rejected OSHA's interpretation of the statute.

In holding that a "significant risk" must be shown, the plurality contended that a contrary interpretation would defy common sense. "In light of the fact that there are literally thousands of substances used in the workplace that have been identified as carcinogens or suspected carcinogens, the Government's theory would give OSHA power to impose enormous costs that might produce little, if any, discernible benefits."[16] Though the plurality left undecided the question whether the agency must also show a reasonable proportion between costs and benefits, it is clear, from the passage just quoted, that the "significant risk" requirement was motivated partly by the desire to ensure some kind of proportionality between benefits and costs, on the theory that the requirement serves to protect against the most egregious disproportions.[17]

In *American Textile Manufacturers' Institute v. Donovan*,[18] however, the Court emphasized what it saw as the ordinary meaning of the word "feasible" in order to hold that OSHA was not required to engage in cost-benefit balancing. In the Court's view, the agency's job is to ensure that all regulated risks are "significant." Once a significant risk is shown, the agency is required to regulate to the point where compliance would no longer be "feasible," in the sense of practicable.[19] The fact that a regulation violated a cost-benefit test is neither here nor there. This holding raises many questions. For the moment, the key point is that the Court's interpretation of OSHA builds on the idea that de minimis exceptions are permitted to reach a conclusion that insignificant risks may not be regulated at all.

No Benefits, No Regulation

In an important case involving hazardous wastes, the court of appeals interpreted the Clean Air Act aggressively, so as to prohibit EPA from imposing regulation without a showing that the regulation would actually clean the air. *Chemical Manufacturers Assn. v. EPA*[20] involved an unusual rule requiring hazardous waste combustors to comply with new emissions standards. The EPA established a bifurcated compliance schedule. Combustors would have three years to modify their existing facilities and processes to come into compliance with the standards. But if combustors decided on "early cessation" and found that it was not cost-effective to make the required changes, they would be required to cease burning hazardous waste entirely within two years.

At first glance, the EPA's program seems to make a great deal of sense. Those attempting to make expensive changes should receive a longer period for compliance than those refusing to make such changes. But EPA itself acknowledged that those who chose "early cessation" would not necessarily clean the air, but would actually redirect hazardous waste to other "facilities to be burned under essentially the same conditions."[21] Thus the early cessation rule would have no significant beneficial effects on hazardous waste or on hazardous waste pollution. "It will instead merely reallocate which combustion facilities process the same hazardous waste under the same conditions."[22] The court held that in these circumstances the rule was unlawful, because it would not promote the purpose of the act, which was to clean the air. In the court's view, it is simply unreasonable "to impose costly obligations on regulated entities" without showing that those obligations would help to promote the act's environmental goals.[23] "Given the absence of environmental benefits—indeed, the possibility of environmental harm," the rule could not be valid.[24]

Chemical Manufacturers Association is a striking application of the principle that regulation should be expected to deliver significant benefits. The court seems to be urging that agencies will not be permitted to require expensive activity without a showing that the expense will improve the environment. We have seen that interest groups often use regulation for their own purposes, and an issue involving interest-group pressure lurks in the background here: Commercial waste incinerators, intervenors in the case, stood to gain a great deal from the rule, because it would transfer business to them. It is reasonable to speculate that the court feared that the EPA was issuing a regulation, nominally based on environmental grounds, that would favor a well-organized private group with an economic stake in the outcome.[25]

There is a general lesson here. Whenever government regulation is producing few benefits, or no benefits, we have reason to fear that interest-group power is involved. The principle in favor of de minimis exemptions can be understood, in significant part, as an effort to reduce that risk. The point holds for other cost-benefit principles as well, as we shall now see.

Substitute Risks

Extensive attention has recently been given to the problem of "risk-risk" or "health-health" trade-offs, which arise when regulation of one health problem creates another health problem.[26] Recall a simple case: More stringent fuel economy standards for new cars, justified partly on environmental and thus health-related grounds, could have the effect of leading automobile manufacturers to produce smaller and more dangerous cars, thus resulting in a significant loss of life in accidents. Is the agency entitled to take this possible effect into account? Or suppose that the FDA is asked to require genetically engineered foods to be labeled as such. If the labels would lead consumers to switch to less-safe substitutes, such as organic foods,[27] may the FDA take that effect into account? Or suppose that the Federal Aviation Administration is asked to require children under the age of three to have their own seats in airplanes. The regulation might be urged on the ground that it would prevent a number of injuries in the air and also produce protection in the event of a crash. In the abstract, it is reasonable to think that children will be helped as a result. But suppose that a consequence of the mandatory purchase of a seat would be to lead many parents to drive rather than fly, on the ground that flying has suddenly become significantly more expensive. It is possible that the overall consequence of the proposed FAA rule would be that more children will die. Is the FAA permitted to take this effect into account? More generally, is the FAA entitled to consider the possibility that steps taken to promote security on airlines might not only increase cost and inconvenience, but also cause people to drive instead, which is less safe?

The Lesser of Two Evils?

The problem of substitute risks is quite general, extending to the situation in which bans gives rise to "replacement risks." A prohibition on asbestos—an admitted carcinogen—will not be so helpful if producers respond by using substances that are equally dangerous. Are agencies allowed to consider the possible consequences of dangerous substitutes? The phasedown of lead from gasoline was a real success, insofar as the benefits clearly exceeded the costs. But the government did not ask a question about substitutes—specifically, about the extent to which aromatics such as benzene would be used instead—and hence failed to anticipate the increased use of serious pollutants, including benzene, toluene, and xylene. An agency that is alert to the use of substitutes might well seek to ensure that any ban is accompanied by restrictions on hazardous replacement risks—or that the ban is softened if the replacement risks are inevitable. Are agencies entitled to think about this kind of thing?

Recent cases suggest an emerging principle of interpretation, in the form of a strong presumption in favor of permitting (and perhaps even requiring) agencies to take account of substitute risks, and hence to undertake health-health trade-offs. In *American Trucking Associations*, for example, it was argued that while ground-level ozone creates certain health risks, it also produces certain health benefits, above all because it provides protection against skin cancer and cataracts.[28] The EPA responded that it lacked authority to consider the risks created by regulation or (to put the point slightly differently) the health benefits of an air pollutant.[29]

Taken on its own, the statutory text seemed to support the EPA's view, or at least to make that view a reasonable interpretation of ambiguous terms. The statute provides that ambient standards must be based on "criteria" documents, which are supposed to include "the latest scientific knowledge useful in indicating the kind and extent of all identifiable effects on public health or welfare which may be expected from the presence of such pollutant in the ambient air, in varying quantities."[30] EPA urged, plausibly, that the phrase "identifiable effects" of "such pollutant" was meant to refer to the adverse effects of the pollutant, not to its beneficial effects.

But the court concluded that the statute could not be interpreted in that way.[31] In a passage that suggests a strong presumption in favor of health-health trade-offs, the court said (unconvincingly) that the statute was unambiguous, and (far more convincingly) that "EPA's interpretation fails even the reasonableness standard. . . ; it seems bizarre that a statute intended to improve human health would . . . lock the agency into looking at only one half of a substance's health effects in determining the maximum level for that substance."[32] What is most striking about this suggestion is that the court seems to have gone beyond the view that the agency is permitted to engage in health-health trade-offs if it chooses, and to require the EPA to do so even if it would choose otherwise. (This aspect of *American Trucking* was not at issue in the subsequent Supreme Court litigation.)

Or consider *Competitive Enterprise Institute v. NHTSA*,[33] where the plaintiffs challenged fuel economy standards precisely on the ground that the agency had failed to take account of the adverse effects of such standards on automobile safety. In the face of an ambiguous statute, the court insisted that a full explanation was required for a decision that, in the abstract, would seem to create serious substitute risks.[34] As a result of this decision, it is now the law that NHTSA must take into account any evidence of adverse safety effects in the process of setting fuel economy standards. On remand, NHTSA confronted the evidence and concluded that the alleged effect could not be demonstrated—a conclusion that the court upheld on appeal.[35] It is not at all clear that the agency was right on the facts; there appears to be good evidence that fuel economy standards can lead to smaller, less-safe vehicles, and that an agency that sets fuel economy standards should be aware of this possibility and attempt to prevent it. But what is important for present purposes is the clear holding that the agency is permitted and even obliged to consider health-health trade-offs in setting fuel economy standards.

The EPA and Drinking Water

In some cases, judicial permission to consider substitute risks has done real violence to statutory language. Consider, for example, the EPA's approach to lead contamination in water. The Safe Drinking Water Act requires the EPA to produce maximum contaminant-level goals (MCLG) for water contaminants.[36] These goals are required to "be set at the level at which no known or anticipated adverse effects on the health of persons occur," with an adequate margin of safety.[37] For lead, the EPA's MCLG was zero, because no safe threshold had been established. Once an MCLG is established, EPA is required to set a maximum contaminant level (MCL), to be set "as close to the maximum contaminant level goal as is feasible."[38] The EPA is authorized not to set a maximum contaminant level, and to require "the use of a treatment technique in lieu of establishing" that level, if it finds "that is it not economically or technologically feasible to ascertain the level of the contaminant."[39]

At first glance, this set of provisions has a familiar structure. The EPA is required to set a standard of performance, and not to require a "technique" for achieving the desired performance, unless it is not feasible to monitor water quality. For lead, then, we would expect EPA to set its MCL as close as "feasible" (economically and technologically) to the MCLG of zero, except if it was not "feasible" to ascertain the level of lead contamination. But this is not what EPA did, because of some distinctive features of the lead problem. Source water is basically lead-free; the real problem comes from corrosion of service lines and plumbing materials. With this point in mind, EPA refused to set *any* MCL for lead. The EPA reasoned that an MCL would require public water systems to use extremely aggressive corrosion-control techniques, which, while economically and technologically "feasible," would be counterproductive, because they would increase the level of other contaminants in the water. What appeared to be the legally mandated solution would make the water less safe, not more so. The EPA therefore chose a more modest approach. Instead of issuing an MCL, it required all large water systems to institute certain corrosion-control treatment, and required smaller systems to do so if and only if representative sampling found significant lead contamination.

Did the EPA violate the Safe Water Drinking Act? At first glance, it seems clear that it did. The EPA did not contend that an MCL was not "feasible" to implement, nor did it argue that it was not "feasible," in the economic or technological sense, to monitor lead levels in water. Nonetheless, the court upheld the agency's decision.[40] The court accepted the EPA's suggestion that the word "feasible" could be construed to mean "capable of being accomplished in a manner consistent with the act." The court said that "case law is replete with examples of statutes the ordinary meaning of which is not necessarily what the Congress intended," and it added that "where a literal meaning of a statutory term would lead to absurd results," that term "has no plain meaning."[41] Because an MCL would itself lead to more contamination, "it could lead to a result squarely at odds with the purpose of the Safe Drinking Water Act."[42] The court therefore accepted EPA's view that "requiring public water systems to design and implement custom corrosion control plans for lead will result in optimal treatment of drinking water overall, i.e. treatment that deals adequately with lead without causing public water systems to violate drinking water regulations for other contaminants."[43]

It should be plain that the court permitted a quite surprising and even countertextual interpretation of the act. The statutory terms seem to make no room for the EPA's refusal to issue an MCL. Nonetheless, the EPA's refusal made good pragmatic sense in light of the risks that would be introduced by any such regulation. The court's decision is probably the clearest example to date of an aggressive default rule, allowing agencies to ensure that regulation does not introduce problems equivalent to those that it is attempting to solve. It is therefore well established that unless Congress has clearly said otherwise, agencies are entitled to consider health-health trade-offs and the substitute risks sometimes imposed by regulation.

Notes

1. 613 F.2d 947 (D.C. Cir. 1979).
2. *Id.* at 955.
3. Alabama Power Co. v. Costle, 636 F.2d 323 (D.C. Cir. 1979).
4. *Id* at 359.
5. *Id.* at 360 n.89.
6. *Id.* at 360.
7. 763 F.2d 120 (D.C. Cir. 1985).
8. 49 U.S.C. 303(c).
9. *Id.* at 130; the case is expressly understood in this way in *Coalition on Safe Transportation v. Dole*, 826 F.2d 60, 63 (D.C. Cir. 1987).
10. *See, e.g.*, Sierra Club v. EPA, 992 F.2d 337, 343-45 (D.C. Cir. 1993); EDF v. EPA, 82 F.3d 451 (D.C. Cir. 1996); Public Citizen v. FTC, 869 F.2d 1541, 1556-57 (D.C. Cir. 1989); Ohio v. EPA, 997 F..2d 1520, 1535 (D.C. Cir. 1993) (suggesting that "the literal meaning of a statute need not be followed where the precise terms lead to absurd or futile results, or where failure to allow a de minimis exemption is contrary to the primary legislative goal").
11. Public Citizen v. Young, 831 F.2d 1108 (D.C. Cir. 1987).
12. 448 U.S. 607 (1980).

13. 29 U.S.C. 655(b)(5).

14. 29 U.S.C. 652(8).

15. 448 U.S. at 633 (Marshall, J., dissenting).

16. 448 U.S. at 617.

17. *Id.*

18. 452 U.S. 490 (1981).

19. *Id.* at 496.

20. 217 F.3d 861 (D.C. Cir. 2000).

21. *Id.* at 864.

22. *Id.*

23. *Id.* at 867.

24. *Id.*

25. *Cf.* BRUCE ACKERMAN & WILLIAM HASSLER, CLEAN COAL/DIRTY Air (New Haven: Yale University Press, 1985) (discussing alliance between environmentalists and eastern coal companies).

26. *See, e.g., Symposium*, 8 J. RISK AND UNCERTAINTY 5 (1994).

27. *See* ALAN MCHUGHEN, PANDORA'S PICNIC BASKET 201-29, 232-37 (New York: Oxford University Press, 2000).

38. 175 F.3d at 1051.

29. *Id.* at 1051-52.

30. 42 U.S.C. 7408(a)(2).

31. 175 F.3d at 1052.

32. *Id.*

33. 956 F.2d 321 (D.C. Cir. 1992).

34. *Id.* at 324.

35. 45 F.3d 481, 484-86 (D.C. Cir. 1995).

36. 42 U.S.C. 300g-1(b).

37. 42 U.S.C. 300g-1(b)(4)(a).

38. 42 U.S.C. 300g-1(b)(4)(2).

39. 42 U.S.C. 300g-1(b)(6)(D).

40. American Water Works v. EPA, 40 F.3d 1266, 1271 (D.C. Cir. 1994).

41. *Id.*

42. *Id.*

43. *Id.*

THE RELEVANCE OF COSTS 4

We now turn to somewhat more aggressive default principles, allowing agencies to consider costs and to weigh them against benefits. As in chapter 2, my purpose here is descriptive. I will attempt to defend these principles in later chapters.

Considering Costs

The presumption that agencies may "consider costs" has emerged in a series of important cases within the D.C. Circuit. Consider some examples.

At issue in *Grand Canyon Air Coalition v. FAA*[1] was an FAA regulation designed to reduce noise from airplanes over the Grand Canyon. The statute required "substantial restoration" of the "natural quiet." The FAA understood this term to require that the park achieve 50 percent of the natural quiet at least 75 percent of the day. In refusing to impose stricter controls, the FAA explained that it took into consideration "the needs of the air tour industry."[2] From the agency's ambiguous explanation, it appears that the FAA sought partly to protect the air tour industry as such, but mostly to protect tourists in their ability to see the Grand Canyon from the air. Not surprisingly, the FAA had been asked to impose both more strict and less strict regulation, and its decision was contested, by different parties, as both too strict and excessively lenient.

Those challenging the rule emphasized that the FAA's task was to ensure "substantial restoration" of the "natural quiet," and that protection of the air tour industry was a statutorily irrelevant factor.[3] The court responded by invoking something like a presumption in favor of considering cost, noting that nothing in the statute "forbids the government from considering the impact of its regulation on the air tour industry."[4] The court's passage is ambiguous, but it appears to be a recognition that in the face of congressional silence, at least one kind of cost—that involving the air tour industry—will be within agency discretion to consider. The narrowest construction of the court's opinion is that statutes should not be taken to be self-defeating, so that the FAA is permitted to conclude that a statute designed to enable people to enjoy the Grand Canyon by reducing noise should not be implemented with regulation so strict as to prevent people from enjoying the Grand Canyon by air.[5] A broader reading is that under ambiguous statutes, agencies will be presumed able to take into account the costs of various implementation strategies.[6]

Support for the broader reading comes from *George Warren Corp. v. EPA*,[7] where domestic companies challenged the EPA's implementation of the reformulated gasoline provisions of the Clean Air Act. A central question for the EPA was how to treat foreign refiners and importers. In resolving that question, the EPA considered not only air quality benefits, but also the comments of the Department of Energy (DOE). That agency expressed concern that certain approaches could increase the price and decrease the quantity of gasoline by making it more difficult for foreign refiners to divert production to the United States in periods of increased demand.[8] The EPA took this point expressly into account in its rule. The result was an outcome more favorable to foreign refiners and less favorable to environmental protection or domestic competitors than EPA might otherwise have chosen. Nonetheless, the court upheld the agency's decision, emphasizing the absence of an explicit legislative ban on consideration of these economic factors.[9] The court appeared to suggest that an express congressional preclusion of economic factors would be necessary in order to make them irrelevant as a matter of law.

By far the most explicit statement on point, however, comes from *State of Michigan v. EPA*.[10] At issue there was an EPA decision to approve a state implementation plan (SIP) for the regulation of ozone. The statutory term provided that SIPs must contain provisions adequately prohibiting "any source or other type of emissions activity within the state from emitting any air pollutants in amounts which will . . . contribute significantly to nonattainment in, or interfere with maintenance by, any other State with respect to any such national primary or secondary ambient air quality standard."[11]

At first glance, this provision might well be read as an absolute ban on "significantly contributing" pollutants. Congress said, after all, that EPA cannot allow emissions that "contribute significantly"; how can cost be relevant to that issue? But the EPA did not understand the provision to ban consideration of costs. Instead the agency reached a more subtle, even creative conclusion: It would adopt a low threshold for deciding whether a contribution was "significant." But the "significant contributors" would be required to reduce their ozone only by the amount achievable via "highly cost-effective controls,"[12] meaning those that could produce large reductions relatively cheaply. In states with high control costs, then, relatively low reductions would be required.

Apparently because of the clarity of the statutory language on that particular point, no one in the case argued that EPA was required to balance costs against benefits before issuing regulations. Challenging the EPA's interpretation, environmental groups claimed that the statute banned any consideration of costs at all. In their view, "contribute significantly" made no room for an inquiry into the costs of compliance. The court rejected the argument, finding no "clear congressional intent to preclude consideration of costs."[13] But the court obviously had a difficult time with the statutory term "contribute significantly," which seems to refer to environmental damage, not to environmental damage measured in light of cost. In upholding the EPA's decision, the court insisted that significance should not "be measured in only one dimension," that of "health alone." In fact, in some settings, the idea of significance "begs a consideration of costs."[14] In the court's view, EPA would be unable to determine "'significance' if it may consider only health," especially in light of the fact that ozone causes adverse health effects at any level. If adverse effects exist on all levels, how can EPA possibly choose a standard without giving some weight to cost?[15]

But there is a serious problem for this conclusion. Taken together, the OSHA cases seem to argue in the opposite direction. As we have seen, the requirement that OSHA show a "significant" risk (a requirement imposed in the Benzene Case) has not been taken to mean that OSHA must or even may consider costs (with cost-benefit balancing apparently banned by the Cotton Dust Case). To this the court responded that in the aftermath of those cases, OSHA has itself attempted to ensure, and invariably claimed, that the costs of safety standards are "reasonably related to their benefits."[16] In any case, "the most formidable obstacle" to a ban on consideration of cost "is the settled law of this circuit,"[17] which requires an explicit legislative statement to preclude consideration of cost. Here, then, is an express judicial endorsement of a cost-benefit default principle, permitting agencies to consider costs if they seek to do so.

We should see *Michigan v. EPA* as a close cousin to *American Water Works*, discussed in chapter 3. In both cases, the court of appeals permitted the agency to read the statutory text aggressively, perhaps even to amend it, on the theory that the agency's approach was so much more sensible than the approach that would be required by textualism. It seems clear that the Congress that enacted the Safe Drinking Water Act could not foresee the special problems creating by removing lead from water—problems that, the EPA plausibly argued, would make a maximum contaminant level counterproductive. So too for the nonattainment program: From every point of view, the EPA's effort to require only cost-effective controls seemed better than an effort to define "contribute significantly" in a cost vacuum. It is not clear whether the Supreme Court would approve the lower court's rejection of textualism in either case. But if we focus on Congress's inability to foresee the many complexities that arise in the context of implementation, we might well have sympathy for both decisions.[18]

Feasibility

Many statutes expressly require regulation to be "feasible."[19] But what if the statute is silent or ambiguous on whether agencies may impose regulations beyond the point of "feasibility"? Sometimes statutes are "technology-forcing," in the sense that they require companies to innovate, and thus to do more than what current technology permits.[20] Often, however, the technology that is "forced" by statutory requirements is entirely feasible—indeed, that is part of the reason that Congress requires it. In fact, technology-forcing can be justified by cost-benefit principles themselves—if the benefits of forcing technology outweigh the costs, as they sometimes do. Companies might fail to innovate with respect to pollution control simply because they do not internalize all of the benefits of the innovation. But technological innovation is sometimes neither feasible nor justified by cost-benefit principles. Because of large costs, regulation will sometimes raise serious questions from the standpoint of feasibility, in the sense that it will drive many companies out of business or require technologies that are not now and cannot soon be made available. Here the question is how to handle legislative silence.

The question arose most prominently in *NRDC v. EPA*,[21] involving the toxic substances provision of the Clean Air Act. That provision, since substantially revised,[22] required EPA to issue regulations that would provide "an ample margin of safety to protect the public health." The principal question was whether cost was relevant to the EPA's judgment. On its face, the statute might seem to block any consideration of cost and indeed to require regulations that would reduce risks to zero. This is so especially because for many toxic substances, safe thresholds simply do not exist. Alert to this point, the EPA urged that it should be allowed to take feasibility into account in setting regulations. The court accepted this conclusion by suggesting that regulations could avoid "zero risk" in two ways. First, the EPA was required to make an initial, benefits-based, cost-blind determination of what is "safe"; but citing the Benzene Case, the court said that "safe" did not mean "risk-free."[23] Thus "the Administrator's decision must be based upon an expert judgment with regard to the level of emission that will result in an 'acceptable' risk to health."[24] Of course, there is a degree of arbitrariness in any particular judgment here, especially if the judgment is cost-blind. But the court was apparently attempting to ensure a degree of visibility and consistency in agency decisions by ensuring that the "accept-able risk" judgment would be made publicly and would be adhered to in a range of cases.

Second, the court said that in deciding how far to go beyond "safety" in order to provide an "ample margin," the administrator was permitted to consider both costs and feasibility.[25] It is clear that the court engrafted these ideas onto a statute that did not expressly include them. In this sense, the decision suggests an interpretive principle to the effect that a statute that is silent or ambiguous on the point will ordinarily be taken to permit the agency to take account of the feasibility of statutory commands.

Costs and Benefits

If the statute is ambiguous or silent on the point, will an agency be permit-ted to decide in accordance with cost-benefit balancing? Is an agency au-thorized to make such balancing the basis for decision?

NRDC v. EPA

An affirmative answer was given in *NRDC v. EPA*[26] (the same title, but not the same case, as that just discussed). At issue there was the EPA's decision whether to classify a source of fugitive emissions as "major" within the meaning of a statutory provision calling for regulation of "major emitting facilities."[27] The EPA concluded that it would not add certain industrial sources, including surface coal mines, on the ground that the social and economic costs of regulation would outweigh the environmental benefits.[28] The statutory language did not require cost-benefit analysis, and the court emphasized that an alternative construction was not barred by statutory language and legislative history.[29] Nonetheless, the court said that it would treat the agency's interpretation as permissible in the face of legislative silence.

Interpretation of OSHA has showed identical thinking. Outside of the area of toxic substances, the statute (with its opaque "reasonably necessary or appropriate" language) is ambiguous on whether CBA may be made the basis for decision. Here a prominent court went out of its way to say that OSHA is permitted to decide on the basis of cost-benefit balancing if it wishes.[30] In a challenge to the agency's lockout/tagout rule, the court of appeals said that such balancing would be a permissible basis for agency decisions. Indeed, the court seemed to suggest that this would be its pre-ferred route.[31] Thus the court emphasized that in the face of statutory am-biguity, the agency would be permitted to engage in cost-benefit balancing if it chose to do so.

On remand, the agency appeared to decline the court's invitation, choos-ing a test based largely on a mixture of the "significant risk" and "feasibil-ity" requirements. With some reluctance, the court upheld the agency's interpretation as reasonable.[32] But the story does not end there. The agency has continued to say—perhaps to insulate itself from a court challenge— that it finds a "reasonable relationship" between costs and benefits, and in its most recent pronouncement on the issue, the court treats this as an authoritative constructive of the statute.[33] It remains to be seen whether an OSHA regulation that does not show such a reasonable relationship might be challenged as unlawful.

The TSCA Wrinkle

An especially aggressive ruling, with a statutory text that is favorable to cost-benefit balancing, is *Corrosion Proof Fittings v. EPA*.[34] What makes this a wrinkle is that, as in the Benzene Case, the court said not merely that the agency is permitted to follow an interpretive principle, but that it is required to do so. At the same time, the *Corrosion Proof Fitting* court's decision is the most elaborate statement to date of the emerging federal common law of CBA.

At issue was the EPA's attempted ban on asbestos, an admittedly carcinogenic substance, under the Toxic Substances Control Act (TSCA).[35] TSCA allows EPA to regulate "unreasonable risks,"[36] and it therefore invites some kind of cost-benefit balancing. But the court went far beyond what the statute unambiguously invited. In addition to allowing EPA to engage in cost-benefit balancing, the court required a high degree of quantification from EPA, including explicit comparisons of the cost-benefit ratios for different degrees of regulation and separate discussions of how regulation would affect different industries using asbestos.[37] The court thus insisted that the EPA go beyond a comparison of "a world with no further regulation" and "a world in which no manufacture of asbestos takes place" to include cost-benefit comparisons under different approaches to regulation.[38]

At the same time, the court objected not to the overall cost-benefit ratio, but to the cost-benefit ratios for some areas in which asbestos was to be banned:

> [T]he agency's analysis results in figures as high as $74 million per life saved. For example, the EPA states that its ban of asbestos pipe will save three lives over the next thirteen years, at a cost of $128-277 million (343-76 million per life saved)...; that its ban of asbestos shingle will cost $23-34 million to save 0.32 statistical lives ($72-106 million per life saved); that its ban of asbestos coatings will cost $46-181 million to save 2.22 lives ($14-54 million per life saved)...[39]

With evident incredulity, the court said that the "EPA would have this court believe that Congress . . . thought that spending $200-300 million to save approximately seven lives (approximately $30-40 million per life) over thirteen years is reasonable."[40] All in all, this is an exceptionally aggressive use of the interpretive principle in favor of cost-benefit balancing. The court not only construes statutory text in a way that mandates such balancing, but also requires a demonstration that particular parts, and subparts, of the relevant regulation satisfy a cost-benefit inquiry.[41]

A general point lies in the background here. With safety and health regulation, there is often (not always) a law of diminishing returns: As government controls get more severe, the benefits of increasing severity diminish, to the point where the "last 10 percent" may do very little at all.[42] When cost-benefit analysis is working well, the marginal costs and benefits are balanced—the last dollar, not the first. If the last $10,000 delivers only trivial benefits, regulators should be permitted and even encouraged to think of other, better ways to protect safety and health. The *Corrosion Proof Fittings* case can be understood as an initial effort to draw attention to this fact.

A Note on American Trucking

In a sense, the cost-benefit default principles were tested before the Supreme Court in its important ruling in *Whitman v. American Trucking Associations*.[43] In that case, the Court was asked to say that the EPA could consider costs in setting national ambient air quality standards. The Court refused the invitation, concluding that such standards must be set without regard to cost. The Court emphasized the evident clarity of the statutory provision at issue, which defined national standards as those "requisite to protect the public health."[44] In context, the reference to "public health" seemed to require a cost-blind judgment, based on health alone.

Does *American Trucking* throw the cost-benefit default principles into doubt? The simple answer is that it does not. The Court concluded that the Clean Air Act was unambiguous; it did not by any means suggest that an ambiguous statute would be taken to disallow consideration of costs. Indeed, the Court itself referred, with evident approval, to several of the decisions discussed here, suggesting that none of those cases involved a section sharing the "prominence" of the "requisite to protect the public health" provision.[45] In his separate opinion, Justice Breyer was careful to add that courts "should read silences or ambiguities in the language of regulatory statutes" to permit consideration of "all of a proposed regulation's adverse effects," at least where those effects would clearly be "serious and disproportionate."[46]

Justice Breyer was clearly concerned that the Court's approach would permit consideration of costs only where Congress had been explicit on the point. But at first glance, Justice Breyer's concern seems baseless. The Court was saying only that in view of the clarity of the main provision of the Clean Air Act, judges would be reluctant to find permission to consider costs elsewhere, since Congress "does not alter the fundamental details of a regulatory scheme in vague terms or ancillary provisions—it does not, one might say, hide elephants in mouseholes."[47] This is a standard approach to statutory interpretation. It does not suggest that where a statute's "fundamental details" are vague, they will be interpreted to forbid consideration of cost.

But it would not be impossible to read the Court's opinion a bit more broadly. In concluding that EPA need not consider costs in issuing national standards, the Court emphasized that some provisions of the Clean Air Act explicitly refer to costs, and explicitly require them to be taken into account. Here the Court was using the canon of construction, *expressio unius est exclusio alterius*: the expression of one thing is the exclusion of another. In the particular context of environmental statutes, the *expressio unius* canon could have explosive implications. When Congress does not explicitly refer to costs, agencies may not consider them, and for one simple reason: Congress often does explicitly refer to costs. If the canon is to govern the future, the cost-benefit default principles are in some trouble.

There is a further point. The Court seems to suggest that a statute should not be taken to confer broad discretionary authority on agencies: "We find it implausible that Congress would give to the EPA through these modest words the power to determine whether implementation costs should moderate national air quality standards."[48] To support the view that *American Trucking Associations* (*ATA*) is best taken to disallow agencies to interpret ambiguous statutes to allow consideration of costs, it would be necessary to make a simple, two-step argument. First: Statutes should be construed so as to give agencies less rather than more in the way of discretion. Second: A construction of a statute that would allow agencies to decide whether to consider costs significantly increases agency discretion. Now, the claim here is not that a statute requiring cost-benefit analysis is itself disfavored on delegation grounds. The claim is instead that an interpretation should be disfavored if the consequence of the interpretation would be to authorize the agency to decide whether to engage in cost-benefit balancing. If this claim is accepted, then the default rule in favor of allowing agencies to consider costs stands as repudiated.

But it is most unlikely that the Court would accept these lines of argument. The *expressio unius* canon can be a useful guide to statutory construction, and the more natural, cost-blind reading of "public health" is certainly supported by the fact that some provisions of the CAA make explicit reference to costs. But here, as elsewhere, the *expressio unius* idea should be taken with many grains of salt. If Congress has not, under some ambiguous statutory term, referred to costs, it will often be because Congress, as an institution, has not resolved the question whether costs should be considered. And if this is so, the agency is entitled to consider costs if it chooses.[49] The fact that Congress explicitly refers to costs under other provisions is not a good indication that, under an ambiguous text, costs are statutorily irrelevant. This would be an extravagant and therefore implausible inference. The use of the *expressio unius* approach in *ATA* is best taken as a sensible way of fortifying the most natural interpretation, and not at all as a way of urging that explicit references to cost in some provisions means that costs may not be considered under ambiguous provisions.

What about concerns about agency discretion? Agencies are typically allowed to interpret statutory ambiguities,[50] and in countless cases in which that principle is invoked, the agency exercises a great deal of discretion over basic issues of policy and principle.[51] To allow an agency to decide to consider costs is not to allow it to exercise more discretion than it does in numerous cases. Where the statute is unclear, agencies should be authorized to seek "rational regulation," and nothing in *ATA* suggests otherwise.

This is especially so in light of the fact, emphasized by both the Court[52] and Justice Breyer,[53] that the Clean Air Act allows EPA to consider costs at numerous stages in the implementation process. Both cost and feasibility are relevant, for example, to states deciding on the mix of control devices used to achieve compliance; those facing economic hardship can seek an exemption from state requirements. The EPA is also permitted to consider costs in setting deadlines for attainment. Congress is also available to extend deadlines if necessary. In fact, noncompliance with national standards has been a persistent pattern under the act, in part because compliance can be so costly. The relevant provision of the CAA might be cost-blind, but this is not at all true for the statute as a whole.

These are extremely significant points, relieving the pressure to interpret the provision at issue to allow consideration of cost and apparently giving the EPA a great deal in the way of flexibility. I conclude that *ATA* is best taken not to question the cost-benefit default principles, and indeed that the most reasonable reading of the opinion is that the Court has explicitly embraced those principles.

Notes

1. 154 F.3d 45 (1998).
2. *Id.* at 48.
3. *Id.* at 49.
4. *Id.*
5. Careful readers will notice that whether this conclusion is necessary to prevent the statute from being self-defeating depends on how the statute's purposes are characterized: If the purpose is to reduce noise for those visiting the Grand Canyon, an interpretation that would ignore the interests of the air tour industry would not be self-defeating at all. Unfortunately, there is no simple purpose to be "found" behind this statute.
6. This is how the case is read in *Michigan v. EPA*, 213 F.2d 663 (2000).
7. 159 F.2d 616 (1998).
8. *Id.* at 619.

9.   *Id.* at 619-20.

10.   213 F.3d 663 (2000).

11.   42 U.S.C. 7410(a)(2)(D)(i)(I).

12.   213 F.3d at 675.

13.   *Id.* at 678.

14.   *Id.*

15.   *Id.*

16.   *Id.* at 677.

17.   213 F.3d at 678.

18.   *See* Cass R. Sunstein, One Case at a Time 227-40 (Harvard Univ. Press, 1999) (discussing reasons for allowing agencies, but not courts, to depart from text in unanticipated cases).

19.   *See e.g.,* 29 U.S.C. 655(b)(5)(1994).

20.   For general discussion, *see* Bruce LaPierre, *Technology-Forcing and Federal Environmental Protection Statutes,* 62 Iowa L. Rev. 771 (1977).

21.   824 F.2d 1146 (D.C. Cir. 1987).

22.   *See* 42 U.S.C. 7412.

23.   824 F.2d at 1149.

24.   *Id.*

25.   *Id.* at 1150-51.

26.   937 F.2d 641 (D.C. Cir. 1991).

27.   42 U.S.C. 7475.

28.   937 F.2d at 643.

29.   *Id.* at 645.

30.   International Union, UAW v. OSHA, 938 F.2d 1310 (D.C. Cir. 1991).

31.   *Id.*

32.   International Union, UAW v. OSHA, 37 F.3d 605 (D.C. Cir. 1994).

33.   *See* Michigan v. EPA, 213 F.3d 663 (2000).

34.   947 F.2d 1201 (5th Cir. 1991).

35.   15 U.S.C. 2600 et seq.

36.   The term appears no less than 35 times in 33 pages of the statute. *See* William Rodgers, *The Lesson of the Owls and the Crows,* 4 J. Land Use & Envtl. L. 377, 379 (1989).

37.   947 F.2d at 1205-07.

38.   *Id.* at 1208.

39.   *Id.* at 1209.

40.   *Id.*

41.   *See also* American Dental Ass'n v. Martin, 984 F.2d 823 (7th Cir. 1993) (upholding OSHA regulations designed to protect against hepatitis and AIDS, and noting that the "rule's implicit valuation of life is high—about $4 million—but not so astronomical certainly by regulatory standards, as to call the rationality of the rule seriously into question, especially when we consider that neither Hepatitis B nor AIDS is a disease of old people").

42.   The point is emphasized in Stephen Breyer, Breaking the Vicious Circle (1993).

43.   121 S. Ct. 911 (2001).

44.   42 U.S.C. 7409(b)(1).

45.   121 S. Ct. at 910.

46.   121 S. Ct. at 921.

47. *Id.* at 910.
48. *Id.*
49. *See* Chevron v. NRDC, 467 U.S. 462 (1984).
50. *See id.*
51. *See, e.g., id.*; Babbitt v. Sweet Home Chapter, 515 U.S. 687 (1995); Young v. Community Nutrition Inst., 476 U.S. 974 (1986).
52. 121 S. Ct. at 910.
53. 121 S. Ct. at 921.

UNDERLYING CONSIDERATIONS | 5

We now see that the cost-benefit default principles are playing a major role in federal regulatory law. But what are the foundations of these principles? What is their rationale? Though the various default principles should be evaluated separately, there are common concerns in the background. Let us begin with statutory interpretation in general.

Ambiguity, Absurdity, and Excessive Generality

There is nothing new or unusual about default principles for statutory interpretation. They are ubiquitous. In fact, they are inevitable.[1] Language has no meaning without default principles of many kinds; everyone uses them every day. Generally such principles are agreed upon, so much so that they do not seem to be principles at all. They are part of what it means to understand the relevant language. They need not even be identified, much less defended. But sometimes the principles are contested, or at least subject to contest, and in such cases they must certainly be identified and defended, and the fact that they are being used is obvious to all.

Three Kinds of Default Principles

We might distinguish three circumstances here.

The simplest cases involve genuine ambiguity, in the sense that without resort to an identifiable default principle, courts really do not know what the statutory term means. Here the default principle will operate as a tie-breaker, authorizing an agency to act when the case is otherwise in equipoise. The use of default principles is uncontroversial in such cases; without such principles, cases cannot be decided.

Less-simple cases involve texts that are most naturally or easily taken to forbid the agency action, but that nonetheless contain ambiguity. Here the default principles are serving as "clear statement" principles—suggesting that the statute will be understood to allow the agency to do what it seeks unless Congress expressly says otherwise. This is a more aggressive use of default principles, pushing statutes away from the disfavored terrain. It appears to be the law, for example, that agencies will be allowed to consider costs unless Congress expressly prohibits them from doing so;[2] this is a clear statement principle, used not only when courts are in equipoise.

The most complex cases involve the sort of interpretive problem that might be understood to involve *excessive generality* or *absurdity*. This is the kind of problem found when, for example, a statute saying "no vehicles in the park" is applied to a war memorial consisting of a tank used in World War II,[3] or when a nephew who has murdered his uncle seeks to inherit under a will that has not been revoked.[4] In many legal systems, courts will look behind the language of the statute to prevent an outcome that makes no sense and that could not possibly have been intended.[5] This was the court's suggestion about the de minimis exception in *Alabama Power*,[6] and the court's requirement that EPA consider health-health trade-offs was clearly understood in similar terms as an effort to prevent an outcome that would be "bizarre" and hence that Congress could not have wanted.[7] In the environmental context, the Supreme Court itself has said that where a statute's literal meaning would produce absurdity, the term "has no plain meaning . . . and is the proper subject of construction by the EPA and the courts."[8] This idea has been expressly invoked in favor of allowing the EPA to consider the substitute risks produced by aggressive regulation of lead in water.[9] The avoidance of absurdity might easily be seen as a clear statement principle; what I am emphasizing here is that the courts are willing to allow some "bending" of apparently unequivocal language to ensure against ludicrous outcomes.

Sense vs. Nonsense

These are the circumstances for using default principles.[10] But what is the appropriate content of such principles? This is a large question, and it makes sense to begin with established understandings.

Where meaning is not clear, many time-honored principles are designed to give sense and rationality the benefit of the doubt. An old interpretive principle, with roots in almost all legal systems,[11] counsels courts to avoid "absurdity"; sometimes this principle has been used to override statutory language. More particular principles, of considerable current importance, disfavor retroactivity;[12] require Congress to speak clearly if it seeks to create exemptions from the antitrust law; give the benefit of the doubt to Native Americans; and say that agencies will not, on their own, be taken to have the authority to apply statutes outside the territorial boundaries of the United States.[13] It was probably inevitable that, confronted with a wide range of regulatory enactments, courts would eventually develop a set of analogues for the regulatory state—principles that give rationality and sense the benefit of the doubt in the particular context of contemporary regulatory law.[14]

Cost-benefit default principles are best defended on just this ground—that they give sense and rationality the benefit of the doubt and that Congress should not be taken to have mandated irrationality or absurdity.[15] On this count, some of the default principles should be less controversial than others. At the very least, it seems sensible to say that agencies are permitted to ignore trivial risks and to balance the health benefits of regulation against the health costs of regulation. Where Congress has left things unclear, agencies should have discretion to move statutes away from (what they reasonably consider to be) the domain of senselessness. Defended in this modest way, the cost-benefit default principles combine substantive ideas about regulatory policy with institutional ones, in the form of a posture of judicial deference, allowing agencies room to maneuver.[16] Because agencies are specialized in the topic at hand, and because they have a degree of political accountability, they are permitted to do what the cost-benefit default principles authorize. If agencies choose to do otherwise, there is, on the rationale as stated, nothing wrong with that.

But we should acknowledge here that it is possible to discern two different strands in the cases establishing the cost-benefit default principles. Call the first strand *antiregulatory* and the second strand *technocratic*. On the antiregulatory strand, the principles are best seen as an effort to block regulation,[17] perhaps on the theory that regulation is frequently illegitimate from the standpoint of liberty, perhaps on the ground that it usually does more harm than good. The antiregulatory strand links the principles with those prevailing in the discredited *Lochner* era,[18] where courts used both constitutional and interpretive principles to limit regulation. By contrast, the technocratic strand embodies no animus against regulation as such. It is neutral on that question, assessing regulation only on the basis of what the data show. Indeed, it sees cost-benefit analysis as a frequent impetus to regulation, as in the phaseouts of lead and chlorofluorocarbons.[19] For technocrats, the impetus toward cost-benefit analysis is as much a check on insufficient regulation as it is a limitation on excessive controls.

To the extent that the cost-benefit principles are approved here, it is because and to the extent that they embody the technocratic strand, enlisting policy analysis in the service of better regulation. The antiregulatory form is illegitimate, a form of judicial hubris. But it should not be denied that both strands are playing a role in the cases. Let us now investigate some details.

De Minimis Exceptions and Acceptable Risks

The idea that agencies may make de minimis exceptions is an outgrowth of the old idea *de minimis non curat lex*. If the risk at issue is tiny, the agency is not required to eliminate it. Much of the rationale here is a kind of implicit cost-benefit balancing. If regulation occurs, both private and public resources will have to be expended in order to ensure compliance. When the benefits of regulation are trivial, the agency is permitted to refuse to regulate, on the ground that the costs are likely to outweigh any benefits.[20] When the benefits of regulation are trivial, no one is likely to have anything to complain about if regulation is foregone. Those who attempt to complain are likely to be well-organized private groups with a self-interested agenda, unrelated to the purposes for which the statute was enacted.[21]

This understanding has the virtue of helping to account for the courts' otherwise puzzling refusal to allow EPA to make a de minimis exception under the color-additive provisions of the Delaney Clause.[22] Perhaps these decisions are best attributed to the fact that the statutory terms seem quite unambiguous. But as one court emphasized, it is unclear if significant costs are actually created by a decision to ban color additives.[23] While the benefits of a ban are low, the costs are, in the particular circumstances, low as well. If the costs of regulation are trivial, perhaps a trivial gain from regulation is justified too. The general point is that trivial risks are unlikely to be worth private and public resources; they need not be controlled unless Congress has explicitly said that agencies must control them. The *Chemical Manufacturers* case, discussed previously, embodies this idea with the suggestion that costly regulations cannot be imposed unless there is a showing of environmental benefits.[24]

Health-Health Trade-offs

In a way, the idea of "health-health trade-offs" is the simplest of all. If agencies are imposing health risks at the same time that they are protecting health, they should, at the very least, be permitted to take this fact into account. What most matters, after all, is whether risks are being reduced on balance (though distributional and equitable concerns can complicate this claim, as discussed below). Other things being equal, it is hardly desirable for government to reduce the respiratory risks of ground-level ozone if ground-level ozone also provides significant protection against cancer and cataracts.[25] The agency should be permitted to ask whether this is what it should do, subject to review for reasonableness.

This does not mean that a sensible legislature will inevitably ask agencies to compare health risks with health benefits. Perhaps an institutional division of labor is sought, so that some agencies deal with some risks, whereas other agencies attend to others.[26] It is imaginable, for example, that an agency entrusted with promoting fuel economy is not supposed to consider safety issues, which are a province of another institution. If the two agencies are not working at cross purposes and are engaged in some effort at coordination, it is possible that this division of labor makes sense. The only claim is that when an agency is aggravating one health problem while it is resolving another, it ought to be permitted to take that factor into account unless Congress has said otherwise. In any case, permission to engage in health-health balancing helps counteract the constant risk of tunnel vision on the part of regulators.

At this stage it might be asked why, to many people, health-health analysis seems so much less controversial than cost-benefit analysis. Many people seem skeptical of the idea that costs should be balanced against lives saved,[27] but few are skeptical of the idea that lives saved should be balanced against lives lost. The simplest explanation is that people have a great deal of difficulty in trading off life against dollars, not only cognitively but also morally, and the very idea of ascribing an explicit monetary value to a (statistical) life remains controversial.[28] When people are asked to weigh health against health, the mental operation is far less troublesome. People generally agree that agencies should attempt to save more lives on balance, rather than fewer. Note that this is a descriptive point about how people tend to think, intended to help explain what might seem to be an anomaly; it is not a normative point at all.

Costs, Feasibility, and Costs vs. Benefits

Why are agencies presumptively entitled to consider costs? The basic idea must be that a "benefits only" approach also reflects a kind of tunnel vision, a myopic focus on only one of the variety of things that matter. Suppose, for example, that one approach to regulation would produce a certain level of air quality benefits, but at a cost of $800 million—and that another competing approach would produce a very slightly lower level of air quality benefits, but at a cost of $150 million. If costs can be made relevant, the agency is permitted to do what seems quite sensible: to save the $650 million on the ground that the benefits of the expenditure would not be high enough to justify the expenditure.

Of course, it would be necessary to know a great deal more to know how to evaluate the particular problem. If the $650 million would mean a significant loss of jobs, and if the lower air quality benefits would not result in significant mortality or morbidity effects, it seems most sensible not to expend the resources. But if the $650 million would mean slightly reduced profits for producers, or slightly increased prices for a dispensable good, and if the air quality benefits would mean a nontrivial reduction in respiratory problems for tens of thousands of asthmatics, the case for more stringent regulation is far stronger. The point is not that a bare accounting of costs and benefits tells officials all of what they need to know.[29] It is only that a sensible agency is entitled to, and does, "consider" the costs of regulation. Congress should not be understood to have banned agencies from doing this. If Congress has a particular reason to require otherwise, it is permitted to do exactly that.

Ideas of this sort help support the closely related idea that agencies are presumptively permitted to compare costs against benefits, and also to consider whether compliance is feasible. As we will see in more detail, the feasibility constraint is both ambiguous and, from the normative perspective, somewhat crude, because there is no identifiable point at which regulation becomes "not feasible." But a feasibility constraint, crude though it is, can be defended in the same basic way as the presumption against mandatory control of insignificant risks: If compliance is not feasible, there is a good chance that regulation is not worthwhile. The least that can be said is that if regulation is so costly that it would force many companies to go out of business, with inevitable adverse effects for workers, the agency ought to have a very strong reason for imposing it.

Notes

1. For discussion from different perspectives, *see* WILLIAM ESKRIDGE, DYNAMIC STATUTORY INTERPRETATION (1996); Cass R. Sunstein, *Interpreting Statutes in the Regulatory State*, 103 HARV. L. REV. 415, 420-35 (1989).

2. Michigan v. EPA, 213 F.3d 663, 678 (D.C. Cir. 2000).

3. *See* H.L.A. HART, THE CONCEPT OF LAW (Oxford: Oxford University Press, 1965).

4. *See* Riggs v. Palmer, 22 N.E. 188 (1889).

5. *See* INTERPRETING STATUTES (D. Neil McCormick et al., eds. 1991).

6. Alabama Power Co. v. Costle, 636 F.2d 323, 360-61 (D.C. Cir. 1979).

7. American Trucking Ass'ns v. EPA, 173 F.3d 1027, 1052 (D.C. Cir. 1999).

8. Chemical Manufacturers Assn. v. NRDC, 470 U.S. 116, 126 (1985).

9. *See* American Water Works v. EPA, 40 F.3d 126, 1271 (D.C. Cir. 1994); American Trucking Ass'ns v. EPA, 173 F.3d 1027, 1052 (D.C. Cir. 1999).

10. I do not explore here the choice between "intentional-mimicking" and "intentional-eliciting" default rules, a choice well elaborated in the law of contract. *See* Ian Ayres and Robert Gertner, *Filling Gaps in Incomplete Contracts: An Economic Theory of Default Rules*, 99 YALE L.J. 87 (1989). In the area of statutory construction, it might be thought that courts should do what they think Congress would have done, if it had made provision on the point (a suggestion that supports the cost-benefit default rules)—and that if courts are unsure what Congress would have done, they should choose a rule that will encourage Congress to be more clear in the future (a suggestion that might argue against some of the default rules, on the ground that without them, Congress will be led to be clearer in the future).

11. *See* INTERPRETING STATUTES, *supra* note 3.

12. Bowen v. Georgetown Univ. Hosp., 488 U.S. 204, 208-09 (1988).

13. *See* Cass R. Sunstein, *Nondelegation Canons*, 67 U. CHI. L. REV. 315 (2000).

14. *Compare* the controversial suggestion, in RICHARD POSNER, ECONOMIC ANALYSIS OF LAW (5th ed. 1999), that the common law embodies principles of economic efficiency. I am suggesting a more modest point—not that courts are pursuing efficiency, economically defined, but that they are converging on a less sectarian, more modest set of ideas,

allowing agencies to move in directions that can be seen as sensible from a wide variety of standpoints.

15. *See* American Water Works v. EPA, 40 F.3d 1266, 1271 (D.C. Cir. 1994).

16. For a powerful attack on unduly complex canons of construction and a plea for simplicity, *see* Adrian Vermeule, *Interpretive Choice*, 75 N.Y. U. L. REV. 74 (2000). I do not deal here with the objection that the cost-benefit default principles make statutory interpretation too unruly. As they operate in the cases, the principles seem reasonably straightforward and not to produce undue complexity. But it is easy to imagine a situation in which these default principles coexisted with a number of others, thus making decisions unnecessarily complex.

17. Of course, there is no avoiding "regulation." What is ordinarily described as "opposition to regulation" is in reality no such thing, but approval of that form of regulation that is embodied in principles of contract, tort, and property law. Nonregulation is not a possibility, short of anarchy. I use the terminology of "regulation" and "antiregulation" to conform to common usage. The real opposition is to specific kinds and forms of regulation.

18. After *Lochner v. New York*, 198 U.S. 45 (1908).

19. *See* RICHARD BENEDICT, OZONE DIPLOMACY 63 (1991); *Cost-Benefit Analysis at EPA* 77-83 (Richard Morgenstern ed. 1998); *id.* at 131-64.

20. Alabama Power Co. v. Costle, 636 F.2d 323, 360-61 (D.C. Cir. 1979).

21. As plausible examples, see Monsanto Co. v. Kennedy, 613 F.2d 947 (D.C. Cir. 1979); Chemical Manufacturers v. EPA. 217 F.2d 861 (D.C. Cir. 2000).

22. Public Citizen v. Young, 831 F.2d 1108 (D.C. Cir. 1987).

23. *Id.* at 1111.

24. 17 F.2d at 865-67.

25. American Trucking Ass'ns v. EPA, 173 F.3d 1027, 1052 (D.C. Cir. 1999).

26. *See* Cass R. Sunstein, *Health-Health Tradeoffs*, *in* FREE MARKETS AND SOCIAL JUSTICE 298 (1997).

27. *See, e.g.*, ELIZABETH ANDERSON, VALUE IN ETHICS AND ECONOMICS (Harvard Univ. Press, 1993).

28. It might well be that the refusal to balance costs and benefits is an overgeneralization of a sound moral posture in ordinary life. In deciding whether to break a promise, or to betray a friend, we do not ordinarily balance costs against benefits, at least not in any simple or direct sense. There is a general understanding that some trade-offs are indeed "taboo," in the sense that certain reasons for action are blocked, not merely outweighed. I speculate that the opposition to CBA, in government policy, is an overgeneralization of moral commitments that work well in the private domain. *See* JONATHAN BARON, JUDGMENT MISGUIDED (Oxford Univ. Press, 1998).

29. *See* Matthew Adler & Eric Posner, *Rethinking Cost-Benefit Analysis*, 109 YALE L.J. 165 (1999) (arguing that CBA is only a decision procedure).

AGENCY PERMISSION VS. AGENCY REQUIREMENTS 6

Thus far we have seen what agencies are *permitted* to do, if Congress is silent on the point. But it is necessary to distinguish between cases in which an agency attempts to do what cost-benefit principles permit and cases in which an agency refuses to do what courts are permitting. We know that for the agency, no legal problem will arise in the first set of cases. What about the second? Might the default principles sometimes require agencies to follow a particular course?

The Framework

To answer this question, some brief background is in order. *Chevron v. NRDC*,[1] the dominant case in the area, sets out the familiar two-step inquiry for judicial review of agency decisions. The first question (step 1) is whether Congress has directly addressed the precise question at issue—more simply, whether Congress has unambiguously banned what the agency proposes to do.[2] Under *Chevron*, agencies are generally permitted to construe ambiguous statutes as they see fit. It follows that even without a cost-benefit default principle, agencies should be permitted to consider costs as long as the statute is ambiguous on the point. When *Chevron* is combined with the default principle, the overall lesson is exceedingly straightforward: Agencies are permitted to consider costs when Congress has not said that they may not.

Under *Chevron*, however, the issue is not finished upon a finding that Congress has not directly addressed the precise question at issue. It remains to ask whether the agency's interpretation of the statute is reasonable (step 2).[3] When the

American Trucking Associations court held that the EPA was required to consider the benefits as well as the risks of a pollutant, it did so partly on the ground that the agency's interpretation to the contrary was not reasonable (because it was, in the court's view, "bizarre"[4]). It is therefore possible that even if an agency's decision does not violate Chevron step one (because the statute is ambiguous), it will nonetheless violate step 2, if the decision can be shown to be arbitrary or "bizarre."

The Framework Applied

If the agency insists that it lacks power to do what the default principles permit it to do, the case is relatively easy. The courts should hold that the agency has the power that it contends it lacks and should remand the case to the agency, instructing it to exercise the power in a reasonable manner. But now suppose the agency has refused to allow a de minimis exemption, or to engage in health-health comparisons, or to consider costs when the statute allows it to do so. If the agency has refused to do what the cost-benefit principles permit it to do, the analysis should address two points relating to *Chevron*, which are explored below.

Congressional Instructions/Judgments

The analysis should consider whether EPA has violated unambiguous congressional instructions or transgressed some judgment made "directly" by Congress. At first glance, the answer, by hypothesis, will be no. The statute is ambiguous rather than clear. The only possible response is that the cost-benefit default rule now operates as a kind of canon of construction, serving as part of the inquiry in *Chevron*, step 1.

The argument is unquestionably adventurous, but not as much so as it might appear. Many canons of construction now work in precisely that way. Consider, for example, the following canons: statutes will not be understood to apply outside the territorial borders of the United States;[5] statutes will not be understood to apply retroactively;[6] statutes will not be taken to raise serious constitutional questions.[7] In all these cases, agency interpretations do not prevail under *Chevron* step 1, not because Congress has expressed its will clearly, but because Congress is required to speak with clarity if it wishes agencies to act in the way that they seek. Perhaps the cost-benefit default principle should be understood in similar terms.

This is indeed possible, but it would require a significant stretch from existing law. The canons discussed above have a degree of longevity—indeed, a straightforward justification from longstanding traditions.[8] The cost-benefit default principles have not yet acquired the status of the canons of construction that operate as part of *Chevron* step 1. It is therefore exceedingly doubtful that an agency's refusal to proceed in the manner suggested by the cost-benefit default principles would be struck down under step 1.[9] At least, it is doubtful at this relatively early stage; perhaps these default principles will coalesce, before long, into agreed-upon background rules, and at that stage they will indeed play a role under step 1.

Reasonableness of the Interpretation

The second point would involve *Chevron* step 2 and consider whether the agency's interpretation of the statute is "reasonable." I believe that the foregoing considerations, supporting the default rules in general, suggest the basis for a particular presumption: The agency's interpretation is to be presumed unreasonable if it interprets the statute to fail to make de minimis exemptions, to disallow health-health trade-offs, not to consider costs or feasibility, to regulate insignificant risks, or to ban cost-benefit balancing. Of these various possibilities, the presumption of unreasonableness is strongest when the agency is attempting to regulate a de minimis risk[10] or refusing to consider health-health tradeoffs.[11] In such cases, the agency's decision seems most obviously unreasonable. Why should expenditures be required for trivial risks? Why should the agency be permitted to increase overall risks? These questions do not have obvious answers.

The argument that agencies would be unreasonable to reject the other default principles is less clear. But even in such cases, any reasonable judgment will ordinarily be based on some kind of weighing of costs and benefits, and not on an inquiry into benefits alone.[12] Return to *Michigan v. EPA*, and suppose that in some states, the costs of reducing the "significant contribution" would be exceedingly high, whereas the benefits would be low, in light of the fact that the risks associated with the relevant concentrations of ozone are not severe. If the costs would be high and the benefits low, on what rationale should be the EPA refuse even to consider the former? Here too there appears to be no good answer.

Notice that what is involved here is a presumption only, and it is rebuttable. It is possible to imagine agency explanations that would show why its view—to reject one or another of the cost-benefit default principles—is reasonable. It is that question to which I now turn.

Rebutting the Presumption

In several contexts, Congress, as well as agencies and courts, could reasonably find the default principles inapplicable. The following sections are intended to identify circumstances in which agencies might sensibly decide not to go in the direction suggested by the default principles—and also in which a reasonable legislature might ban agencies from going in that direction.

Regulating de Minimis Risks

Suppose that an agency has discretion to interpret the relevant statute so as to allow exemptions of de minimis risks for (as an illustration) carcinogenic color additives in food. Suppose that the agency refuses to interpret the statute this way, because (a) the benefits of color food additives are generally low (noncarcinogenic color additives will do about as well), (b) as a matter of science, it is not always simple to distinguish between weak and strong carcinogens, and (c) a flat rule will be simpler to administer. At least at first glance, this sort of explanation seems fully reasonable. It would distinguish the case from one in which the agency attempts to interpret the OSHA statute in such a way as to call for costly regulation of insignificant risks.

Suppose that the agency attempts to regulate risks that (it agrees) cannot be shown to be significant. Suppose that it contends not that it will understand the statute to cover demonstrably insignificant or demonstrably de minimis risks, but instead to cover risks that, in light of existing scientific information, might be small but might also be large—a distinction that cannot be made with existing tools and in light of existing scientific understandings. In other words, the agency interprets the statute to allow regulation where the benefits might be significant, but cannot be shown to be significant given existing knowledge. This, in short, is a case where there is a wide range of expected benefits, from quite low to quite high, and where science cannot choose a probable "point" along the range (not an uncommon situation).

This does not seem to be an unreasonable interpretation of an ambiguous statute. Certainly the agency should be required to identify the range of potential benefits to ensure that the possible gains, discounted by the probability that they will be realized, are sufficient to make regulation worthwhile. The basic point is that when scientific understanding is primitive, it can be perfectly reasonable to regulate risks that might be small but might be large. Indeed, such regulation might even survive cost-benefit balancing, notwithstanding the real possibility that when more is known, the risk will turn out to be de minimis.

Disregarding Costs

Might it be reasonable for an agency to interpret a statute not to allow consideration of costs? In some cases, this would indeed be reasonable. Recall that under the Clean Air Act, the EPA is supposed to set standards at the level that, with an "adequate margin of safety," are "requisite to protect the public health."[13] At first glance it might appear quite unreasonable for the agency not to consider costs if it has the discretion to do so. Whether it is worthwhile to produce a certain level of benefits would seem to depend, at least in part, on the cost of achieving those benefits. But suppose that the EPA urges (as it has for a number of years, and as the Supreme Court has approved[14]) that costs will be considered not in setting standards in the first instance (where health is the sole consideration), but at other, later stages, in the development of state implementation plans and in insistence on deadlines for compliance. In such a system, the EPA would say that national ambient air quality standards are based only on an inquiry into issues of health, that this is a benefits-based judgment, but that the decision how and when to meet those standards, made through complex procedures at the state and federal levels, will consider costs as well as benefits.

In fact, this is how the Clean Air Act now operates.[15] National standards are issued in what is at least nominally a cost-blind manner, but costs emphatically and openly play a part at other stages of the process, in the design and enforcement of state implementation plans. Whether or not it is ultimately convincing, this kind of procedural defense of "health only" judgments seems at least plausible. From this it follows that even if the relevant provisions of the Clean Air Act are taken to be ambiguous,[16] it would be reasonable, under *Chevron* step 2, to understand national standard setting to be cost-blind, not because cost-blindness is itself reasonable (it is not), but because costs are taken into account at later stages of a multistage inquiry.[17] Whether it would be better for costs to be considered throughout is an issue on which reasonable people can differ. This is a highly pragmatic question on which general enthusiasm for cost-benefit balancing is not decisive.

Disregarding Particular Costs

There are other arenas in which costs might reasonably be disregarded by agencies. Suppose, for example, that the FAA concluded that the needs of the air tour industry were entitled to no weight in issuing regulations controlling noise at the Grand Canyon. Under a different administration, the FAA might believe that the statute is best understood to ensure that those who enjoy the Grand Canyon can do so with a minimum of noise— and that the adverse effects on the air tour industry are irrelevant, even if this means that fewer people will be able to enjoy the Grand Canyon. At first glance, this is an entirely reasonable judgment. Where Congress has been unclear, administrations and administrators might make different decisions on that question.

Disregarding Feasibility

Is it ever reasonable for an agency to ignore the question whether regulation is feasible for the industry? Might the FAA choose to interpret an ambiguous statute so as to impose an air quality regulation that would not be feasible for the air tour industry over the Grand Canyon, so that the relevant companies could not stay in business? At first glance, feasibility seems relevant, but it is possible to imagine cases in which an agency might reasonably choose to interpret a statute to allow rules that are not feasible. The agency might believe that it is more important to reduce noise levels than to allow the continued operation of the air tour industry. When judgments of this kind are made, the agency is effectively engaging in a kind of cost-benefit balancing, one that justifies regulation that is not feasible. Of course, an agency might engage in technology-forcing, though usually this approach depends on a judgment that regulation is indeed feasible, because more advanced technologies are feasible to develop.

Rights and Irreversibility

Thus far the discussion has emphasized pragmatic or instrumental considerations. But are there contexts in which the cost-benefit default principles are inapplicable in principle? In many domains, cost-benefit balancing fails to describe the operation of law; rights-based thinking often "blocks" resorts to costs, or at least costs of a certain kind. Ordinarily, ideas of this sort play a role in constitutional law,[18] where certain "costs" are off-limits. For example, the costs undoubtedly associated with politically controversial speech are not a legitimate basis for regulating such speech. Those costs are entitled to no weight at all; it is not as if they count but are insufficiently high.

Such thinking is not foreign to regulatory policy. The most vivid example is the Endangered Species Act,[19] which forbids the agency from engaging in action that would threaten members of endangered species even if a balancing test would appear to justify the action.[20] In holding that the statute disallows balancing, the Court relied on what it said was the unambiguous meaning of the text.[21] But as Justice Powell urged in dissent, the language was perhaps not so clear as to disallow invocation of a strong default principle, one that would justify a degree of balancing.[22] Can the outcome in the case be explained in a legal system pervaded by cost-benefit default principles?

Perhaps it cannot be. Perhaps the Court's decision is an anachronism, inconsistent with the more contemporary judicial enthusiasm for balancing. But there is another explanation. The Endangered Species Act is concerned with preventing genuinely irreversible losses, and at least in the context of human activities that cause extinction, perhaps the statute is best taken to be rooted in a theory of rights, one that rebuts the presumption in favor of cost-benefit balancing. It is possible that some kind of "meta" balancing justifies a flat prohibition on actions that would destroy members of an endangered species. Perhaps that higher form of cost-benefit balancing calls for a refusal to engage in cost-benefit balancing in particular cases. The benefits might be thought to be so high, and the costs usually so low, as to support such a prohibition. But this way of understanding the statute seems to misconceive its foundations, which lie in a judgment that human beings should not knowingly bring about the extinction of other species,[23] at least in the absence of truly extraordinary circumstances.[24]

It is possible to generalize from this example. Where regulatory policy is designed to ensure against irreversible damage, or otherwise to prevent the violation of rights, the cost-benefit default principles might well be displaced. In most domains of regulatory policy, however, what is involved is not the danger of irreversible loss but instead issues of degree, and hence the presumption remains intact.

Notes

1 467 U.S. 837 (1984).

2. *Id.* at 842.

3. *Id.*

4. 173 F.3d 1027, 1052.

5. EEOC v. Arabian American Oil, 499 U.S. 244, 248 (1991).

6. Bowen v. Georgetown Univ. Hosp., 488 U.S. 204, 208-09 (1988).

7. DeBartolo v. Florida East Coast, 485 U.S. 568 (1988).

8. *See* ANTONIN SCALIA, A MATTER OF INTERPRETATION (Princeton Univ. Press, 1997) (defending canons if and only if they are vindicated by tradition).

9. Evidence to this effect comes from *International Union, UAW v. OSHA,* 37 F.3d 605 (D.C. Cir. 1994) (upholding agency decision not to make CBA the basis for decision under a statute that, in the court's view, would have allowed the agency to do this).

10. This is the apparent holding of *Chemical Manufacturers, supra,* at 866-67, holding that the agency is not permitted, under step 2, to impose a regulation that has no environmental benefits.

11. This appears to be the court's holding about the benefits of ground-level ozone in American Trucking Ass'ns v. EPA, 175 F.3d 1027, 1051 (D.C. Cir. 1999).

12. *But see id.* (upholding a significant risk/feasibility reading of the Occupational Safety and Health Act, notwithstanding a previous decision suggesting that cost-benefit balancing would have been a permissible reading).

13. 42 U.S.C. 7409(b).

14. Whitman v. American Trucking Ass'ns, 531 U.S. 457 (2001).

15. *See* 42 U.S.C. 7410.

16. I do not believe that they are, for reasons given in *Lead Industries, supra,* and followed in *American Trucking Ass'ns, supra* note 11.

17. From this it follows that the Supreme Court properly rejected the plea for cost-consciousness in *American Trucking Ass'ns, supra,* not by rejecting cost-benefit default rules, but by invoking the clarity of the statutory text and the fact that, taken as a whole, the system for implementing national ambient air quality standards is far from cost-blind. Of course, this is not a claim that, as a matter of policy, the current system is optimal.

18. *See* Richard Pildes, *Why Rights Are Not Trumps,* 27 J. LEGAL STUD. 725 (1999).

19. 16 U.S.C. 1531 et seq.

20. TVA v. Hill, 437 U.S. 153 (1978).

21. *Id.* at 162.

22. *Id.* at 166 (Powell, J., dissenting).

23. *See* ROBERT PERCIVAL ET AL., ENVIRONMENTAL REGULATION 1085-89 (2000).

24. In the wake of *TVA v. Hill*, Congress amended section 7 of the act to establish a special committee, known as the "God Squad," to make exemptions, and thus to permit action to go forward, under extraordinary circumstances. In the decades since the amendment, no wholesale exemption has ever been granted.

Unsettled Questions | 7

Cost-benefit default principles leave many open questions. They are abstract and general. Courts have done extremely little to particularize them; agencies have done somewhat more, but they have made only a start.[1] The Office of Management and the Budget (OMB) has set out "best practices" for agency use;[2] because of the importance and generally high quality of OMB's guidance, excerpts are included as Appendix C. It is here that a great deal of law will be made in the next decades. Following is a discussion of the crucial issues.

The Incipient Common Law of Acceptable Risks

What makes a risk "significant" or "de minimis"? Here the law is extremely ill-developed. Perhaps we can find some agreed-upon standards for labeling a risk de minimis. If the risk is less than that created by eating a moderate number of peanuts with legally permitted aflotoxin levels, or from living in Denver rather than New York for a week every year, the case seems relatively easy. Risks this slight are the kind that people ignore each day. But how should we evaluate, say, a cancer risk, from a lifetime exposure to a certain carcinogenic substance, of one in 1 million? One in 100,000? One in 10 million? Does it matter if the exposed population is large or small?

These are the pivotal questions. For guidance, it might be noted that the International Commission on Radiological Protection recommends that environmental factors should not be allowed to cause an incremental cancer risk, for those exposed over a lifetime, of 3 in 1,000 or more.[3] But the practice of American agencies is highly variable, with the EPA's acceptable range varying, under different programs, from 1 in 10,000 to 1 in 1 million.[4] In the Benzene Case, the plurality of the Supreme Court attempted to provide some clarification, making a distinction between two quantitatively different levels of risk. If the risk of getting cancer from drinking a glass of water is one in a billion, the plurality said, it could not possibly be considered significant. [5] By contrast, a fatality risk of 1/1000 from regular inhalation of gasoline vapors "might well" be considered significant.[6] OSHA has built on this simple idea in issuing its own regulations. Thus the agency has said that a lifetime risk of 1.64/1000 will be counted as significant, whereas a lifetime risk of 0.6 in 100,000 "may be approaching a level that can be viewed as safe."[7]

The effort to look at the statistical risk faced by members of the exposed population is certainly a start, and in light of the Supreme Court's statements, perhaps OSHA's approach is sufficient to survive judicial scrutiny, while the EPA's one-in-one-million standard might be questionable.[8] An effort at quantification is a helpful way of clarifying the basis for the agency's decision, especially laudable in light of the slipperiness of the idea of "significance." But many questions might be asked. In deciding whether a risk is trivial or significant, it would seem important to ask not only about the level of the risk faced by each person, but also about the size of the exposed population.[9] If two people in the United States face a lifetime risk of 2/10,000, perhaps the risk should not be deemed significant in light of the fact that it is overwhelmingly likely that no fatalities will be suffered. We could easily imagine a challenge to a decision to treat such a risk as "significant" as a matter of law. Certainly the agency should explain any failure to take account of the small number of exposed people—even though it would probably be reasonable, as a matter of law, for the agency to concern itself with probabilities faced by individuals, at least if it is not permitted to engage in cost-benefit balancing.

At the same time, a statistically small risk, if faced by large numbers of people, might well be deemed significant. If 20 million people face a lifetime risk of 1/200,000, 100 people are expected to die—far from a trivial number. If 200 million people face a risk of 1/1 million, 200 people are also expected to die; is this number insignificant merely because the statistical risk, for each person, is small? We could easily imagine a challenge to an agency decision to treat the latter risks as "insignificant"; indeed, that challenge might even be convincing. The point raises serious doubts about the Supreme Court plurality's confidence that a risk of one in a billion, from drinking a glass of water, could not be deemed significant. If each person drinks five glasses of water per day, and if there are 260 million Americans, the one-in-a-billion risk no longer seems so small, converted into expected annual fatalities (474.5, hardly an insignificant number). We should therefore conclude that it is at least reasonable for agencies to consider risks to be "significant," and not de minimis, if the probability is very low but the exposed population quite large. It is also reasonable to suggest that if the probability is very low but the exposed population sufficiently large, a high number of expected fatalities should require the agency to consider the risk "significant" as a matter of law.

There is an additional problem. Both OSHA and the Supreme Court seem to focus on the "lifetime" risk—that is, the risk that would come from being exposed to a substance for all of one's working life. Under OSHA, it does seem that this focus is required by the statute, at least for toxic substances, for which the relevant provision is expressly drawn in terms of lifetime exposure. But in the abstract, and under other provisions, we should not be focusing on the risk of fatality or anything else that would come from a lifetime of exposure, *except to the extent that all, most, or many people actually have a lifetime of exposure.* Imagine, for example, that almost all workers in the relevant industry are exposed, not for their lifetimes, but for five years or less. What risk do they face? This is the crucial question. Perhaps the risk, for them, is a small fraction of the lifetime risk. Sensible policy requires the government to reduce the risks that people actually face, not the risk that people fancifully face. When an agency has discretion, it should look not at lifetime risk, but at actual risk.

What all this suggests is that when agencies are asking whether risks are significant, they ought to move in the direction of setting out a range of "expected benefits" in terms of mortality, morbidity, and other relevant variables.[10] These variables could be aggregated into some sort of total number, below which a risk would be treated as insignificant. Of course, there will be a large degree of guesswork in generating the relevant numbers. There will also be a degree of arbitrariness in choosing the precise point at which risks are no longer significant. But without movement in the direction of quantification, it will not be possible to produce informed, transparent, and consistent policy.[11] Thus an effort to quantify the level of risk that would be deemed acceptable would replace the current system, with its high degree of inconsistency and guesswork, with something like a common law of acceptable risks.[12]

The Meaning of Feasibility: No "On-Off" Switch

What does it mean to say that regulation must be "feasible"? In the abstract, a requirement that regulation be "feasible" might seem to invite cost-benefit balancing. In the private sector, a "feasibility study" is essentially an exercise in cost-benefit balancing. But as we have seen, a feasibility requirement involves no balancing of costs and benefits.[13] It amounts instead to a cost-only inquiry into whether achievement of the regulatory goal is "practicable."[14]

Assume, for example, that a regulation would cost $800 million, and that in the process it would save 10 lives per year; assume also that the exposed population is relatively small, so that each of the exposed workers faces a lifetime risk of well over 1 in 1,000. It is easy to imagine that this regulation would be entirely feasible, in the sense that the industry would face no technical problems in meeting it, and also in the sense that it would be practicable for industry to bear the cost. But it is also easy to imagine that such a regulation would fail CBA, in the sense that the $800 million expense would not be justified by the (relatively lower) monetized savings. If a statistical life is valued at $5 million, for example, the benefits ($50 million) would be only one-eighth the cost.

But it would be wrong to think that CBA is more "antiregulatory" than a feasibility constraint. We can easily imagine a regulation that might not be feasible, but that might satisfy a requirement of cost-benefit balancing. Suppose, for example, that a regulation would cost $2 billion, that industry could not bear that cost without many business failures, but that the regulation would save 5,000 lives. In some cases, the cost-benefit requirement is more protective, not less protective, of intended beneficiaries of regulatory programs.

So far, perhaps, things are clear enough. But there is a problem here as well. Most important: Feasibility is not an on-off switch. Any significant increase in costs is likely to prove "not feasible" for at least some companies. As the costs increase, the number of companies for whom the regulation proves "not feasible" will increase, too. In these circumstances, it seems extremely artificial to say that at a certain point, regulation becomes "not feasible." Perhaps there is a set point at which regulation, by virtue of its stringency, establishes a sudden, large-scale increase in the number of companies that cannot bear the cost of regulatory controls and continue in business. But it is more likely that as the costs grow, the number of companies that cannot bear the cost grows too, perhaps with several specific points at which that number spikes upward. In these circumstances, what sense is made by a "feasibility" constraint? At first glance, very little. Just as safety is not an absolute but a matter of degree, so too for feasibility. Law that says otherwise appears to substitute a comforting but misleading formula for a serious confrontation with the issues at stake.

Perhaps there is an intelligible answer here. Perhaps Congress wants to say that for most regulations, companies must comply, unless a large number of them can show that they cannot comply and continue. And certainly this is a relatively simple inquiry in most cases. What makes little sense is the suggestion that agencies can pick a single point that is "feasible" and go to, but not beyond, that point.

In these circumstances, how can we account for the evident popularity of requirements that regulation be "feasible" or "achievable"? There are several possibilities, suggesting that the feasibility standard might be justified by reference to institutional considerations. From the standpoint of those concerned with safety and the environment, a cost-benefit standard might be thought to introduce undue opportunities for industry to stall the process, perhaps because of the prospect and actuality of judicial review.[15] A requirement that regulation must be "feasible" greatly improves the agency's chances in court. In fact, this conclusion is well-supported by the record of agencies on appeal; no agency has *ever* lost a challenge to the feasibility of its regulation, while cost-benefit requirements have proved troublesome for agencies in court.[16]

This is a point about the goals of supporters of environmental regulation. From the standpoint of Congress, there is a separate point. A statute that expressly refers to cost-benefit balancing seems to invite complaints about the decision to trade off lives for dollars; hence statutes that embody CBA are unpopular in many circles. (It is noteworthy here that *none* of the actual and seriously considered enactments involving cost-benefit balancing has *ever* set out numbers for valuing regulatory benefits.) Legislators who seek to avoid complaints about CBA, while also seeking to impose a constraint on excessive regulation, might naturally be drawn to feasibility requirements. From the standpoint of industry, perhaps "feasibility" statutes are not so troublesome if it is possible to maintain control over the agency's docket and over appropriations, so as to ensure that draconian statutes are, in practice, far less than that.

These points help explain the appeal of feasibility constraints. But they still do not tell us what such constraints mean. The best answer, not entirely satisfactory, is that a regulation becomes infeasible if it would result in significant dislocations in the industry, in the form of large numbers of business failures, substantial losses of jobs, or the equivalent.[17] Ideas of this sort are qualitative rather than quantitative, and in implementation they leave a great deal of discretion to agencies. What might be expected in the future is a more quantitative account from agencies implementing regulations that are said to be feasible, or refusing to impose regulations said to be infeasible.

Considering Costs

What of principles or statutes that ask agencies to "take into consideration" costs (and other relevant factors)? Statutes of this kind typically include an "achievability" constraint as well, one that operates, in practice, in the same way as a feasibility requirement. What is added by the idea that agencies should also take costs into consideration?

The answer seems to be that such provisions give agencies the discretion not to go to the full extent of feasibility if the costs of doing so are disproportionately high. Suppose, for example, that a regulation would cost $800 million and that it would save 10 lives annually. Suppose too that it is entirely feasible. If the agency is permitted to take costs into consideration, presumably it is permitted to impose a less intrusive regulation, or perhaps not to regulate at all. The foregoing sentence is qualified because the idea that costs must be taken "into consideration" does not say how much *weight* costs must have; it does not say, by itself, to what extent agencies must treat costs as relevant to the ultimate decision. Presumably it would be unlawful for an agency to ignore costs altogether. If the agency were permitted to do this, the "consideration" requirement would be empty. At a minimum, then, the agency must discuss cost and explain its decision in light of cost. Similarly, an agency that is allowed to "consider" costs but need not take account of feasibility is authorized to soften regulation by selecting less expensive and also less effective means.[18] Hard questions would arise if an agency authorized to "consider" costs chooses means that are much less expensive but also much less effective.

This is a procedural understanding of the "consideration" requirement, one that has precedent under other statutes.[19] But is there a substantive requirement as well? Must an agency give some kind of weight to costs, in addition to discussing them? The best answer is yes to both questions. An agency decision would be unlawful if it gave no weight whatsoever to costs, as, for example, through the choice of a regulation that would do only trivially more good than one that would be 50 percent less costly. An agency decision would also be doubtful if it made costs an overriding factor, such as, for example, by choosing a regulation that is slightly less expensive (say, $1 million annually) but also much less effective (say, because it would allow 30 additional deaths annually).

In this view, a requirement that an agency take costs into consideration falls short of CBA, in the sense that the agency is expected to give principal weight to the initially identified factor, and from there to make adjustments because of costs.[20] An agency would run into difficulty if it transformed costs into the overriding statutory factor *or* if it gave costs no substantive consideration at all. These are the polar cases for administrative illegality. Cases that fall between the poles should present hard line-drawing questions, but no serious conceptual issues.

Of Costs and Benefits

It remains to discuss the largest problem of all. If cost-benefit balancing is required, what is an agency permitted to do? What is it prohibited from doing? There are hard issues of valuation here. If an agency values a life at $10 million, it will produce outcomes very different from those that would follow if it valued a life at $500,000. Is an agency permitted to value a life at, say, $100 million, or at $50,000?[21]

Basic Issues of Valuation: The Standard Approach

For several decades, agencies have undertaken cost-benefit analysis of major regulations, even when CBA is not the basis for decision but is merely a matter of informing the public about the consequences of proposed courses of action.[22] But how are costs and benefits to be calculated? In principle, the issue is often easier to resolve on the cost side, though the practical problems here can be very serious, especially in light of industry's incentive to overestimate costs. With respect to benefits, the now-standard approach involves an effort to calculate people's "willingness to pay" for the various goods at stake.[23] Sophisticated (though still controversial) methods are available for this purpose.[1]

There remains a good deal of variation across agencies, with statistical lives being valued at between $1.5 million and $6.1 million.[24] With respect to statistical lives, consider the table in Exhibit 7-1.[25] Notwithstanding these variations, willingness to pay is the general basis for undertaking calculations. It is on the basis of this sort of analysis that the EPA compiled the table in Exhibit 7-2,[26] which can be taken as representative. To become intelligible, of course, these numbers must be combined with an assessment of the problems that would be averted with various approaches to regulation. As an example of such an assessment, consider the table in Exhibit 7-3.

A simple exercise of multiplication, putting these tables together, will generate monetized benefits, which can then be compared with monetized costs. Of course, it is possible to challenge the numbers in the tables. Perhaps the agency has understated or overstated the number of lives saved or chronic bronchitis cases; perhaps it has overvalued or undervalued the dollar value of life or other health benefits. In fact, evidence suggests that prospective estimates are bound to contain serious errors. The Office of Technology Assessment, asked in 1992 to evaluate the accuracy of OSHA's prospective estimates, found many mistakes.[27] But the basic method increasingly dominates administrative practice.

Legal Floors and Ceilings

When would a given cost-benefit ratio be held to be unlawful? The simplest answer is that when the costs significantly exceed the benefits (when these are properly measured). A reasonable agency might begin with numbers near the middle of both market valuations[28] and government valuations[29]—in the case of a statistical life, somewhere between $3 million and $7 million. If an agency seeks to deviate from those numbers, it should explain why. The basic idea is that there should be a presumption in favor of adherence to the normal range, with an explanation of departures from the numbers thus indicated. And if the agency seeks to go forward with a regulation whose costs significantly exceed benefits, it should have to explain why.

A legitimate risk in allowing departures is that the stated rationale will conceal an effort to placate powerful private groups not having a strong claim to governmental assistance.[30] Notwithstanding this risk, there are several possible grounds for making adjustments. Both the EPA and its Science Advisory Board have explored the possibility of adjusting the ordinary numbers because of equitable factors, including the involuntariness and uncontrollability of the risk.[31] For example, an agency might make a

(continued on page 80)

Exhibit 7-1 Valuations of Life

Agency	Regulation	Citation	Value ($ mil.)
Department of Transportation—Federal Aviation Administration	Proposed Establishment of the Harlingen Airport Radar Service Area, TX	55 FR 32064 Aug. 6, 1990	1.5
Department of Agriculture—Food Safety and Inspection Service	Pathogen Reduction: Hazard Analysis and Critical Control Point Systems	61 FR 38806 July 25, 1996	1.6
Department of Health and Human Services—Food and Drug Administration	Regulations Restricting the Sale and Distribution of Cigarettes and Smokeless Tobacco to Protect Children and Adolescents	61 FR 44396 Aug. 28, 1996	2.5
Department of Transportation—Federal Aviation Administration	Aircraft Flight Simulator Use in Pilot Training, Testing, and Checking and at Training Centers	61 FR 34508 July 2, 1996	2.7
Environmental Protection Agency	Protection of Stratospheric Ozone	53 FR 30566 Aug. 12, 1988	3
Department of Health and Human Services—Food and Drug Administration	Proposed Rules to Amend the Food Labeling Regulations	56 FR 60856 Nov. 27, 1991	3
Department of Transportation—Federal Aviation Administration	Financial Responsibility Requirements for Licensed Launch Activities	61 FR 38992 July 25, 1996	3
Department of Agriculture—Food and Nutrition Service	Proposed National School Lunch Program and School Breakfast Program	59 FR 30218 June 10, 1994	1.5, 3.0

Exhibit 7-1 Valuations of Life *(continued)*

Agency	Regulation	Citation	Value ($ mil.)
Environmental Protection Agency	National Ambient Air Quality Standards for Particulate Matter	62 FR 38652 July 18, 1997	4.8
Environmental Protection Agency	National Ambient Air Quality Standards for Ozone	62 FR 38856 July 18, 1996	4.8
Department of Health and Human Services—Food and Drug Administration	Medical Devices: Current Good Manufacturing Practice	61 FR 52602 Oct. 7, 1996	5
Department of Health and Human Services—Public Health Service, Food and Drug Administration	Quality Mammography Standards	62 FR 55852 Oct. 28, 1997	5
Environmental Protection Agency	Requirements for Lead-Based Paint Activities in Target Housing and Child-Occupied Facilities	61 FR 45778 August 29, 1996	5.5
Environmental Protection Agency	National Primary Drinking Water Regulations: Disinfectants and Disinfection Byproducts	63 FR 69390 Dec. 16, 1998	5.6
Environmental Protection Agency	Arsenic in Drinking Water	66 Fed. Reg. 7014 Jan. 22, 2001	6.1
Environmental Protection Agency	Radon in Drinking Water Health Risk Reduction and Cost Analysis	64 FR 9560 Feb. 26, 1999	5.8

reasonable upward adjustment if it believes that children are largely at risk—perhaps because more life-years are at stake, perhaps because chil-

Exhibit 7-2   Willingness-to-Pay Estimates (Mean Values)

Health Endpoint	Mean WTP Value per Incident (1990 $)
Mortality Life saved Life year extended	$4.8 million $120,000
Hospital Admissions: All Respiratory Illnesses, all ages Pneumonia, age < 65 COPD, age > 65 Ischemic Heart Disease, age < 65 Congestive Heart Failure, age > 65 Emergency Visits for Asthma	 $12,700 $13,400 $15,900 $ 20,600 $ 16,600 $9,000
Chronic Bronchitis	$260,000
Upper Respiratory Symptoms	$19
Lower Respiratory Symptoms	$12
Acute Bronchitis	$45
Acute Respiratory Symptoms (any of 19)	$18
Asthma	$32
Shortness of Breath	$5.30
Sinusitis and Hay Fever	Not monetized
Work Loss Days	$83
Restricted Activity Days (RAD) Minor RAD Respiratory RAD	 $38 Not monetized
Worker Productivity	$1 per worker per 10% change in ozone
Visibility: residential	$14 per unit decrease in deciview per household
Recreational	Range of $7.30 to $11 per unit decrease in deciview per household (see U.S. EPA, 1997a)
Household Soiling Damage	$2.50 per household per g/m^3

dren are unable to protect themselves and hence have a special equitable claim to government resources.[32] A downward adjustment would similarly be lawful if the agency finds that mostly old people are at risk, so that any extensions of lives would produce a low level of savings in terms of life-years. Or the agency might reasonably conclude that special attention should be given to risks faced by poor people or African-Americans, on the ground that existing injustice is compounded in a situation in which health and environmental dangers are thus concentrated. In its arsenic rule, the EPA offered an analysis of how the benefits would be reassessed if the involuntariness and uncontrollability of arsenic were considered, suggesting that this would produce a 7 percent increase in benefits.[33] In an important essay, Richard Revesz has claimed that the government's failure to make upward adjustments for uncontrollable, involuntary, and dread risks results in a

Exhibit 7-3 Proposed PM$_{10}$ Standard (50/150 _g/m³) 99th Percentile National Annual Health Incidence Reductions
Estimates are incremental to the current ozone and PM NAAQS: (year = 2010)

Endpoint		Partial Attainment Scenario
	Annual PM$_{2.5}$ (_g/m³)	50
	Daily PM$_{2.5}$ (_g/m³)	150
1. Mortality: short-term exposure		360
long-term exposure		340
2. Chronic Bronchitis		6,800
Hospital Admissions:		
3. All respiratory (all ages)		190
All respiratory (ages 65 +)		470
Pneumonia (ages 65 +)		170
COPD (ages 65 +)		140
4. Congestive heart failure		130
5. Ischemic heart disease		140
6. Acute Bronchitis		1,100
7. Lower Respiratory Symptoms		10,400
8. Upper Respiratory Symptoms		5,300
Shortness of breath		18,300
Asthma attacks		8,800
9. Work Loss Days		106,000
10. Minor Restricted Activity Days (MRADs)		879,000

substantial understatement of the monetized benefits of regulation.[34] We could easily imagine a creative legal challenge to rules as insufficiently stringent and insufficiently explained if adjustments are not made, at least if the agency fails to explain itself.

Agencies should also be permitted to take into account the fact that people care about *relative* economic position, not only absolute economic position, and thus to adjust market valuations upward. And the agency could reasonably employ "incidence analysis" to conclude that regulation should go forward notwithstanding the fact that benefits exceed costs (see the reference to distributional considerations in OMB's "best practices" document in Appendix C). If, for example, the benefits are $800 million but are enjoyed mostly by low-income workers, whereas the costs are $900 million but are faced mostly by consumers generally, it seems reasonable for the agency to go forward, at least if Congress has not expressly precluded that judgment.

There is a larger point here. In addition to knowing the benefits and costs of regulation, it is necessary to know *who* bears those costs and enjoys those benefits, and also the particular *nature* of those costs and benefits. Suppose, for example, that an occupational safety and health regulation would have a total cost of $600 million, and that the monetized benefits would be $400 million (including, let us say, 40 lives saved per year, and hence $200 million in monetized savings from fatalities averted). Is it clear that this regulation should not go forward? For various reasons it is not. If the people who are saved are children or teenagers, the uniform-lives-saved number might undervalue the relevant benefits. Equally important: What does the $600 million mean, concretely? Does it mean that prices will increase, by a little, for many people? That cost might be worth incurring. So too if the consequence of the $600 million expenditure would be a reduction in annual profits for companies that already make billions. Or does the cost mean that poor people will lose their jobs? An ideal CBA would tell us something about the *incidence* of both costs and benefits. It makes sense to say that the "bottom line" numbers will not be decisive when an incidence analysis shows that those numbers should be adjusted to take account of the identity of the winners and losers. Of course, it is possible to think that we lack the tools to engage in a good incidence analysis, or that an assessment of distributional issues will be subject to interest-group manipulation, and hence that the "bottom line" numbers should be used for pragmatic reasons.[35]

While these points give agencies a degree of flexibility, they do not give them carte blanche, because they operate in limited domains, and because they come with a duty of reasoned explanation. This duty is procedural, but it is far more than that. In the *Corrosion Proof Fittings* case, for example, it is hard to see how the agency could have justified the extreme cost-benefit ratios that applied to certain bans on asbestos.[36]

The Discount Rate

Perhaps the most difficult issue here, from the theoretical point of view, involves the selection of the appropriate discount rate. How should the agency value future gains and losses? In terms of ultimate outcomes, the choice matters a great deal. If an agency chooses a discount rate of 2 percent, the outcome will be very different from what it would be if it chose a discount rate of 10 percent; the benefits calculation will shift dramatically as a result. If a human life is valued at $8 million, and if an agency chooses a 10 percent discount rate, a life saved 100 years from now is worth only $581.[37] "At a discount rate of five percent, one death next year counts for more than a billion deaths in 500 years."[38] OMB suggests a 7 percent discount rate (see Appendix C), but this is highly controversial. A key question, then, is: What legal constraints should be imposed on the agency's choice?[39]

My basic conclusion is that it is much harder to untangle the theoretical issue than to identify the appropriate posture of reviewing courts. In this highly technical area, courts should generally adopt a posture of deference, requiring agencies only to produce a reasonable explanation for their choice and to show a degree of consistency. Part of the reason for deference is the extreme complexity of the underlying issues. Part of the reason is the risk that an aggressive judicial posture would contribute to the "ossification" of rulemaking[40]—a particular problem in this setting, because any particular discount rate will be easy to challenge, with reasonable arguments suggesting that it is too low or too high.[41] To understand these points, some details are in order.

Usually statutes are silent on the question of appropriate discount rate. In fact, I have been unable to find *any* statute that specifies a discount rate for agencies to follow. On judicial review, the question will therefore involve a claim that the agency's choice is arbitrary. Here the national government shows strikingly (and inexplicably) variable practices. As noted, the Office of Management and Budget suggests a 7 percent discount rate,[42] departing from a 10 percent rate in the 1980s.[43] But agencies are not bound by OMB guidelines, and they have ranged from as low as 3 percent (Food and Drug Administration, Department of Housing and Urban Development) to as high as 10 percent (EPA).[44] In fact, the same agency sometimes endorses different discount rates for no apparent reason—with EPA, for example, selecting a 3 percent rate for regulation of lead-based paint as compared to 7 percent for regulation of drinking water, and a 10 percent rate for regulation of emissions from locomotives.[45] Here government practice seems extremely erratic.

From the purely economic standpoint, there are serious conundrums here.[46] The impetus for discounting future effects stems from the judgment that in the context of money, discounting future benefits and losses is entirely rational, even simple: A dollar today is worth more than a dollar tomorrow. There are two reasons: investment value (or opportunity cost) and pure time preference.[47] A dollar today can be invested, and for this reason it is worth more than a dollar a year from now. An emphasis on the investment value of money yields a discount rate of roughly 5 percent to 7 percent. Quite apart from this point, people generally seem to have a preference for receiving money sooner rather than later. People value current consumption more than they value future consumption; for this reason alone, $1,000 is worth more today than it is in a decade. An inquiry into pure time preference produces discount rates of 1 percent to 3 percent. Though they lead to different numbers, both points justify discounting future income gains and losses.

So far, so good. The problem is that notwithstanding conventional wisdom among economists, these points are not easily taken to justify a discount rate for the nonmonetary benefits of regulation (see Appendix A, Table A-5 for an overview of such benefits). If a regulation will save 10 lives this year and 10 years annually for the next 10 years, it cannot plausibly be urged that the future savings are worth less than the current savings on the ground that a current life saved can be immediately "invested." The point about investment value or the opportunity cost of using capital seems utterly irrelevant here. With time preference, things are less clear. Perhaps people would rather save 10 lives today than 10 lives in a decade. But it is unclear that this is so; and even if it is, what moral status would such a time preference have? Almost certainly it makes sense to say that it would be worse for you to lose your limb now than to lose it in 10 years; in the latter case, you will have 10 years of use of the limb. And probably it makes sense to say that agencies should attend to life-years saved, not only lives saved. But holding all this constant, the death of a 35-year-old in 2004 does not seem worth more than the death of a 35-year-old in 2044. And since different people are involved, the moral problem is serious: The preference of the chooser in 2002 is certainly relevant to determining that chooser's own fate and the timing of risks that might come to fruition for that chooser; but the chooser's preference cannot easily be used to determine the fate of someone not yet born.

These points illustrate that, as Richard Revesz suggests, it is important to distinguish two issues that go under the name of "discounting" and that have yet to be separated in administrative practice: (a) latent harms, in the form of exposures whose consequences will occur late in someone's lifetime; and (b) harms to future generations.[48] It is reasonable to say that latent harms should count for less than immediate ones, since they remove fewer years from people's lives, and because people do seem to prefer, other things being equal, a harm in the future to a harm in the present. For latent harms, some kind of discount rate is sensible. Consider, for example, the case of arsenic. In its regulation, the EPA treats an arsenic death in the future as equivalent to an arsenic death in the present, even though an

arsenic death is likely to come, if it does come, many years after exposure.[49] On this count, the EPA's judgment seems wrong, even arbitrary;
some kind of discount rate is clearly appropriate here.[50] It would be easy to
imagine a challenge to the failure to discount the latent harms here. On the
other hand, OMB's 7 percent figure, based on the investment value of
money, is probably too high.[51] There is no reason to believe that the discount rate for future health harms is equal to the discount rate for future
income effects, and considerable reason to believe otherwise.[52] Indeed, the
use of a 7 percent discount rate, if it decisively affects the ultimate decision, would seem to be legally doubtful—arbitrary in its own way.

But the case of harms to future generations, or people not yet born, is
altogether different, and in that case the usual grounds for discounting
monetary benefits are quite inapplicable. For this reason some people think
that no discounting is appropriate for the nonmonetary benefits of regulation.[53] In this view, a life-year saved is a life-year saved, and it does not
matter, for purposes of valuation, when the saving occurs.

But there is a major objection to this way of proceeding: It would
appear to require truly extraordinary sacrifices from the present for the
sake of the (infinite) future. Perhaps the "failure to discount would leave
all generations at a subsistence level of existence, because benefits would
be postponed perpetually for the future."[54] On the other hand, it is not clear
that the assumption behind this objection is convincing. Technological and
other advances made by the current generation benefit future generations
as well, and hence impoverishment of the current generation would inevitably harm those who will come later.[55] In any case there is a hard ethical
question here—how much the current generation should suffer for the benefit of the future—and a judgment against discounting would not answer
that question unless we were sure that as a matter of policy, we should be
engaging in maximizing some aggregate welfare function.[56] It is not at all
clear that this form of maximization is the appropriate choice to make.

At this point it should be clear that these issues are exceedingly complex and that agencies asked to engage in CBA have no clear path to an
appropriate choice of discount rate for future generations. My principal
topic, however, is not regulatory policy, but the implementation of the
cost-benefit default principles. In the face of the underlying conundrums,
the most that a reviewing court can require is a rationale for the agency's
choice that is both articulated and reasonable. There are several possibilities here,[57] suggesting what courts should and should not do.

1. Courts should not require costs and benefits to have the same discount rate, at least not if costs are to be absorbed in terms of dollars
and benefits will come in terms of fatalities and illnesses averted. It
follows that in the *Corrosion Proof Fittings* case, the court of appeals was quite wrong to tell EPA to produce an "apples-to-apples

comparison, even if this entails discounting benefits of a non-monetary nature."[58]

2. Courts should not simply defer to agency decisions as a "policy choice," as did one court in an unusually complex setting.[59] What is necessary is some kind of explanation for the choice.

3. For latent harms, it is hard to justify a refusal to apply any discount rate at all. A discount rate of 2 percent or 3 percent seems to make the best sense. If the agency refuses to discount, it should be prepared to explain itself. At the same time, an agency's use of a 7 percent discount rate for latent harms would be hard to defend, because that figure comes from the investment value of money.

4. In the case of future generations, courts should acknowledge that good explanations can be given for a wide range of choices—between, say, a discount rate of 0 percent (for future generations, not latent harms) and 7 percent (OMB's suggestion for future generations). As long as the agency gives a sensible rationale and departs from it only on the basis of articulated reasons, courts should respect the choice. The value judgments here can be reasonably disputed, and they should be made democratically, not judicially. It follows that in the context of discount rates, as elsewhere, the common law of CBA is to be developed at the administrative level, subject only to judicial review for reasonableness.

Conclusion

I have attempted to identify the cost-benefit default principles, to defend their use, and to explore their meaning for the future. In the face of statutory ambiguity, courts are now permitting agencies to refuse to regulate when a significant risk is not shown; to refuse to regulate beyond the point where regulation is not feasible; to consider costs; and to engage in a form of cost-benefit balancing. At their least intrusive, the cost-benefit default rules *allow* the agency to go in the suggested direction when the statute is unclear. At their most intrusive, the principles *require* the agency to act in the way they suggest unless Congress has unambiguously said otherwise.

I have argued on behalf of both the least and most intrusive versions of the cost-benefit default rules by suggesting that they are likely to give sense and rationality the benefit of the doubt. At the same time, I have urged that the argument on their behalf is presumptive only, and that in certain contexts agencies have good reasons for embarking on a different course. The question is whether agencies have been able to offer a reasonable defense of their decision to that effect.

I have also attempted to set out some guidelines for the future, both under the cost-benefit default principles and under statutes that point in the same direction. It is necessary for agencies to particularize the idea of "significant" and "de minimis" risks through quantitative guidelines. A large point here is that the statistical probability of harm is not all that matters; the size of the exposed population is important as well. "Feasibility" is not an off-on switch, and here too agencies should specify what they understand the term to mean, beginning with the admittedly vague notion that massive dislocations would be both necessary and sufficient to show that regulation is not feasible. We have seen that with respect to valuation of life and health, market measures can provide a good start, from which agencies are entitled to make reasonable adjustments. We have also seen that the most difficult issue involves selection of the appropriate discount rate. Reviewing courts should not require agencies to apply the same discount rate to life and health that they apply to money; with respect to discounting, there are good reasons to distinguish money from other goods. The most that courts can do is to impose ceilings and floors on agency judgments by requiring a good rationale for whatever discount rate is chosen.

Suitably specified and understood, the cost-benefit default principles should be regarded not as a technique for stalling desirable regulation, but as a pragmatic effort to ensure that regulation responds to serious problems rather than to trivial or imaginary ones. And if they are seen in these terms, the cost-benefit default principles operate not only as a foundation for deterring regulation that promises to do less good than harm, but also as a basis for producing regulatory action where an assessment of the consequences shows that regulation is desirable.

Notes

1. *See* the overview at http://www.whitehouse.gov/media/pdf/2000fedreg-report.pdf; see also the discussion of agency practice in Matthew Adler & Eric Posner, *Implementing CBA When Preferences Are Distorted*, 29 J. LEGAL STUD. 1105, 1146 (2000).

2. *Available at* http://www.whitehouse.gov/omb/inforeg/riaguide.html.

3. March Sadowitz & John Graham, *A Survey of Permitted Residual Cancer Risks*, 6 RISKS 17 (1995).

4. *Id.*

5. *See* 448 U.S. at 655.

6. *Id.*

7. 52 Fed. Reg. 46,168, 46,234 (1987).

8. *See* Robert PERCIVAL ET AL., ENVIRONMENTAL REGULATION 440 (3d ed. 1999).

9. Agency attention to the size of the exposed population is strongly urged in JAMES HAMILTON & W. KIP VISCUSI, CALCULATING RISKS (MIT Press, 1999).

10. This is the direction suggested in *ATA v. EPA*, 175 F.3d 1027, 1039-40 (1999).

11. *See* JAMES HAMILTON & W. KIP VISCUSI, *supra* note 9.

12. *See* Sadowitz & Graham, *supra* note 3.

13. *Id.*

14. For evidence, *see* Corrosion Proof Fittings v. EPA, 947 F.2d 1201 (5th Cir. 1991) (invalidating asbestos ban).

15. *See, e.g., id.*

16. *See, e.g.,* United Steelworkers v. Marshall, 647 F.2d 1189 (5th Cir. 1980); Building and Construction Trades v. OSHA, 838 F.2d 1258 (D.C. Cir. 1988); NCP v. Brock, 825 F.2d 482 (D.C. Cir. 1987).

17. Michigan v. EPA, 213 F.3d 663, 678 (D.C. Cir. 2000).

18. Most notably the National Environmental Policy Act. *See* Stryker's Bay v. Karlen, 444 U.S. 223 (1980).

19. *See* API v. EPA, 52 F.3d 1113, 1119-20 (D.C. Cir. 1995), holding that the factors that follow the "taking into consideration" language must be treated as secondary.

20. *See* Corrosion Proof Fittings v. EPA, 947 F.2d 1201 (5th Cir. 1991).

21. For an overview, *see* Richard Pildes & Cass R. Sunstein, *Reconceiving the Regulatory State*, 62 U. CHI. L. REV. 1 (1995).

22. This approach is challenged in many places. *See, e.g.*, ELIZABETH ANDERSON, VALUE IN ETHICS AND ECONOMICS (Harvard Univ. Press, 1995).

23. *See* W. KIP VISCUSI, FATAL TRADEOFFS (Oxford Univ. Press, 1992).

24. *See* Matthew Adler & Eric Posner, *supra* note 1.

25. Borrowed from Matthew Adler & Eric Posner, *Implementing CBA When Preferences Are Distorted, in* COST-BENEFIT ANALYSIS 269 (Matthew Adler & Eric Posner eds., Univ. of Chicago Press, 2001).

26. INNOVATIVE STRATEGIES GROUP, ENVIRONMENTAL PROTECTION AGENCY, REGULATORY IMPACT ANALYSIS, OZONE AND PARTICULATES (1998).

27. *See* OMB, 1999 Report to Congress, at 40-43.

28. *See* W. Kip Viscusi, *Risk Equity, in* COST-BENEFIT ANALYSIS 7 (Matthew Adler & Eric Posner eds., Univ. of Chicago Press, 2001).

29. *See* STEPHEN BREYER ET AL., ADMINISTRATIVE LAW AND REGULATORY POLICY 30-31 (1999); Matthew Adler & Eric Posner, *supra* note 1.

30. *See* VISCUSI, *supra* note 23.

31. *See* 66 Fed. Reg. at 7013-17.

32. *See* the acknowledgment of the relevance of life-years in *American Dental Ass'n v. Martin*, 984 F.2d 823, 827 (7th Cir. 1993).

33. 66 Fed. Reg. at 7016.

34. Richard Revesz, *Environmental Regulation, Cost-Beneft Analysis, and the Discounting of Human Lives*, 99 COL. L. REV. 941 (1999).

35. *See* Viscusi, *Risk Equity, supra* note 28.

36. 947 F.2d 1201 (5th Cir. 1991).

37. *See* Michael Gerrard, *Demons and Anegls in Hazardous Waste Regulation*, 92 N.W. L. REV. 706, 742-43 (1998).

38. DEREK PARFIT, REASONS AND PERSONS 357 (Oxford Univ. Press, 1984).

39. Valuable treatments include Richard Revesz, *Environmental Regulation, Cost-Beneft Analysis, and the Discounting of Human Lives*, 99 COL. L. REV. 941 (1999); Comment, *Judicial Review of Discount Rates Used in Regulatory CBA*, 65 U. CHI. L. REV. 1333 (1998).

40. Thomas McGarity, *Some Thoughts on "Deossifying" the Rulemaking Process*, 1992 DUKE L.J. 1385.

41. I am therefore disagreeing with the endorsement of "hard look" review in the excellent Comment, *supra* note 39.

42. *See* OMB, Benefit-Cost Analysis of Federal Programs, 57 Fed. Reg. at 53,520 (1992).

43. *See* Appendix C for details; see also Revesz, *supra* note 34, at 950.

44. *See* Comment, *supra* note 39, at 1336-37.

45. *Id.* at 1337.

46. *See id.* at 1341-50; *see also* Appendix C for excerpts from OMB's own account.

47. *Id.* at 1341-46.

48. As argued, convincingly, in Revesz, *supra* note 34.

49. 66 Fed. Reg. at 7013.

50. *See* Revesz, *supra* note 34; JASON BURNETT & ROBERT W. HAHN, EPA's ARSENIC RULE: THE BENEFITS OF THE STANDARD DO NOT JUSTIFY THE COSTS (unpublished manuscript 2001).

51. Revesz, *supra* note 34.

52. *Id.*

53. *Id.* at 987-1009 (offering a qualified version of this view).

54. *See* DAVID PEARCE & R. KELLY TURNER, ECONOMICS OF NATURAL RESOURCES AND THE ENVIRONMENT 223-24 (1990).

55. Revesz, *supra* note 34, at 994.

56. Tyler Cowen & Derek Parfit, *Against the Social Discount Rate, in* JUSTICE BETWEEN AGE GROUPS AND GENERATIONS 149 (Peter Laslett & James Fishkin eds., 1992).

57. For a good discussion, *see* DANIEL FARBER, ECOPRAGMATISM (Univ. of Chicago Press, 1999).

58. *Corrosion Proof Fittings, supra* note 20 at 1218.

59. 880 F.2d at 465.

PART III
CLEANING THE AIR

In issuing and revising a national ambient air-quality regulation under the Clean Air Act, the Environmental Protection Agency (EPA) should provide a detailed benefits analysis. To this end, it should undertake two tasks. First, it should specify the range of benefits that it believes will result from the regulation, along with a specification of the range of benefits that it believes would result from at least two reasonable alternative approaches, one stricter and one more lenient. In the process, EPA should identify the *residual risk* left under the competing regulatory regimes; it should also acknowledge scientific uncertainty, to the extent that uncertainty exists and requires guesswork. This proposal is an effort to strengthen the role of sound science in environmental protection. Second, the EPA should explain why it believes that the chosen rule is preferable to the alternatives— why the set of benefits to be received from the selected rule justifies that rule, whereas the set of benefits to be received from the less and more stringent rules does not. In the process, it should explain why the residual risk left by the selected rule is acceptable, while the residual risk left by the less stringent rule is not. This proposal is an effort to strengthen the role of democratic forces in environmental protection.[1]

If necessary, reviewing courts should require the EPA to perform these tasks. Taken together, the two proposals should increase the level of consistency across regulations, reducing the power of well-organized private groups and also diminishing the risks associated with both insufficient and excessive environmental regulation. If the EPA has undertaken the two tasks and carried them out in a reasonable way, judicial review is at an end; courts should uphold the EPA's decision.

Ideas of this kind have potentially broad implications, extending well beyond the Clean Air Act and even the EPA to the work of the Occupational Safety and Health Administration, the Consumer Product Safety Commission, and the National Highway Traffic and Safety Administration as well. They would mark a key moment in the movement toward a system of environmental protection that is at once more democratic and better informed. At the same time, they would accelerate the continuing shift of 1970s environmentalism, and indeed 1970s regulation in general, away from recognizing the existence of problems of safety and health and toward assessing their magnitude, in such a way as to reduce both regulatory paranoia and regulatory neglect, and to put a premium on the acquisition of information.

A note at the outset: With respect to ambient air-quality standards, I am making a plea for "benefits analysis"—not for cost-benefit analysis, for which I have been arguing throughout. There are two reasons for limiting my plea to the analysis of benefits. The first is narrowly legalistic: The relevant provisions of the Clean Air Act simply do not permit the EPA to consider costs. The second reason is pragmatic: When the EPA sets national standards, it merely initiates a process, and costs are indeed pertinent when states actually implement those standards (see chapter 6). Ambient air-quality standards represent health-based goals for all states to achieve, but the methods of achieving those goals are intended to be highly sensitive to costs. As we shall see, there is, in practice though not in law, a great deal of flexibility for states facing extremely high compliance costs. When compliance is expensive, compliance will not be required in the real world—a claim supported by the fact that tens of millions of Americans live in areas failing to meet national standards. Those areas could not comply without facing exceptionally high costs.

It is possible to think that the relevant provisions of the Clean Air Act should be amended to allow the EPA to engage in cost-benefit balancing when setting standards in the first instance, as we will discuss in the following chapters. My basic argument is that even if the EPA is focusing on public health alone, it should try to be as quantitative as possible to ensure sense, and transparency, in the government's decision to regulate to one point rather than another. In this way, we shall see that quantitative risk analysis—more simply, benefits analysis—is appropriate even under statutes that ban consideration of cost.

Notes

1. Of course, costs are important too; the two proposals are based on the current understanding that benefits, but not costs, may be taken into account in issuing primary standards. The question of costs is taken up later in this book.

THE CLEAN AIR ACT: DIFFICULTIES AND PROBLEMS

8

Introduction

The Clean Air Act may well be the most important of all environmental statutes. Its effects include a wide range of beneficial consequences for human health and well-being and extremely high costs to the private sector. The Environmental Protection Agency (EPA) estimates overall compliance costs at $0.5 trillion.[1] The act's claim to success rests on enormous improvements in ambient air quality and corresponding health benefits. The EPA estimates that the act prevents at least 45,000 deaths annually and that it also prevents a minimum of 13,000 heart attacks and 7,000 annual strokes.[2] On a standard (though not undisputed) view, the benefits of the act, ranging between $5.6 trillion and $49.4 trillion, far exceed its costs.[3]

Criticism of the Act

The act has nonetheless been subject to telling criticism. The foundation of clean air regulation consists of the EPA's issuance of nationally uniform ambient air quality standards[4]; but in light of the extraordinary diversity of the 50 states, it is not clear that the idea of national standards can be rationally defended.[5] Federal courts and the EPA both seem to think that the standard-setting process does not and cannot involve consideration of costs.[6] But does it make sense, or is it even feasible, to say that national standards will be founded on an assessment of benefits alone, conducted in a cost vacuum?[7] If an improvement in ambient air quality would produce health benefits that are small but not trivial, is it not clear that the improvement is justified if compliance costs are trivial, but

93

perhaps not if the costs are very high? There is reason to think that at least in some cases, an understanding of costs has affected the EPA's decision about appropriate standards—but that the cost-benefit balancing has been left implicit and free from public scrutiny and review.[8]

Perhaps the largest question involves the criteria by which EPA decides whether one or another level of regulation is (in the statutory phrase) "requisite to protect the public health."[9] For most pollutants, air quality at various levels is not either "safe" or "not safe"; there are diminishing degrees of risk associated with diminishing degrees of exposure. On what basis is a particular level of residual risk said to be the appropriate one? What judgments do, or should, enter into that conclusion? The EPA has been criticized for sometimes suggesting, in an unhelpful and conclusory fashion, that it chooses the "safe" level, as if this were solely a technocratic judgment and as if "safety" were an on-off switch,[10] when its decision about permissible levels rests instead on a series of political, scientific, and economic judgments and compromises.

Pressing Problems

There are two problems with this state of affairs. The first involves democratic deliberation.[11] If the EPA does not give a clear sense of the range of adverse effects, and if it does not say why one set of such effects calls for regulation and another does not, the public and its representatives are not informed of the nature of the underlying questions, and they are unable to evaluate the choices actually made. Under the EPA's articulated position, a purely technical issue (Would a certain level be safe?) is sometimes substituted, at least publicly, for the real and more complicated ones (What level of safety is appropriate in light of all the relevant factors? Why should one level of regulation be preferred to another?).

The second problem involves sound regulatory policy. Any proposed national standard could be loosened or tightened, and the question is whether the agency has chosen the optimal, or at least a reasonable, regulatory "point." Without a clear and (to the extent possible) quantified presentation of the expected environmental benefits of the various alternatives,[12] there can be no assurance that the agency has chosen that point rather than one that is too strict or too lenient.

Addressing the Difficulties

My most general goal is to understand current difficulties with environmental policy, the Clean Air Act, and EPA promulgation of ambient air-quality standards, and to see how courts might perform a constructive role in making things better rather than worse. My simplest claim is that the EPA should undertake the two tasks identified above; it should specify the range of benefits that it believes will follow from the regulation it seeks to impose, including a discussion of the benefits from more lenient and more stringent alternatives and a treatment of the residual risks under the various regulatory regimes. It should also explain why it believes that the chosen regulation is preferable to the alternatives.

I also discuss possible improvements in the operation of the Clean Air Act at the legislative, administrative, and judicial levels, improvements that might respond to various concerns about EPA performance. I attempt to explain how the act seems based on the (false) assumption that pollutants generally have "safe thresholds," and how this assumption has seriously impaired both regulatory policy making and democratic deliberation. In particular, I emphasize that EPA should engage in more specific and quantitative assessments of the hazardous effects of pollution at various levels so as to increase the transparency of its decisions. It would even make sense for EPA to move in the direction of the "quality-adjusted life years" approach designed to provide a concrete sense of the benefits of regulatory alternatives. Under such an approach, EPA would attempt to specify the range of "quality-adjusted life years" likely to be saved by a regulation, and it would also indicate the degree of savings that would justify a regulation. But because of the harmful side effects of aggressive judicial review, courts should play only a secondary and catalytic role. The central point is that EPA should undertake such inquiries on its own.

Notes

1. J. Clarence Davies and Jan Mazurek, *Pollution Control in the United States* 130 (WASHINGTON: RESOURCES FOR THE FUTURE, 1998).

2. *Id.* Judgments about benefits, nonmonetized but especially monetized, are highly sensitive to contentious assumptions, and hence the "bottom line" numbers should be taken with many grains of salt. *See* Randall Lutter, *An Analysis of the Use of EPA's Benefit Estimates, in* OMB's DRAFT REPORT ON THE COSTS AND BENEFITS OF REGULATION (October 1998), urging the use of plausible alternative assumptions and arguing that EPA's benefit calculations are inflated. *See also* Lisa Heinzerling, *Regulatory Costs of Mythic Proportions*, 107 YALE L.J. 1981 (1998) (urging that cost per lives saved are inflated, also because of contentious assumptions). Though coming from different directions, Lutter and Heinzerling both argue, convincingly, that characterization of both benefits and costs can shift dramatically with small changes in assumptions.

3. *See* J. Clarence Davies & Jan Mazurek, *supra* note 1 at 130, 147 (1998).

4. 42 U.S.C. 7409(a).

5. *See* James E. Krier, *The Irrational National Air Quality Standards: Macro- and Micro-Mistakes*, 22 UCLA L. REV. 323 (1974). For an instructive recent discussion of how the "slippage" between law on the books and law in the world actually allows a degree of flexibility and converts seemingly rigid standards into a basis for negotiation and pragmatism, *see* Daniel Farber, *Taking Slippage Seriously*, 23 HARV. ENV. L. REV. 297 (1999).

6. *See* Lead Industries v. EPA, 449 U.S. 1042 (D.D.C. 1980); Whitman v. EPA, 531 U.S. 457 (2001), *affirming* American Trucking v. EPA, 175 F.3d 1027 (D.C. Cir. 1999).

7. *See* MARC K. LANDY, MARC J. ROBERTS & STEPHEN J. THOMAS, THE ENVIRONMENTAL

PROTECTION AGENCY: ASKING THE WRONG QUESTIONS FROM NIXON TO CLINTON 49-82, 279-83 (Harvard Univ. Press, 1994).

8. *See id; see also* Boyden Gray, *The Clean Air Act Under Regulatory Reform*, 11 TUL. ENVTL. L.J. 235 (1998).

9.   42 U.S.C. 7409.

10.   *See* Landy et al., *supra* note 7, at 379-83. The criticism is not sound as applied to the particulates and ozone regulations, but here too the EPA's explanation leaves many open questions.

11.   *See id.*

12.   Costs are important too. The prevailing view forbids EPA from considering costs, and my basic proposal does not challenge that prevailing view. I do, however, raise some doubts about it.

THE CLEAN AIR ACT: COSTS AND BENEFITS 9

Taken as a whole, the benefits of the Clean Air Act seem clearly to outweigh the costs.

—J. Clarence Davies
and Jan Mazurek[1]

Congress should not preclude decisionmakers from considering the economic benefits and costs of different policies in the development of regulations.

—Kenneth Arrow et al.[2]

Most environmental initiatives of the past seemed expensive and questionable at the time, and today every one of them appears a bargain in retrospect. Looking back on the present a few decades hence, society will consider every environmental program running now to have been a bargain, and wish more programs had been started sooner.

—Gregg Easterbrook[3]

Setting National Standards

The Clean Air Act was enacted in 1970. Though many hundreds of pages in length, some of them mind-numbingly specific and detailed,[4] the act offers two remarkably brief provisions designed to set the statutory program in motion.

Standards for Air Quality

The first of these provisions, and the central focus here, involves primary national ambient air quality standards.[5] Here

97

the EPA is asked to set standards "the attainment and maintenance of which in the judgment of the Administrator," based on air-quality criteria documents "and allowing an adequate margin of safety, are requisite to protect the public health."[6] The second of these provisions involves secondary national ambient air quality standards, which the EPA must set at levels "requisite to protect the public welfare from any known or anticipated adverse effects associated with the presence of such air pollutant in the ambient air."[7] "Welfare" is defined to include "effects on soils, water, crops, vegetation, manmade materials, animals, wildlife, weather, visibility, and climate, damage to and deterioration of property, and hazards to transportation, as well as effects on economic values and on personal comfort and well-being."[8] For secondary standards, involving welfare rather than health, there is no provision for an "adequate margin of safety." But the secondary standards are anticipated to be more stringent than the primary ones; notice in particular the statutory emphasis on plant and animal lfe.

These provisions have three especially noteworthy features. First, they seem not to contemplate any consideration of cost in the standard-setting process.[9] Primary standards are based on health, apparently to be assessed in a cost vacuum, while secondary standards are based on welfare, also apparently to be assessed without regard to cost. This is not an entirely inevitable reading of the relevant provisions; perhaps the level "requisite to protect the public health" and "welfare" is a function of cost, not only benefit. But the prevailing interpretation is otherwise.[10] Second, the standards are fully national—even though political judgments about air quality vary greatly from state to state, and even though the effects of improved air quality (on the cost and benefits sides) are highly variable from one state to another. Finally, both provisions appear to contemplate the existence of "safe thresholds." The basic idea is that the EPA should ensure that air is "safe" and that public welfare is "protected." What makes this idea distinctive is its artificiality. To be sure, we could imagine pollutants for which the evidence indicated a point of "no risk" or "de minimis risk." At least in theory, it is possible to construct a dose-response curve for which risks effectively vanish at a certain defined point. But for most pollutants, there are diminishing degrees of risk, associated with diminishing degrees of pollution.[11] "Safety" is not an off-on switch; it is a matter of degree. When it is said that a certain level of pollution is "safe," what is really meant is that the residual risk is acceptable or tolerable—not that there is no risk at all. Consider, for example, this commendably direct testimony from the chair of EPA's Scientific Advisory Committee's panel on ozone and particulates, unambiguously confessing the impossible nature of the task imposed on the EPA by the act:

> Based on information now available, it appears that ozone may elicit
> a continuum of biological responses down to background concentra-

tions. It is critical to understand that a biological response does not necessarily imply an adverse health effect. Nevertheless, this means that the paradigm of selecting a standard at the lowest-observable-effects level and the providing of an "adequate margin of safety" is not possible. It further means that risk assessments must play a central role in identifying an appropriate level.[12]

How might we explain the enactment of provisions that seem at once so vague, rigid, and artificial? Much of the answer lies in the distinctive political dynamic of environmental debates in the late 1960s and early 1970s, in which citizens wanted air to be "safe" and politicians who failed to respond were at great risk.[13] This is part of what I have been describing as "1970s environmentalism," a form of thinking that accomplished a great deal of good by producing rapid decreases in pollution levels, but that also seems increasingly anachronistic, even counterproductive. In the 1970s in particular, politicians would proceed at their peril if they asserted that "safety" could be compromised by other goals.[14] At the same time, politicians were affected by, and doubtless catered to, the pervasive psychological urge for certainty, as confirmed by evidence that people are willing to pay a great deal for "no risk" and much less for "substantially less risk."[15] The idea that the Clean Air Act would produce "safety" rather than "reduced risk" made it far easier to support and far harder to challenge.

Undoubtedly Congress believed that it was delegating to EPA the power to be reasonable rather than unreasonable, and in any case the act allowed various safeguards in the event that compliance proved to be excessively costly.[16] As we will see, the most important safeguard consisted in a form of (implicitly authorized) civil disobedience on the part of all relevant actors, including the EPA, which was simply not prepared to shut down automobile traffic in Los Angeles, a step that would have been necessary to produce compliance with national air-quality standards.[17]

Problems and Puzzles

All of these points have created serious difficulties for the EPA in practice. For nonthreshold pollutants, it seems both natural and sensible to assess further reductions in terms of their cost. If, for example, the expense of reducing sulfur dioxide from 0.3 ppm to 0.2 ppm is trivial, then the reduction is almost certainly worthwhile (unless the dose-response curve has a most peculiar shape[18]). Even if there is little direct evidence of adverse human health effects at 0.2 ppm, this is likely to be because of the limited data, rather than because of an absence of such effects. But matters look very different if the cost would run into the tens of billions of dollars. When benefits are highly uncertain, it is peculiar to say that EPA cannot consider cost, especially since health gains are almost inevitable as permissible exposure levels decline.[19]

In light of this point, some critics have suggested that some kind of cost-benefit balancing inevitably occurs at EPA.[20] At least publicly, EPA denies this claim.[21] Consider Administrator Browner's suggestion:

> Costs of meeting the standards and related factors have never been considered in setting the national ambient air quality standards themselves.... [T]he focus has been entirely on health, risk, exposure and damage to the environment.... And the American public deserves to know whether the air in its cities and counties is unsafe or not; that question should never be confused with the separate issues of how long it may take or how much it may cost to reduce pollution to safe levels. Indeed, to allow costs and related factors to influence the determination of what levels protect public health would be to mislead the American public in a very fundamental way.[22]

Only insiders know for certain whether EPA does in fact consider costs in issuing national ambient air quality standards.[23] But consider, by way of contrast and as a possible clue, the administrator's explanation of the 1979 revision of the ozone standard:

> The Clean Air Act, as the Administrator interprets it, does not permit him to take factors such as cost or attainability into account in setting the standard; it is to be a standard that will adequately protect public health. He recognizes that controlling ozone to very low levels is a task that will have significant impact on economic and social activities. This recognition causes him to reject as an option the setting of a zero-level standard.... However, it is public health, and not economic impact, that must be the compelling factor in the decision.[24]

This explanation, difficult to follow though it is, is most naturally taken as a suggestion that despite the nominal irrelevance of costs, they do matter in the context of standard setting for nonthreshold pollutants.

With respect to state-by-state variations, there is little question that the exceedingly high costs of attainment will, for many states, produce frequent violations of national requirements—and this has in fact turned out to be the case.[25] Several decades after the initial issuance of ambient air quality standards for ozone, for example, over 50 million people live in areas that are frequently in violation of national standards.[26] Smaller numbers—but still many millions—of people live in nonattainment areas for other pollutants.[27] Indeed, it is contemplated, by the 1990 revision of the act, that one of the nation's largest urban areas, Los Angeles, will not be in compliance until 2010 at the earliest.[28]

The upshot is that in theory, the act requires nationally uniform standards; but in practice, it authorizes an enormous amount of variation among states. National standards have mostly served not as real law, but as targets or *aspirations*[29]—flexible goals to which the federal government can point without, however, insisting on compliance unless or until it is reasonable. The aspirational quality of national standards has led Congress to enact an increasingly complex set of provisions for nonattainment areas, provisions that anticipate compliance in certain areas over a period of many years and that, in practice, therefore recognize the existence of reasonable variations across states.[30]

This point leads to a more general one, bearing on cost-benefit balancing as well as federalism. The EPA's official position that standard setting is cost-blind is complemented by explicit statements to the effect that cost, efficiency, and feasibility are relevant in making choices about compliance.[31] In a way these statements are puzzling, for the Supreme Court has held that cost, and infeasibility, are irrelevant to the EPA's decision whether to approve state implementation plans.[32] But the EPA appears to acknowledge that state implementation plans will themselves consider control costs, and also that cost will be relevant in setting schedules for compliance.[33]

Finally, EPA must make hard choices about how safe is safe enough—choices that involve not merely the facts, but also evaluative judgments about acceptable degrees of risk. A central question has to do with the ingredients of any judgment that a certain risk is too high. There are many important questions here, including:

- The size of the population at risk, that is, whether 100,000, a million, or tens of millions of people are at risk.[34]
- The nature of the population at risk—for example, whether it involves a large number of children, whether only elderly people are affected, whether those affected have a preexisting condition, such as asthma.[35] An important question is whether any "lives saved" number would involve young people or old people; there is less need for a policy that would (say) increase life expectancy by one year for those over 80 than for a policy that would increase life expectancy by sixty years for those under 10. This point suggests that the EPA might reasonably concern itself not with lives saved, but with life-years saved.
- The likelihood of harm for particular members of the affected population—that is, whether the likelihood of incurring harm is one in 1,000, one in 10,000, or one in a million.[36] Thus, for example, the plurality of the Supreme Court held, in the Benzene Case,[37] that OSHA ought to regulate only "significant risks," and that a risk of one in a billion could not count as significant.[38] OSHA now concludes that a lifetime annual risk of 1/1,000 would count as significant.[39] But undoubtedly the importance of addressing such a risk will depend on other factors, notably including the size of the affected population.

- The severity of the risk—for example, whether it involves cancer or mortality risks, or increased hospital admissions, bronchitis, respiratory symptoms, lost workdays, or what the EPA calls minor restricted activity days (MRADs).[40]

EPA considers all of these questions in issuing national standards.[41] But the agency has developed no clear guidelines to discipline its judgment about when one or another level of regulation is appropriate. It has not said, for example, that if 100,000 people face a cancer risk of 1/1,000, regulation is presumptively desirable, but if 10,000 face a 1/1,000 chance of minor respiratory problems, regulation is presumptively not desirable.[42] A reading of EPA's voluminous documents on the major air pollutants provides an enormous amount of data, but little information on the answers that would trigger a decision to increase or decrease regulation. As we will see, all of the various points noted above might reasonably be turned into a kind of global figure, "quality-adjusted life years," attempting to quantify the various benefits from regulation.[43]

One final note: An obvious and important question has to do with the *distributional* effects of national ambient air quality standards. Who bears the costs? Who receives the benefits? Full information is not available. But an early study finds that under the act, poor people and African-Americans are net gainers, whereas wealthy people and whites are net losers[44]—perhaps not a shocking finding in light of the fact that many of the adverse effects of air pollution are concentrated in large cities. A recent study finds that poor people and African-Americans have indeed gained a great deal from regulation of air pollution.[45]

Notes

1. J. Clarence Davies & Jan Mazurek, Regulating Pollution: Does the U.S. System Work? 51 (1997).
2. Kenneth Arrow et al., Benefit-Cost Analysis in Environmental, Health, and Safety Regulation: A Statement of Principles (American Enterprise Institute, 1996).
3. Greg Easterbrook, A Moment on the Earth 210 (1995).
4. Consider the acid deposition program, which goes so far as to list, by name, every plant entitled to emit sulfur dioxide, 42 U.S.C. 7651c, and its permitted emissions level (a sample: 13,570 tons for Colvert generator 1 in Alabama, 15,430 tons for the Armstrong plant, generator number 2, in Pennsylvania)—alongside an exceptionally specific program for the granting and trading of emissions rights.
5. 42 U.S.C. 7409 (b).
6. 42 U.S.C. 7409(b)(1).
7. 42 U.S.C. 7409(b)(2).
8. 42 U.S.C. 7602(h).
9. *Whitman v. American Trucking Ass'ns* confirms this reading. *See* 531 U.S. 457 (2001). For the initial holding to this effect, see *Lead Industries Ass'n, Inc. v. EPA*, 647 F.2d 1130 (D.C. Cir. 1980).
10. *See* Whitman, *supra* note 9; Lead Industries Ass'n, Inc. v. EPA, *supra* note 9.

11. *See* MARC K. LANDY, MARC J. ROBERTS & STEPHEN J. THOMAS, THE ENVIRONMENTAL PROTECTION AGENCY: ASKING THE WRONG QUESTIONS FROM NIXON TO CLINTON 49-82 (Harvard Univ. Press, 1994).

12. Prepared Testimony of George T. Woolf, Chair, EPA's Clean Air Scientific Advisory Committee's Panel on Ozone and PM, Before the House Judiciary Committee, July 29, 1997.

13. *See* Bruce Ackerman, John Millian & Donald Elliott, *Toward a Theory of Statutory Evolution: The Federalization of Environmental Law*, 1 J. L. ECON. & ORGANIZATION 313 (1985).

14. *See id.*

15. *See* Daniel Kahneman & Amos Tversky, *Prospect Theory: An Analysis of Decision Under Risk*, 47 ECONOMETRICA 263 (1979); GEORGE LOEWENSTEIN ET AL., RISK AS FEELINGS (unpublished manuscript 1999).

16. For an outline, *see* Union Electric v. EPA, 427 U.S. 246 (1977).

17. *See* James E. Krier, *The Irrational National Air Quality Standards: Macro- and Micro-Mistakes*, 22 UCLA L. REV. 323 (1974).

18. For example, one that would show no health benefits from a reduction from 0.3 ppm to 0.2 ppm, notwithstanding health benefits from a reduction from 0.4 ppm to 0.3 ppm.

19. There is reason to think that costs were relevant to the EPA's decision not to reduce the particulates standard further than it did, since the data indicated significant benefits from further reductions. See Table A-7, Appendix A.

20. *See* George Eads, *The Confusion of Goals and Instruments: The Explicit Consideration of Cost in Setting National Ambient Air Quality Standards, in* TO BREATHE FREELY: RISK, CONSENT, AND AIR (Mary Gibson ed., 1985). See also the suggestion in Daniel Farber, *Taking Slippage Seriously*, 23 HARV. ENV. L. REV. 297 (1999), about the distinctive "slippage" between law and reality in the context of environmental law.

21. *See* 45 Fed. Reg. 55,066 (1990).

22. Testimony of Carol Browner before the Senate Environment and Public Works Committee, Feb. 12, 1997.

23. As noted, some evidence is provided by the EPA's failure to require more stringent regulation of particulates, in spite of the fact that on the EPA's own numbers, more stringent regulation might have provided $4 billion in increased benefits. See Table A-7, Appendix A. If this was possible, why did the EPA not require it, if not because of some cost-consciousness?

24. *See* 45 Fed. Reg. at 55,072.

25. There are many discussions. *See, e.g.*, Farber, *supra* note 20; John Dwyer, *The Practice of Federalism Under the Clean Air Act*, 54 MD. L. REV. 1183 (1995); James Krier, *On the Topology of Unifom Environmental Standards in a Federal System—And Why It Matters*, 54 MD. L. REV. 1226 (1995); Eads, *supra* note 20; see James A. Henderson, Jr. & Richard N. Pearson, *Implementing Federal Environmental Policies: The Limits of Aspirational Commands*, 78 COLUM. L. REV. 1429 (1978).

26. *See* Davies & Mazurek, *supra* note 1, at 17.

27. *Id.* (showing about 9 million people live in areas not meeting national standards for particulates; about 11 million live in areas not meeting national standards for carbon monoxide; and about 5 million live in areas not meeting standards for lead).

28. 42 U.S.C. 7511 et seq. (nonattainment program).

29. *See* George Eads, *The Confusion of Goals and Instruments: The Explicit Consideration of Cost in Setting National Ambient Air Quality Standards, in* TO BREATHE FREELY:

RISK, CONSENT, AND AIR (Mary Gibson ed., 1985); James A. Henderson, Jr. & Richard N. Pearson, *Implementing Federal Environmental Policies: The Limits of Aspirational Commands*, 78 COLUM. L. REV. 1429 (1978).

30. 42 U.S.C. § 7511.

31. *See* Statement of Carol Browner, *supra* note 22.

32. *See* Union Electric v. EPA, 427 U.S. 246 (1976).

33. *See* the outline of the EPA's "Common Sense Implementation Plan" in ROBERT PERCIVAL ET AL., ENVIRONMENTAL REGULATION, 1998 Supplement 123-24 (1998).

34. *See* the discussion of lead in R. SHEP MELNICK, REGULATION AND THE COURTS (1983).

35. *See id.*

36. *See* Statement of Carol Browner, *supra* note 22.

37. Industrial Union Dept. v. American Petroleum Inst., 448 U.S. 607 (1980).

38. *Id.* at 612.

39. *See* Building and Construction Trades v. Brock, 838 F.2d 1258, 1265 (D.C. Cir. 1988).

40. United States Environmental Protection Agency, Regulatory Impact Analysis 12-43 (1996).

41. *See, e.g.,* Testimony of Carol Browner Before the House Science Energy and Environment Subcommittee, May 21, 1997: "I determined that setting an appropriate air quality standard for a pollutant for which there is no discernible threshold means that factors such as the nature and severity of the health effects involved, and the nature and size of the sensitive populations exposed, are very important." *See also* the discussion of lead in MELNICK, *supra* note 34; the discussion of ozone in LANDY ET AL., *supra* note 11, at 44-82.

42. *Compare* OSHA, which has said that if a risk is 1/1,000, regulation will be presumed desirable and the risk will be found significant.

43. Richard Zeckhauser & Donald Shepard, *Where Now for Saving Lives?*, 40 L. & CONTEMP. PROBS. 5 (1976).

44. *See* Henry M. Peskin, *Environmental Policy and the Distribution of Benefits and Costs, in* CURRENT ISSUES IN ENVIRONMENTAL POLICY (Paul Portney ed., 1978).

45. *See* Matthew E. Kahn, *The Beneficiaries of Air Pollution Regulation*, 24 REGULATION 34 (2001).

REVISING NATIONAL STANDARDS—AND THE TYRANNY OF THE STATUS QUO 10

EPA's Key Standards

In 1971, EPA issued six national standards governing ozone, particulates, carbon monoxide, nitrogen oxides, and particulates 2.5. In 1978, as a result of a court order, EPA issued a seventh standard involving lead. These seven regulations amount to the centerpiece of EPA's regulatory system for the control of national ambient air quality.

It would be extremely surprising if the standards originally adopted in 1971 and 1978 turn out to survive new scientific evidence, and many people have urged adjustments. Congress has thus created an "agency-forcing" mechanism designed to require EPA reconsideration of primary and secondary standards. Under the act, EPA is required to review the relevant criteria and standards at least once every five years and to revise them "as appropriate" under the statutory guidelines.[1] EPA is specifically required to consider, and to explain any significant departures from, the recommendations of Clean Air Scientific Advisory Committee (CASAC), an independent committee established specifically to advise the administrators on air-quality criteria and standards.[2]

So much for the statutory requirements; the possibility of litigation raises further complexities. The most general point is that EPA is highly vulnerable to suits by those seeking more stringent controls and new regulations based on apparent evidence of hazards at existing levels.[3] If the agency does not act within the statutory period, or if it decides not to impose more stringent controls, it will predictably be faced by a suit from an environmental organization—one that, in view of likely scientific evidence, has a reasonable chance of success.[4] This is so especially in light of a recent judicial suggestion that the administrator may be barred from declining "to establish a margin of safety in the face of documented adverse health effects."[5] But the EPA is also highly vulnerable to challenges by industry whenever it tightens a standard. Creative lawyers have a quite good chance of successfully challenging an EPA regulation whether it has tightened, or refused to tighten, existing standards.[6]

It is therefore possible to venture an only slightly tongue-in-cheek prediction: The day will eventually come when the same court of appeals holds that the EPA has behaved unlawfully both for regulating *above* a certain level and also for not regulating *below* that level! The basic point is that the centrality of litigation to environmental protection creates a new form of tyranny of the status quo—a great deal of inertia in favor of the existing regulatory framework, whatever its content. The general problem for modern administrative law is that because of the complexity of the scientific evidence, skilled advocates are highly likely to be able to find a serious problem in the agency's rationale, a factor that makes rulemaking extremely cumbersome and increasingly encourages agencies to avoid it altogether.[7]

The Record

Thus far it might be tempting to be quite skeptical of the act—to think that it rests on false assumptions, that it foolishly ignores costs and state-by-state variations, that it invites excessive litigation, and that it is an extremely crude foundation for regulatory policy. There is considerable sense in these skeptical reactions. But it must also be acknowledged that the act has done a great deal of good—indeed, that reductions in air pollution can plausibly be counted among the substantial success stories in regulatory government in the last half century.[8] The good news is that for all of the pollutants, there have been large improvements in ambient air quality. Consider the table in Exhibit 10-1 and the data in Exhibit 10-2.

As we have seen, even the cost-benefit ratio appears to be quite good, at least according to most studies. A general review contains many criticisms of American efforts at environmental protection but concludes that "the benefits of the Clean Air Act seem clearly the outweigh the costs."[9] Thus a study of EPA rule between 1990 and 1995 found that the costs outweighed the benefits by no less than $70 billion.[10]

On the other hand, improved tools could have produced similar results at a far lower cost. Thus there is evidence that with better tools, especially economic incentives, EPA could have achieved that same benefits at one-quarter of the costs[11] (more about this important issue below). There is also

Exhibit 10.1 Air Quality and Emissions Trends 1986-95

	Air quality change (%)	Emissions change (%)
Carbon monoxide	-37	-16
Lead	-78	-32
Nitrogen dioxide	-14	-3 (nitrogen oxides)
Ozone	-6	-9 (VOCs)
PM-10*	-22	-17
Sulfur dioxide	-37	-18

*PM-10 changes are based on 1988-95 data

Source: U.S. Environmental Protection Agency. *National Air Quality and Emissions Trends Report, 1995.* Office of Air Quality Planning and Standards Research, Research Triangle Park, North Carolina.

Exhibit 10.2 Percent Decreases in National Air Quality Concentrations

1980-1999		1990-1999
57%	Carbon Monoxide	36%
94%	Lead	60%
25%	Nitrogen Oxide	10%
20%	Ozone	4%
—	Particulate Matter (PM10)	18%
50%	Sulfur Dioxide	36%

Source: U.S. Environmental Protection Agency. *National Air Quality and Emissions Trends Report, 1999.* Office of Air Quality Planning and Standards Research, Research Triangle Park, North Carolina.

a problem of poor priority setting. EPA's own studies suggest that it is not devoting resources to the most serious problems and indeed that inadequate priority setting is a particular problem for clean air regulation, where large problems (such as indoor air pollution) receive relatively little attention.[12] An important task for the future is to ensure that EPA devotes limited public and private resources to the most serious environmental hazards.

Particulates and Ozone at EPA

These issues are hard to understand in the abstract; it will be useful to consider them in light of the EPA's efforts to revise its regulations governing particulates and ozone. Notably, the origins of the new particulates standards can be found not in an independent decision by the EPA, but in a 1993 suit by the American Lung Association, which sought to compel EPA to complete its review of the particulate matter (PM) standard. The district court ordered EPA to issue a proposed rule by November 29, 1996, and a final rule by July 18, 1997.

The final rules for particulates and ozone were based on a massive amount of evidence involving thousands of pages of documents. A general review of the evidence suggests that there would be both high benefits and high costs from the new particulates standard. For the new ozone standard, both costs and benefits would be significantly lower. EPA offered a great deal of detail about the harms apparently caused by particulates and ozone at existing levels. It also acknowledged uncertainties in the evidence. There are extensive discussions of the scientific literature.

EPA ultimately chose a standard of 15/65 for particulates—more specifically, an *annual* standard, for PM sub2.5, of 15 mg/m3, based on the three-year average of annual arithmetic PM sub2.5 concentrations; it also set an *hourly* standard of 65 mg/m3, based on the three-year average of the 98th percentile of 24-hour PM sub2.5 concentrations.

EPA set a 0.08 ppm standard for ozone averaged over an eight-hour period, replacing the previous 0.12 ppm standard averaged over a one-hour period. In an illustrative comment, Administrator Browner publicly defended the 0.08 ppm standard for ozone "because, though it is in the middle of the range recommended for consideration by CASAC and the EPA staff paper, as a policy choice it reflects the lowest level recommended by individual CASAC panel members and it is the lowest level tested and shown to cause effects in controlled human-exposure health studies."[13] In its explanation of the final rules, the EPA did not defend these selections against plausible alternatives. The regulatory impact analysis (RIA), required by Executive Order 12866, also discusses a more stringent and a less stringent alternative—particulates standards of 16/65 and 15/50, and ozone standards of 0.08 5th max and 0.08 3rd max (see Appendix A for details). This discussion was designed to give a sense of the cost and benefits of the alternatives.

The EPA's own public justification is extremely long and detailed but in important respects vague and conclusory. It is filled with legalistic arguments, with reports on specific studies having unclear implications for the particular issue of what standard to select, and with qualitative judgments that leave a great deal of uncertainty about the magnitude of the effects.[14]

Keys to the EPA's Analysis

The heart of the EPA's analysis is as follows.[15] (I discuss particulates as an illustration.) The EPA begins by referring to "the greatly expanded body of community epidemiological studies."[16] This evidence shows a range of adverse health effects, including premature mortality, and there is also evidence that children, the elderly, and asthmatics are most vulnerable to these effects. More particular evidence emerges from quantitative risk estimates from two "example cities," estimates that include a judgment that existing standards create residual risks of "hundreds of premature deaths each year, hundreds to thousands of respiratory-related hospital admissions, and tens of thousands of additional respiratory-related symptoms in children."[17] (In an inadvertently hilarious qualification, the EPA adds that the "epidemiological findings cannot be wholly attributed to inappropriate or incorrect statistical methods, misspecification of concentration-effect models, biases in study design or implementation, measurement errors" and the like.) But the EPA notes that the results "should be interpreted cautiously" and should be taken to "provide ample reason to be concerned that there are detectable health effects attributable to PM at levels below the current NAAQS (national ambient air quality standards)."[18]

The EPA's basic claim is that "the increase in relative risk is small for the most serious outcomes" but "significant from an overall public health perspective, because of the large number of individuals in sensitive populations that are exposed to ambient air as well as the significance of the health effects involved."[19] International evidence, and evaluations by over 1,000 experts, supported the view that the existing standard was insufficiently protective.[20] Much of the EPA's discussion involves the fact that existing evidence does not reveal mechanisms to explain the range of reported adverse effects.[21] And frequently the EPA repeats what appears to be a key phrase, almost a mantra, to the effect that the data "provides the basis for decisions on standard levels that would reduce risk sufficiently to protect public health with an adequate margin of safety, recognizing that such standards will not be risk-free."[22]

To the EPA's credit, it does offer some discussion of both less stringent and more stringent alternatives.[23] But the discussion is quite brief, especially considering the centrality of the comparative question. As against the less stringent possibilities, EPA says that "despite well recognized uncertainties, the consistency and coherence of the epidemiological evidence and the seriousness of the health effects require a more protective response."[24] As against those who argued for more stringent regulation, EPA said that "the inherent scientific uncertainties are too great" and also that such regulation "might result in regulatory programs that go beyond those that are needed to effectively reduce risks to public health."[25] Studies "provide some suggestion of risks extending to lower concentrations, but they do not provide a sufficient basis for establishing a lower annual standard level."[26] Because this point is so important, it is worthwhile noting that the EPA spoke in similar terms for ozone, saying that more stringent regulation would prevent "certain . . . effects, [that] while judged to be adverse, are transient and reversible, and the more serious effects, with greater immediate and potential long-term impacts on health, are less certain, both as to the percentage of individuals exposed to various concentrations who are likely to experience such effects and as to the long-term significance of these effects."[27]

Hence any reader is likely to be puzzled about exactly why EPA chose the particular regulations it did—about why it did not regulate either somewhat more or somewhat less. A special puzzle is why the EPA did not impose more stringent controls on particulates; the regulatory impact analysis shows that a more stringent regulation would have produced $4 billion in increased health benefits.[28] The problem is not that the EPA was careless or off-hand; its exhaustive documentation was anything but that. The problem is that in the explanation accompanying the final rules, EPA did not attempt to quantify the risks under competing standards, nor did it show the basic value judgment that would deem one risk too high, another risk acceptable, and another risk too low (that is, below the level requisite to protect the public health).

In many ways, the most informative document is the RIA. This is the most informative document because it provides actual numbers on the benefit (including nonmonetized and monetized quantities) and cost sides. It is also a tribute to Executive Order 12866, requiring cost-benefit analysis even when CBA cannot be the basis for decision. The problem is that in its justification, EPA made little use of this document. Indeed, the RIA was written by a contractor, not by EPA personnel, and it had little or no influence on the ultimate decision. Some of the benefits calculations appear to have been rejected by EPA itself. Nonetheless, the RIA provides the only systematic discussion of the consequences of the approach chosen and of alternative approaches.

According to the RIA, new particulates regulation would prevent 350 annual mortalities; 6,800 cases of chronic bronchitis; 1,100 cases of acute bronchitis; about 1,200 hospital admissions from, for example, congestive heart failure and respiratory problems; 106,000 lost workdays; and 879,000 minor restricted activity days.[29] (Note that in both cases the RIA specifies a range, which is a tribute to candor in the midst of scientific uncertainty.) For the selected ozone standard, it finds that the new regulation would prevent 0-80 deaths, 130 emergency department visits for asthma, 29,840 acute respiratory symptoms, 0-530 chronic bronchitis cases, 0-20 hospital admissions for congestive heart failure, 0 to 50,440 lost workdays, and 0 to 420,300 minor restricted activity days.[30]

All these benefits are monetized: $4.8 million per life saved, $120,000 per life-year saved, $12,700 per respiratory illness, $16,600 per congestive heart failure for those over 65, $9,000 for emergency department visits for asthma, $260,000 for chronic bronchitis, $83 per lost workday, and $38 per minor restricted activity day.[31]

Costs and Benefits: The Bottom Line

The overall cost-benefit analysis[32] shows, for the health regulation of ozone in 2010, benefits of $0.4 billion (low-end estimate) to $2.1 billion (high-end estimate) and costs of $1.1 billion. For particulates, the benefits range from $19 billion to $104 billion, whereas the costs are anticipated to be $8.6 billion. A noteworthy point is that the ozone rule might have negative net benefits of -$0.7 billion, if the low-end estimate is correct; note also that if the health benefits of ground-level ozone (discussed below) are included in the calculation, the negative net benefits—or, more simply, net costs—of the rule are higher still. (In an unfortunate typographical error in the crucial table, the net benefits are described as $0.7 billion to $1.0 billion, rather than $-0.7 billion to $1 billion.[33])

The RIA also suggests the costs and benefits of the two alternatives.[34] The more stringent particulates standard would have high-end benefits of $108 billion and costs of $9.4 billion; the less stringent would have high end benefits of $90 billion and costs of $5.5 billion.[35] The less stringent ozone standard would have high-end benefits of $1.6 billion and costs of $0.9 billion; the more stringent would have high-end benefits of $2.9 billion and costs of $1.4 billion.[36] The most noteworthy point here is that by the EPA's own accounting, the more stringent particulates standard would have produced $4 billion in greater benefits (on the high-end estimate). This would seem to count as a substantial improvement in public health, especially considering the fact that each life is valued at $4.8 million; translated into lives, the more stringent regulation would prevent more than 200 additional deaths each year. EPA did not square this conclusion with its decision not to choose more stringent regulation. Indeed, it seems clear that EPA's own calculations showed that a tighter particulates standard would have produced far greater health benefits than the ozone standard; this leaves a serious unexplained anomaly in the two standards taken together.[37] A possible explanation for not tightening the particulates standard is that the consensus of CASAC members did not support doing so, a consensus that raises questions about the RIA itself; but EPA did not offer a benefits analysis that would resolve these uncertainties.

A serious gap in the RIA is that it does not give low-end estimates for the benefits associated with the alternatives; only high-end estimates are given for these. For the options actually chosen, a range is specified, which greatly assists assessment of the EPA's judgment. But without the range, it is hard to compare the options not chosen. An additional problem, reflected in the EPA's explanation as a whole, is the absence of a detailed assessment—even a wholly benefits-based assessment—of why the options that were chosen were deemed superior to those that were not chosen.

In this light, what overall evaluation would be reasonable? If the EPA's conclusions are correct, the particulates regulation promises significant benefits and the ozone regulation promises relatively small benefits. The basic problem is that the agency did not explain, in concrete terms, why it chose one level of regulation rather than another. To see how the agency should approach the question of choice, it is necessary to examine the meaning of the relevant provisions of the Clean Air Act.

Notes

1. 42 U.S.C. 7409(d)(1).
2. *Id.* 7409 (d)(2)(B), 7607 (d)(3).
3. For recent evidence, *see, e.g.*, American Lung Association v. EPA, 134 F.2d 388 (D.C. Cir. 1998); American Trucking Co. v. EPA, 175 F.2d 1027 (D.C. Cir. 1999); Corrosion Proof Fittings v. EPA, 947 F.2d 1201 (5th Cir. 1991).
4. *See, e.g.*, American Lung Association v. EPA, 134 F.3d 388 (D.C. Cir. 1998) (requiring EPA to give a better justification for its failure to establish a new standard for sulfur dioxide emissions).
5. *Id.* at 393 (leaving the issue undecided on the ground that the administrator did not adequately explain her judgment that no public health threat exists).
6. *See, e.g., American Trucking, supra* note 3.
7. *See* Richard Pierce, *Seven Ways to De-Ossify Agency Rulemaking*, 47 AD. L. REV. 59, 60-62 (1995).
8. *See, e.g.*, GREGG EASTERBROOK, A MOMENT ON THE EARTH 181-83 (1996).
9. J. Clarence Davies & Jan Mazurek, *Regulating Pollution: Does the U.S. System Work?* 31 (RESOURCES FOR THE FUTURE, 1996).
10. *Id.*
11. *See* TOM TIETENBURG, EMISSIONS TRADING (1985).
12. Davies & Mazurek, *supra* note 9, at 24-30.
13. *See* Clean Air Act: Hearings Before the Subcommittee on Clean Air, Wetlands, Private Property, and Nuclear Safety, 105th Cong. 282 (1997) (statement of Carol M. Browner).
14. 62 Fed. Reg. 38,650-681.
15. 62 Fed. Reg. 38,652 (1997).
16. *Id.* at 38,655.
17. *Id.*
18. *Id.* at 38,656.
19. *Id.* at 38,657.
20. *Id.*
21. *See, e.g., id.* at 38,664-665.
22. *Id.* at 38,665.
23. *Id.* at 38,674-677.
24. *Id.* at 38,665.
25. *Id.* at 38,675.

26. *Id.*

27. 62 Fed. Reg at 38,868/2.

28. See Appendix A, table A-7. Note that this compares the highest benefit estimate; unfortunately, the RIA does not give lowest bound benefits estimates for the two alternatives.

29. Appendix A, Table A-2.

30. Appendix A, Table A-3.

31. Appendix A, Table A-4.

32. Regulatory Impact Analysis at 13-4.

33. *Id.*

34. *Id.* at 13-2, 13-3.

35. *Id.* at 13-3.

36. *Id.* at 13-4.

37. *See* Randall Lutter & Christopher DeMuth, *Ozone and the Constitution at EPA, in* ON THE ISSUES 3 (July 1999).

LAW AND POLICY   11

[A]n agency wielding the power over American life possessed by EPA should be capable of developing the rough equivalent of a generic unit of harm that takes into account population affected, severity and probability.
— *American Trucking Associations v. EPA*[1]

What the Clean Air Act Means

Does the act authorize the EPA to set national ambient air quality standards at whatever level it wishes? Or does it set ceilings and floors? What does it require the EPA to do, and what does it ban the EPA from doing?

The most reasonable interpretation is that EPA's health-based judgment (a) cannot call for regulation of small or trivial risks (such regulation would not be "requisite to protect the public health"), and (b) must call for regulation of risks that are serious and substantial. Thus if the residual risk of a pollutant is trivial or de minimis—if, for example, the risk involves minor respiratory problems but no more than that—then EPA is not obligated to regulate it. Indeed, EPA regulation of a trivial or de minimis risk should be held unlawful, on the ground that such regulation is not requisite to protect the public health, even with an adequate margin of safety. If EPA seeks to reduce exposure to ground-level ozone below a level that already ensures protection against all serious risks faced by almost everyone, it is acting unlawfully. On the other hand, EPA is required (not merely permitted) to regulate any substantial or significant risk. If, for example, 10,000 people are

115

likely to die each year as a result of exposure to a certain level of lead, EPA must act; it is not authorized to allow that level of risk.

These points go a long way toward creating floors and ceilings and resolving a wide range of cases. Suppose, for example, that existing evidence shows increased mortality risks from sulfur dioxide at levels above 0.8 ppm, and increased hospital admissions at levels about 0.6 ppm, but no mortality risk from sulfur dioxide levels below 0.4 ppm, and no increase in hospital admissions below 0.4 ppm—and also that there is chronic plant injury at 0.1 ppm, and that respiratory problems increase among a small, sensitive subpopulation at 0.15 ppm. On the facts as stated, EPA's discretion is confined. It could not issue a primary standard above 0.6 ppm or so, and it could not issue a standard below 0.5 ppm or so—unless it could make extrapolations from the evidence that would suggest a substantial risk at lower levels. Of course, this is a stylized and artificial example, and often the evidence will allow a range of reasonable judgments. But that is a product of the uncertain science. Indeed, EPA itself has asserted that on the evidence, it was required to set the ozone standard somewhere between 0.07 ppm and 0.09 ppm.

Benefits Analysis

These points suggest that the relevant provisions of the Clean Air Act require EPA not to produce a cost-benefit analysis, but nonetheless to move in the direction of something quantitative, in the form of a "benefits analysis." To explain this idea, we should deal with some details.

I have emphasized that notwithstanding its commendable detail about the underlying evidence, the EPA's explanation of its particulates and ozone rules leaves much to be desired. This is not uncommon for agency explanations in the area of safety and health; similar problems can be found in the OSHA context and also in EPA action under other statutes.[2] For particulates and ozone, the agency's extensive discussion is abstract and conclusory on the key points. It does provide evidence that ozone and particulates can have adverse effects at current levels. But it does not give a sufficiently clear sense of the level of those adverse effects, nor does it explain why the particular, selected regulation was optimally suited to new information about health effects. The most informative document is the agency's regulatory impact analysis, which could be used as the basis for a simple statement of the anticipated benefits of increased regulation at various levels.

The resulting problems have both technocratic and democratic dimensions. Without specification of the range of benefits to be anticipated from various approaches, there is a weak role for sound science in standard-setting. The best that science can do is to give a range of likely health and welfare gains from alternative initiatives, and the proper role of technocratic factors cannot be served if the EPA speaks in vague, conclusory, or wholly qualitative terms. What is necessary is to have some sense of the magnitude of gains from competing approaches. From the democratic point of view, what is missing is an opportunity for the public to have a sense of those gains and to receive an account of why the government has chosen one set of gains rather than another. Any particular choice reflects an important social judgment; officials should be clear about the values that underlie that choice.

By way of response, I suggest that in issuing national ambient air quality standards, EPA should endeavor to provide a detailed benefits analysis designed to strengthen both technocratic and democratic forces. In order to improve the role of science, the benefits analysis should attempt to describe, in both qualitative and quantitative terms, the various savings from the selected regulation and at least two alternatives, one more stringent, the other less so. This is an effort to strengthen the role of technocratic forces by ensuring that EPA is acting pursuant to a clear understanding of the health and welfare effects of reasonable options. In the process, EPA should identify the residual risk left, under alternative approaches, by the pollutant in question and explain why that residual risk is not above the level "requisite to protect the public health." The EPA should thus take steps to identify the size of the population affected, the severity of the various risks, and the likelihood that members of any particular group will suffer the relevant effects. To the extent possible, it should attempt to quantify each of these items.[3] It might say, for example, that 40 million people are at risk, that 10 million of these people are under the age of 18, that 5 million are over the age of 60, that there is a 1/1,000 chance of cancer as a result of exposure, and that the relevant risks range from respiratory problems to hospitalization and missed workdays to cancer (each of which might be quantified; see Appendix A).

The EPA should also explain why one set of savings, thus quantified, justifies regulation, whereas other sets of savings do not. Here there is an inevitable judgment of value, and no purely technocratic exercise. EPA might conclude, for example, that one approach leaves an excessive risk to health, because it would result in between 500 and 1,500 annual deaths as compared with the chosen approach—whereas another initiative would go beyond the level required to protect the public health, because it would result in between 0 and 150 annual deaths, most of them involving the elderly. This is an effort to strengthen democratic forces in regulation by ensuring that the relevant value judgment is made publicly and exposed to democratic view.

EPA should also attempt to reduce its own discretion by showing that, at least as a presumption, risks above a certain level will not be tolerated (risk ceilings) and that risks below a certain level (risk floors) will be acceptable. It should, in short, explain why a standard for ozone of 0.08 is to be preferred to a standard of 0.09 or 0.07, and do so by reference to generalizable criteria. If—as seems clear—the risks prevented by the new ozone regulation are far smaller than the risks that would be prevented by more stringent regulation of particulates, EPA should explain the apparent anomaly in terms of statutorily relevant factors. A chief advantage of this approach is that it should ensure inter-regulation consistency in such a way as to combat, simultaneously, interest-group power, public torpor, and public overreaction with respect to certain pollutants.

Problems and Possibilities

A proposal of this kind raises several problems. An obvious difficulty is connected with specifying the set of alternatives. Any agency could "frame" the alternatives so as to make its own choice seem plausible, even inevitable. In the context of ozone, for example, the choice of 0.08 would have seemed entirely reasonable if EPA had compared that option to 0.12 (much worse on health grounds) and 0.04 (regulating apparently trivial risks). Thus it is necessary to ensure that the alternatives be reasonable ones—that they be within the domain, or "strike zone," indicated by the scientific evidence. Recommendations created by advisory bodies could provide a great deal of help here. They would specify the range of options that experts consider plausible, and if EPA compares its choice to both more and less stringent alternatives within the approximate domain suggested by the relevant advisory bodies, the problem of "framing" should be adequately addressed.

Of course, any analysis of expected benefits will depend on contentious assumptions. The most serious problem here is that in many cases, scientific uncertainty will confound any attempt to quantify with anything like precision (see the discussion of dose-response curves in Appendix B). In these circumstances EPA's real question is one of timing: Does it act now, or does it wait until the scientific information provides more clarity with respect to health effects? Inaction would create potential problems, possibly even a significant number of preventable deaths; but action could create problems too, in the form of high costs for trivial health benefits. This is certainly a plausible reading of the situation with respect to both particulates and (especially) ozone; in both cases we do not know enough to assign specific numbers to different exposure levels. When existing evidence does not justify any particular number, then EPA should do the best that it can to specify a reasonable range. (See Appendix A for examples, taken from the regulatory impact analysis.)

But scientific uncertainty is not the only problem. A projection of benefits must depend on a baseline about what would have happened without regulation, and might also require use of the contingent valuation method, for which estimates are highly vulnerable to the nature of the particular questions asked.[4] Perhaps most important, the estimate of benefits will turn partly on the discount rate for future savings; a discount rate of 8 percent will produce very different numbers from a discount rate of 2 percent (see chapter 6). In these circumstances, the benefits analysis should be clear about the assumptions chosen, and should indicate the range of benefits and the numbers that would emerge from different assumptions.

In terms of intergovernmental design, it makes sense to ensure that the analysis of the rule, and the alternatives to the rule, are developed in conjunction with another institution in the executive branch, such as the Office of Management and Budget, which already plays a role of this sort under Executive Order 12866.[5] The purpose of intergovernmental review of this kind would be to ensure a form of internal "peer review" designed to overcome possible biases and errors on the part of any particular bureaucracy. An external check is well-suited to accomplishing this goal.

An Analogy

A promising approach to the evaluation of benefits comes from the health field, where much attention has focused on evaluating preferences for healthy conditions (or aversion to unhealthy ones) in terms of what are called quality-adjusted life years (QALYs).[6] A QALY is a measure of health based on people's attitudes toward various conditions. It rejects the concept of monetary evaluation of health; instead, it focuses on how people value various health states. It seeks to generate a means of comparing various states of health through a single metric, so that comparisons and trade-offs can be made for public policy purposes. The measure attempts to take into account both quantitative benefits of health improvement, such as increase in life expectancy, and more qualitative improvements, such as quality-of-life benefits.

The QALY approach works by asking people through interview techniques to express their strength of preference for various health states. The most advanced methods disaggregate the process by asking people to describe how they would value a health improvement along several dimensions: mobility, physical activity, social activity, and the kinds of symptom effects involved.[7] The answers to these questions are combined into a single scale, ranked 0.0 (for death) to 1.0 (for optimum functioning). The result is an index of utility for health states measured on an interval (or cardinal) scale. By independently determining the cost of various treatments and their likely outcomes, reseachers can suggest a cost per QALY of various public programs. Alternative programs can be ranked in what is essentially a utility-based cost-effectiveness scale.[8]

In the context of the Clean Air Act, it makes little sense to engage in surveys about how people rank various health risks. In the governing RIA, EPA has already attempted to measure willingness to pay to reduce various risks (see Appendix A), and it could easily adapt these figures to generate numbers for overall risk reductions, defined in terms of quality-adjusted life years. Lives saved might, for example, be converted into a life-years-saved number, and to this EPA could add various numbers representing the other health gains to be brought about by the regulation. The approach to particulates might be compared to, and squared with, the approach to ozone, and these approaches might also be rationalized with existing regulation of lead, sulfur dioxide, nitrogen oxides, and carbon monoxide (again, see Appendix A).

A Common Law of Regulatory Protection

Through such a route EPA could begin to develop what it should have provided at least a decade ago: a common law of public health protection. This would reflect a system of judgments indicating when a given set of harms is sufficient to trigger additional regulation, and also when a set of harms is too trivial to count as a legally cognizable public health problem. And eventually it should be possible to have quite disaggregated data, showing the geographical areas in which health problems are most concentrated. For example, the health risks of lead were concentrated in the inner city; the same may well be true of particulates. If this is so, a careful "benefits analysis" could pave the way toward an understanding of where regulatory activity would accomplish the most good, in a way that would diminish some of the problems associated with a nationally uniform policy. Such an approach could also help to invigorate local processes for environmental protection, so as to allow a higher degree of coordination between the national government and states and localities.

This final point raises a general question about the content of any such common law: the status, for purposes of law and policy, of *inter-regulation inconsistency*. Suppose, for example, that the EPA leaves a much higher residual risk for particulates than for ozone, as indeed it plainly appears to have done here. Is this indefensible, or even unlawful? As we have seen, one of the virtues of the approach suggested here is that it attempts to promote consistency in the rulemaking process, in such a way as to reduce the power of well-organized private groups. It might seem to follow that if EPA allows a much higher residual risk for one substance than for another, it should be vulnerable on judicial review, and so too if it allows a much lower residual risk for a particular pollutant. This does indeed follow. The question is whether EPA can defend apparent inter-regulation inconsistency in statutorily relevant terms (as, for example, by showing that children are at particular risk from one problem or another). If it cannot, it has acted unlawfully.

There is a still broader point in the background here. The case for clear standards is strongest in a "mass justice" situation—a context in which an agency must decide a wide range of cases. In such situations, lack of standards is unacceptable, a recipe for abuse, and breeds unequal treatment of the similarly situated.[9] When an agency is making a one-shot decision, or two or three decisions, the argument for binding standards is less insistent. The point helps explain the decision of the court of appeals in *American Trucking*, where two regulations were before the court, not easily reconciled with one another, and where many years of NAAQS decisions made the situation resemble more closely a "mass justice" problem. In these circumstances, the proposal for benefits analysis is designed to ensure a set of relatively uniform and transparent standards more suitable to the future of environmental protection, when the whole area will achieve a degree of maturity. The development of a common law of regulatory protection, generated in the first instance by agencies rather than judges, would be a crucial step in this endeavor.

Throughout this chapter, I have been speaking of benefits analysis, not cost-benefit analysis. The focus on benefits is mandated by the unusual nature of the statutory provisions governing national ambient air-quality standards; as we have seen, these provisions are cost-blind. But in chapter 2, I urged that regulations should generally be accompanied by an analysis of both costs and benefits, and that agencies should generally go forward only if the benefits of regulation justify its costs. These basic ideas might easily be brought into contact with the general suggestions offered in this chapter. Under ordinary circumstances, agencies should undertake analysis of costs as well as benefits, for the option under consideration and at least two alternatives, one more stringent and one less so. The general advantages of benefits analysis would be even greater if agencies expanded their viewscreen to include costs as well.

Does Benefits Analysis Survive Cost-Benefit Analysis?

There is a final point, one that is difficult to resolve in the abstract: Does benefits analysis survive cost-benefit analysis? An elaborate analysis is, in principle, always preferable to a superficial analysis, but it is difficult, and expensive, to produce an elaborate analysis. As an abstract matter, we cannot be sure that the benefits analysis would be worth the candle. The point applies to cost-benefit analysis itself, which I mean to endorse throughout this book. What makes us so sure that cost-benefit analysis survives cost-benefit analysis?

The answer is that we cannot be sure. But the current situation is not nearly as good as it could be, and if the analysis is done well, there is every reason to expect that it will lead to improvements. With particulates and ozone, the EPA should not be taking stabs in the dark; but without something approaching a benefits analysis, its choices cannot be much more than a guess. EPA already engages in the kind of data collection that would be used in a benefits analysis, and there is no reason to think that the production of that analysis would be a huge burden. We do not have a systematic study of whether cost-benefit analysis passes cost-benefit analysis. But within EPA, cost-benefit analysis appears to have produced significant improvements, contributing to more stringent regulation of lead in gasoline and ozone-depleting CFCs, as well as more cost-effective regulations in general.[10] The current record suggests that benefits analysis in particular, and cost-benefit analysis in general, are likely to improve the current situation. Of course, the proof can only come from the practice.

Notes

1. American Trucking Ass'ns v. EPA, 175 F.3d 1027 (D.C. Cir. 1999).

2. *See Corrosion Proof Fittings v. EPA,* 847 F.2d 1201 (1991), where the court rightly found a number of unanswered objections to an agency rule banning asbestos—a rule that would probably have produced far more gain than harm on balance. (No one contradicted the agency's conclusion that the rule would have saved well over 300 lives per year at a reasonable overall cost.) The court's decision eliminated the asbestos regulation, a 10-year effort, and seems in the process to have brought EPA's rulemaking efforts under the Toxic Substances Control Act to a complete halt. A possible answer to this problem would have been for the court to remand without vacating the rule.

3. An argument against quantification is provided in Lisa Heinzerling, *Regulatory Costs of Mythic Proportions,* 106 YALE L.J. 2042-069 (1998). Even if we accept Heinzerling's argument against the form of monetizing quantification that is embodied in cost-benefit analysis, it is far from clear that the argument has weight against an attempt to quantify (rather than to monetize) benefits.

4. *See* Randall Lutter, *An Analysis of the Use of EPA's Benefit Estimates, in* OMB's DRAFT REPORT ON THE COSTS AND BENEFITS OF REGULATION 6-10 (October 1998).

5. C.F.R. 638 (1993).

6. The measure was first described in Richard Zeckhauser & Donald Shepard, *Where Now for Saving Lives?,* 40 L. & CONTEMP. PROBS. 5 (1976).

7. An important work in the development of these multidimensional measures is Robert M. Kaplan & James W. Bush, *Health-Related Quality for Life Measurement of Evaluation Research and Policy Analysis,* 1 HEALTH PSYCH. 61 (1982). For a general survey of QALY approaches, *see* George W. Torrance, *Measurement of Health State Utilities for Economic Appraisal: A Review,* 5 J. HEALTH ECON. 1 (1986).

8. An important advantage of the QALY method is that it eliminates the distribution-of-income problems of other methods. The QALY approach rests on a strict egalitarian premise: the value of various states of health should be independent of the economic status of the particular people in those states. Willingness to pay and contingent valuation treat health like any other market commodity, while QALY approaches view health as a distinct good that should be distributed according to a nonmarket logic. Costs are still relevant, of course, but they are not brought in at the level of individual decisions.

9. See JERRY MASHAW, BUREAUCRATIC JUSTICE (Yale Univ. Press, 1983).

10. *See* ECONOMIC ANALYSES AT EPA 455-56 (Richard Morgenstern ed., 1998).

THE ROLE OF COURTS

12

Introduction

For the future, a major question is how a plaintiff might be able to challenge a national standard if costs cannot be considered. We know that if the regulation is less stringent than is "requisite to protect the public health," with an "adequate margin of safety," it will be unlawful. We also know that if the regulation is more stringent than is "requisite," it will also be unlawful. In the easy cases, at least, the lessons are clear. A regulation will be subject to challenge if it allows significant adverse health effects, at least if the agency cannot reasonably explain that the adverse effects are insignificant. If we accept the EPA's evidence (see Appendix A, Table 1), it would therefore be reasonable to argue that the EPA was required, and not merely permitted, to produce a new regulation for particulates. A regulation will also be subject to challenge if significant adverse effects cannot be expected at levels that the EPA forbids. On a reasonable reading of the evidence governing ozone (see Appendix A, Table 2), the new EPA regulation might be unlawful for that reason.

For reviewing courts, there are several major routes to follow, and each of them would be entirely sensible. As an illustration of how these issues might be resolved, I would suggest that the particulates rule should probably be upheld, but that the ozone standard should probably be remanded, so that the EPA can give a better, more quantitative explanation of why it chose the particular regulatory "points" that it selected. What is more important than the particular conclusion is an appreciation of the grounds on which the three possibilities might be criticized and defended. The analysis here of the particulates and ozone standards might be applied, with suitable modifications, to any national ambient air-quality standard and indeed more broadly.

Preliminaries: A Health-Health Trade-off

Let us begin with a particular claim with respect to EPA's ozone regulation: that ground-level ozone has health benefits, and that these benefits were not taken into account by the agency. There is evidence that ozone reduces the risk of both cataracts and cancers.[1] The science here is disputed, but if taken into account, the health benefits of ground-level ozone might even be roughly equivalent to the health costs of ozone. But the EPA refused to consider those health benefits. In an interesting application of "health-health" analysis, the court of appeals held that the refusal was unlawful.[2]

In general, it is right to say that agencies should be required to take account of the health problems sometimes produced by regulation designed to reduce health problems. This kind of health-health trade-off can take many different forms.[3] In typical cases, the regulation of one risk, like those associated with asbestos, may give rise to further risks as a result of the substituted products. The most adventurous claims for "health-health" comparisons arise when a costly regulation imposes health risks simply by virtue of its cost. If a regulation produces less employment and more poverty, it may result in worse health as well.[4] But these are adventurous claims, because they depend on contentious projections about the disemployment effects of particular regulations.

For the ozone rule, the argument for taking those problems into account seemed especially insistent, for the claim was far from indirect, and there was nothing speculative or abstruse about the causal chain. If ozone protects against cancers and cataracts, it is possible that a regulation of ozone will cause serious health problems. The text of the Clean Air Act is not unambiguous on the point, and the court was wrong to say that it unambiguously required the agency to address the beneficial effects of some pollutants.[5] But the court was right to hold that even if it was ambiguous, the agency interpretation was unreasonable (see chapter 3). The rule was properly found inadequately explained on this ground, and it may well be that after remand, the agency will be unable to explain its failure to take account of the effects of ozone in combatting cataracts and cancer.

There is a large and general lesson here. Sometimes statutes ban cost-benefit balancing and are focused only or primarily on health. But such statutes might well be interpreted to allow, and even to require, agencies to compare health benefits against health costs, and thus to engage in at least a constrained form of balancing. We saw in chapter 4 that courts have created an interpretive principle in favor of allowing consideration of health-health trade-offs. That principle is fully operative in the context of the

Clean Air Act. Now let us turn to potential approaches to the particulates and ozone standards in general.

A Soft Look

A reviewing court might say that there is substantial scientific evidence to support the view that both pollutants produce significant adverse health effects at currently permitted levels—and hence the new controls are, in the administrator's reasonable judgment, "requisite to protect the public health." The statutory requirement of an "adequate margin of safety" might well be taken to support this view. As I have emphasized, the evidence supporting regulation of ozone seems a good deal weaker than the evidence supporting regulation of particulates, especially if we take into account the fact that ground-level ozone seems to have nontrivial health benefits. But perhaps a court should say that there is much scientific uncertainty here, and that the EPA should be allowed to resolve the doubts as it sees fit. If the court took this route, it would be following the direction established in the *Lead Industries* case, in which the EPA was given a great deal of room to maneuver.[6]

There are several advantages to this approach, especially if we consider the institutional role of the courts. A serious problem with intense judicial review of agency action is that it creates delay—and hence ensures a bias in favor of the status quo.[7] In light of the inevitable scientific uncertainties, it should exceptionally easy for a skillful advocate to challenge almost any national standard as either too high or too low.[8] On the basis of EPA's own data, an environmental group would have had a quite plausible argument that the regulation of particulates was insufficiently stringent under the statute.[9] In order to allow agencies room to maneuver in the face of scientific uncertainty, it would be reasonable to say that on the basis of minimally plausible evidence, courts should simply uphold the relevant decisions. A special virtue of this approach is that the Bush Administration would be permitted to come to a different conclusion from the Clinton Administration, and vice versa, because different judgments of value could lead to different conclusions about how to proceed in the face of ambiguous science.

Evidentiary Review

Another possibility, hinted at above, would be to invalidate the ozone regulation while upholding the regulation of particulates. The simple claim here would be that on the evidence given, the new particulates standard was requisite to protect the public health—but the new ozone standard was not, especially if we take into account the health benefits of ground-level ozone.[10] We have seen the possibility that, all things considered, the regulation would increase rather than reduce health problems.

Even if this is overstated, Justice Breyer's opinion in the *American Trucking*[11] case rightly suggests that under the "requisite to protect the public health" language, the EPA is not supposed to remove all risks from the air, or to make the air "risk-free," and that the EPA should take account of context to compare the risk at hand to risks that people face in ordinary life. It does appear that the statistical risks from low levels of ozone are smaller than statistical risks that people find acceptable in multiple domains (see Appendix A, Table A-2). The Clean Air Scientific Advisory Committee (CASAC), an independent panel of scientists that examines the evidence used in EPA's review of the air-quality standards, concluded that the level chosen by the EPA did not provide "significantly" more protection than the existing standard—an observation that raises serious questions about whether the new standard is "requisite to protect the public health." Particulates are very different on this count. Here the existing hazards do seem high, on a plausible reading of the evidence. Indeed, CASAC agreed that scientific evidence for PM 2.5's adverse health effects provided an adequate basis for the new standard. By upholding the particulates standard and asking the EPA to explain itself more thoroughly with respect to ozone, the court would be contributing to the development of a kind of common law of acceptable risks of the sort that Justice Breyer seemed to be encouraging.

The approach I am suggesting—upholding the particulates standard as requisite, while invalidating the ozone standard as not shown to be requisite—would certainly be reasonable. The principal objection would be institutional; it would involve the special limitations of judicial review. The evidence shows the possibility of nontrivial health gains from the ozone regulation, and in the face of scientific uncertainty, the agency should be permitted to make whatever (reasonable) policy choices it likes. Especially in view of the risk of status quo bias, perhaps the court should refuse to invalidate a judgment like that in the ozone case, even if the judgment seems wrong.

There is a further set of questions. Suppose that the new particulates standard should be, and is, upheld. At that stage, EPA will have to decide what, exactly, to regulate; and to do this, it will have to decide what fine particulates consist of. This is not a simple question. Currently EPA is focusing on nitrogen oxides and sulfur oxides but ignoring mobile sources, even though mobile sources appear to be emerging as the principal source of fine particulates (as well as of aromatics). Ideally, the EPA should be able to create a trading system for the precursors for fine particulates, just as it has for ozone, and just as the Clinton Administration proposed for control of global warming.[12] But EPA has refused to attempt this step, and for one simple reason: It does not know what the precursors are, or at least how they relate to one another. There are many complexities here. Ideally, an agency that is sensitive to the need for high benefits and low costs will try to design a system that promotes regulatory goals at the lowest possible expense. But in view of the technical complexities, it is not clear how much a court can do to require such an approach here.

Requiring a Clear Standard

A final possibility would be to invalidate both regulations as arbitrary or as inadequately justified, not because the risks are too low, but because EPA did not explain on what grounds it chose these particular regulations rather than ones that would be somewhat more strict or somewhat more lenient. The Supreme Court's holding, in the *American Trucking* case, that the Constitution does not require this form of specificity says nothing about whether such specificity might be required as a matter of administrative law.[13] If the EPA cannot explain, in concrete terms, why it chose the particular levels it chose, how can courts know that the agency's decision was not arbitrary?

In doctrinal terms, judicial invalidation on these grounds might take one of two routes. First, the court might invoke the statutory language and say that it cannot know whether the particular level chosen is "requisite to protect the public health" unless it has a clear sense of why the EPA reached that conclusion. Without numbers and criteria, it is impossible to obtain any such sense. Second, the court might put the statutory language to one side and say that it cannot tell whether the agency's action is arbitrary or capricious, within the meaning of the Administrative Procedure Act,[14] unless the EPA has given a more detailed explanation of its choice. Either of these conclusions would be relatively conventional, and neither would mark a huge departure from current law.

But there would nonetheless be a genuine innovation here. Thus far, courts have not required anything like a quantitative basis for health and safety regulation. Sometimes they have required agencies to show that the costs are not grossly disproportionate to the benefits;[15] sometimes they have prohibited agencies from acting when it seems as if there are no benefits at all.[16] But the relevant decisions have been more qualitative than quantitative, and when they have been quantitative, the overall judgment has seemed overwhelmingly clear.[17] It would be a significant step from these decisions to a holding that agencies must quantify the effects of pollutants at various levels so as to explain, in specific terms, why one level was chosen rather than another.

Would the step be worthwhile? While I cannot discuss the issue in detail, I believe that it would be, at least for the ozone rule, where the evidence of harm is relatively thin.[18] Such a ruling would not impose an unacceptable informational burden on EPA. In fact, EPA routinely gathers enough information to provide the necessary explanation. At the same time, such a requirement would provide a useful spur to the agency, one that would also produce a higher degree of rationality and coherence. The result would be to show when, and why, environmental groups or industry would be able to mount a successful challenge to an ambient air-quality standard.

In sum: On remand, the court should probably uphold the particulates standard, on the ground that on a reasonable view of the evidence, the agency had sufficient basis to conclude that that standard was "requisite to protect the public health," even without an attempt to quantify. At the same time, the court should probably remand the ozone rule, on the ground that the EPA has not given an adequate explanation of why that rule is "requisite." The court should encourage the EPA to be as quantitative as possible. And on remand, the EPA should take up the invitation, attempting in the process to give a clear sense, for the first time, of why it has chosen one regulatory "point" rather than another.

My principal goal, however, has not been to urge any particular result in the cases of particulates and ozone, which will obviously turn on close engagement with the record. I have attempted instead to give a sense of the proper judicial approach to ambient air-quality standards. Cost-benefit analysis is not permitted under the relevant provisions of the Clean Air Act, but it is nonetheless possible for both the EPA and federal courts to attempt a more rational system for assessing air-quality problems. As an initial step, I have argued on behalf of a high degree of quantification to ensure that the government addresses the large pollution problems and does not spend significant resources on the small ones.

Notes

1. *See* Randall Lutter, *An Analysis of the Use of EPA's Benefit Estimates, in* OMB's DRAFT REPORT ON THE COSTS AND BENEFITS OF REGULATION (October 1998).

2. 175 F.3d at 1027.

3. *See* JOHN GRAHAM & JONATHAN WIENER, RISK VS. RISK (Harvard Univ. Press, 1997); Cass R. Sunstein, *Health-Health Trade-Offs, in* CASS R. SUNSTEIN, FREE MARKETS AND SOCIAL JUSTICE (Oxford Univ. Press, 1997).

4. *See* ROBERT HAHN ET AL., DO FEDERAL REGULATIONS REDUCE MORTALITY? (AEI, 2001).

5. *See* 175 F.2d at 1027.

6. *See* Lead Industries Association v. EPA, 647 F.2d 1130 (D.C. Cir. 1980).

7. *See* JERRY MASHAW & DAVID HARSFT, THE STRUGGLE FOR AUTO SAFETY (Yale Univ., 1993).

8. *See* the discussion of arsenic in Sunstein, *supra* note 3.

9. This is because a more stringent standard would, on the EPA's own number, produce substantial health benefits. See Table A-7 of Appendix A.

10. I am not attempting here to reach definitive conclusions about the scientific data. I am simply suggesting how a reviewing court might reasonably respond to the data that the EPA has compiled.

11. Whitman v. American Trucking Ass'ns, 531 U.S. 457, 475 (2001) (Breyer, J., concurring in part and concurring in the judgment).

12. On the advantages of economic incentives and trading systems, *see* CASS R. SUNSTEIN, RISK AND REASON, chapter 10 (forthcoming).

13. *See* Whitman v. American Trucking Ass'ns, *supra* note 11.

14. 5 U.S.C. 706.

15. Corrosion Proof Fittings v. EPA, 947 F.2d 1201 (5th Cir 1991).

16. *See* Chemical Manufacturers Assn. v. EPA, 217 F.3d 861 (D.C. Cir. 2000).

17. *See Corrosion Proof Fittings*, at 1205-11.

18. For a detailed discussion, see SUNSTEIN, *supra* note 3.

THE ROLE OF CONGRESS 13

Should Congress consider amending the national ambient air-quality provisions of the Clean Air Act? I believe that it should. The analysis thus far suggests three possibilities: more guidance on safety and health, an instruction to use better tools, and an instruction to consider costs. Let us discuss these possibilities in sequence.

How Safe Is Safe Enough?

As emphasized throughout, a crucial defect of the national ambient air-quality provisions is that they seem to assume that whether air is "safe" can be assessed solely on the basis of the facts. The truth is that the facts might be able to show the degree of risk (at least within a range), but they cannot show whether any particular degree of safety is "safe enough." Whether pollutants lack safe thresholds, "the paradigm of selecting a standard at the lowest-observable-effects level and then providing an 'adequate margin of safety' is not possible."[1] The result of the statutory framework is to misframe the key question and also to give EPA little guidance for asking and answering that question. As we have seen, EPA has greatly struggled with the resulting difficulties.

Congress should amend the statute to identify the specific factors that EPA should consider in making the judgment about appropriate national standards. Congress might offer substantive guidance by saying, for example, that the EPA must consider the severity of the risk, the size of the affected population, and the anticipated adverse effects at various exposure levels.

Congress might, in short, require a benefits analysis of the sort I have been urging, including a requirement that EPA identify the range of scientific uncertainty. Congress might also say that a benefits analysis should always include a comparison between the chosen alternative and reasonable alternatives, both more and less stringent. The EPA might thereby be instructed to consider reasonable alternatives to the option being recommended, and for all of the options, to identify, to the extent possible, the nature of the risks that it is reducing while quantifying the relevant risk reductions. Appendix A shows that this is now possible. At the same time, the EPA should be told to produce standards to say why and when a certain level of health protection would be deemed "requisite to protect the public health," and why and when more stringent regulation would not be deemed requisite. Congress might say in the process that EPA should regulate all significant or substantial risks, and should not regulate risks that are trivial, de minimis, or at the level that most people customarily and unhesitatingly run in ordinary life.

The strongest argument against an amendment to this effect is that it is unnecessary; if the EPA moved in the directions suggested above, it would essentially be interpreting the current statute as if it contained instructions of exactly this sort. But an amendment of this kind, suggested by important amendments to the Safe Drinking Water Act,[2] would at least provide a clear legislative signal. It would also move EPA judgments in the direction of greater transparency. And it would tell the EPA to take steps that courts might be reluctant to require on their own.

Better Tools

We now know that significant cost savings can be achieved by using more flexible, market-oriented instruments.[3] Indeed, some of the most important changes in federal regulatory law have involved a shift to such instruments, which promise to achieve regulatory goals at a far lower cost than can be achieved by national "command-and-control."[4] In the United States, the most dramatic program of economic incentives can be found in the 1990 amendments to the Clean Air Act.[5] The act now explicitly creates an emissions-trading system for the control of acid deposition. In these amendments, Congress has made an explicit decision about aggregate emissions level for a pollutant. Whether it is the correct one may be disputed. But surely there are large democratic benefits from ensuring that public attention is focused on that issue.

There are other beneficial features to the acid deposition provisions. Congress has said that polluters may obtain allowances for emissions avoided through energy conservation and renewable energy. In this way, avoidance of this kind is turned into dollars, in the form of an increased permission to pollute. This provision creates an incentive to shift to conservation and renewable sources without causing further environmental degradation. Polluters are explicitly permitted to trade their allowances; this is a first in national legislation. In this way, people who are able to reduce their pollution below the specified level receive economic benefits. Again incentives are created for environmentally beneficial behavior. An especially intriguing provision allows spot and advance sales of sulfur dioxide allowances, to be purchasable at $1,500 per ton. Through this route, polluters must—for the first time—pay a fee for their pollution. Even more intriguing is a provision calling for auction sales of specified numbers of sulfur dioxide allowances. Here the market is permitted to set the price for polluting activity.

The acid deposition program has turned out to be a terrific success.[6] Compliance with the program has been nearly perfect. Considerable trading has occurred; an effective market in permits developed, just as anticipated. As compared with a command-and-control system, the trading mechanism is estimated to have saved $357 million annually in its first five years. For the next 15 years, the mechanism is predicted to save $2.28 billion annually, for an overall savings in excess of $20 billion. Since enactment of the program, the price of transporting coal has been reduced dramatically because of deregulation, and the program proved able to handle this surprise, with permits trading for far less than anticipated. Indeed, it is fair to say that the acid deposition program ranks among the most spectacular success stories in all of environmental regulation. Because the costs of the program have been so much lower than anticipated, the cost-benefit ratio seems especially good, with compliance costs of $870 million compared to annual benefits ranging from $12 billion to $78 billion—including reductions of nearly 10,000 premature deaths and over 14,500 cases of chronic bronchitis.

Sometimes, however, the EPA is banned from using economic incentives, and sometimes it does not choose such instruments even when it is legally authorized to do so. We should hope that in the future, Congress will build on the acid deposition model, using economic incentives to control environmental harms. Wherever feasible, the EPA should use economic incentives rather than a "command-and-control" approach.[7] It is clear that an approach of this kind could save substantial resources, and if the instruments are properly chosen, it should do so without compromising air-quality goals.[8] An effort to encourage the EPA to select less burdensome alternatives could send a desirable signal to attempt the least-cost methods of obtaining regulatory goals and might in addition spur creative experimentation.

Costs and Benefits

A possible lesson of EPA experience with national standards is that EPA should be required or at least permitted to consider costs when setting such standards. It is worth giving serious consideration to a statutory change.

The basic reasoning here is straightforward. If a reduction in some pollutant from 0.8 parts per million to 0.7 parts per million would be a trivial expense, surely it should be required. If it would cost trillions of dollars, there had better be good grounds to believe in very substantial health benefits. If the ozone regulation would have relatively low costs, it would seem to be justified, notwithstanding the fact that the accompanying benefits do not appear to be large. The overall assessment would be quite different if the costs would be exceptionally high. Recall that high costs are important not for their own sake, but because they can have concrete consequences for real people, including lower wages, fewer jobs, higher prices, more poverty, even worse health, and more deaths. In these circumstances, it seems reasonable to suggest that Congress should require EPA to consider costs as well as benefits in setting national standards.

A possible argument to the contrary is that national standards operate as aspirations, not ordinary law, and aspirations, at least, should be set on a health-only basis—not because there is a magic place where air quality is "safe," but because it is valuable to obtain, and use, a technocratic judgment that people should have air quality of a certain specified sort.[9] But the problem is that it is difficult to assess safety in a cost vacuum. Much of the time, air pollutants lack safe thresholds. Because there is no set point when things become safe, no purely technocratic judgment can be made about the appropriate level of air quality. There are different increments of safety, depending on the level of regulation. A judgment of value must be made about the appropriate increment. In order to make that judgment, both costs and benefits are relevant. If the cost of achieving an additional increment of safety is low, the situation is different from what it is if the cost of achieving that additional increment is high. This simple point weakens the suggestion that aspirations should be set, via the EPA, on the basis of health alone.

A more convincing argument against an amendment to require cost-benefit analysis is that the statute, complex as it is, actually embodies a better accommodation of costs and benefits than would a statute that required cost-benefit analysis at the level of standard setting (see chapter 7 for an outline). On this view, the optimal system is one in which EPA makes an initial, purely health-based judgment, and then the process of implementation allows costs to play a role at various stages, emphatically including an expectation that implementation will not be immediate and will in fact be a product of a continuing inquiry into whether compliance is worthwhile, all things considered. A possible virtue of this state of affairs is precisely the aspirational quality of the health-based standard, setting a target against which various state performances can be measured. The aspirational quality can also contribute to technology forcing, an important and often highly desirable phenomenon in environmental protection,[10] and a phenomenon to which cost-benefit analysis is, at least in practice,[11] unlikely to contribute.

This pragmatic argument against a statutory amendment is certainly reasonable. But in the abstract, it is hard to know whether the argument is valid.[12] What is clear is that the statutory scheme, pragmatically defensible as it may be, is far from transparent and provides a set of confusing signals to the American public. In the overall system for improving the quality of the ambient air, costs are certainly relevant and cannot sensibly be ignored.

Identifying Gains

Whenever an agency issues a regulation designed to diminish risks to health, safety, or the environment, it should attempt to identify the gains sought by the particular regulation it has chosen, and it should compare these gains to those under at least two reasonable alternative regimes, one stricter and one more lenient. In this light, the most serious problem with the EPA's performance in issuing national air-quality standards is that it usually fails to explain, in simple, concise terms, its decision to require a particular level of ambient air quality. Sometimes the EPA acts as if it were pursuing "safety" and ensuring "safe levels" without sufficiently acknowledging that for most pollutants, the serious question is what degree of safety. To its credit, the EPA invariably offers extensive discussions of the underlying data, demonstrating that there is a genuine health risk at current levels. But to the extent that it provides an explanation of its particular choices, the discussion often involves little more than evidence of nontrivial adverse effects at those current levels—evidence that may well argue for a reduction from current levels, but does not by itself call for any particular regulatory standard.

In general, the EPA (and other agencies involved in similar tasks) should offer a detailed cost-benefit analysis. This requirement, formally recognized by executive order, has been been taken insufficiently seriously by federal agencies. Where costs are not relevant under the law, and when agencies must concentrate on health or safety alone, the government should nonetheless undertake two tasks. First, it should undertake an analysis of both benefits and costs, so that the public will know what is at stake. Second, it should explain its decision on the basis of a careful exploration, both qualitative and quantitative, of the benefits that it hopes to obtain.

The central goal of this approach would be to create a kind of federal common law of environmental protection, generated in the first instance by administrative agencies, and designed to promote consistency and rationality in the protection of health and safety. Ordinary judicial review should require any national ambient air-quality standard to be accompanied by an adequate explanation of why that level, rather than one more or less stringent, has been selected. By itself, this requirement calls (to the extent feasible) for a high degree of quantification from EPA; it also bears on the performance of other regulatory agencies entrusted with the task of promoting health, safety, and the environment. A requirement of this kind would mark a key moment in the shift from the rigidity and simplicity of 1970s environmentalism toward a new and more promising approach—one that places a high premium on assessing the magnitude of problems, ensuring consistency across regulations, limiting interest-group power, acquiring better information, and authorizing democratic control of regulatory choices.

Notes

1. *See* Randall Lutter & Christopher DeMuth, *Ozone and the Constitution at the EPA*, ON THE ISSUES 3 (July 1999).
2. 42 U.S.C. § 300g-1(b).
3. *See generally* NATIONAL ACADEMY OF PUBLIC ADMINISTRATION, THE ENVIRONMENT GOES TO MARKET (1994).
4. *See* A. DENNY ELLERMAN ET AL., MARKETS FOR CLEAN AIR (Cambridge Univ. Press, 2001).
5. 42 U.S.C. 7651 et seq.
6. *See generally* A. DENNY ELLERMAN ET AL., *supra* note 4.
7. *Cf.* Statement of Jonathan Wiener Before the Committee on Governmental Affairs, March 8, 1995 (urging general amendment to allow agencies to choose incentive-based regulation).
8. *See* Robert Hahn & Gordon Hester, *Marketable Permits: Lessons for Theory and Practice*, 16 ECOLOGY L.Q. 361 (1989).
9. *See* the discussion from Administrator Browner, in Clean Air Act: Hearings before the Subcommittee on Clean Air, 105th Cong. 262 (1997). Administrator Browner goes on to say: "While cost-benefit analysis is a tool that can be helpful in developing strategies to implement our nation's air quality standards, we believe it is inappropriate for us to set the standards themselves. In many cases, cost-benefit analysis has overstated costs. In addition, many kinds of benefits are virtually impossible to quantify—how do I put a dollar value on reductions in a child's lung function or the premature aging of lungs or increased susceptibility to respiratory infection?" Ironically, the Regulatory Impact Analysis required by Presidents Reagan, Bush, and Clinton engages in monetization of just this kind.
10. Technology forcing is not desirable if the costs of the forcing greatly exceed the benefits—if, for example, the new technology contributes little to air quality but substantially increases prices and diminishes wages.
11. In principle, a competent cost-benefit analysis would include the costs of new technological developments, and indeed this issue is discussed in the particulates and ozone regulatory impact analysis. The problem is that government is likely to have very little information about the cost of technological innovation, and industry is likely to overstate those costs by a significant amount.
12. *See* the valuable discussion in James Krier, *On the Topology of National Standards in a Federal System—And Why It Matters*, 54 MD. L. REV. 1226 (1995), a staunch and long-time defender of cost-benefit analysis for the Clean Air Act, who acknowledges the pragmatic possibility.

COSTS AND BENEFITS FOR EVERYONE 14

My goals in this book have been to investigate the rise of the cost-benefit state, to defend it, and to see how it bears on some central questions in regulatory law and policy. A great virtue of cost-benefit analysis is that it promises to promote a better understanding of the actual consequences of regulation. At the same time, cost-benefit analysis often helps to identify the best tools for achieving social goals. A significantly reformed system of regulation could save many lives and also many billions of dollars. In a society that is concerned about both safety and economic growth, there is every reason to adopt reforms that will produce such savings.

When the public is becoming fearful of an imaginary danger, an effort to tabulate the costs and benefits can overcome unjustified panic—and prevent the government from imposing high costs for little good. As we have seen, cost-benefit analysis can operate to reduce general concern by showing that highly publicized problems may be greatly exaggerated. When the public is indifferent to serious risks in daily life, an analysis of costs and benefits can counteract unjustified neglect. As we have seen, the Office of Information and Regulatory Affairs has responded to this problem with the idea of "prompt letters," trying to encourage agencies to issue regulations that will actually do some good. When people are not attuned to the potential harms of attempting to address genuine problems, cost-benefit analysis can place the full range of effects on the public viewscreen. When regulation actually increases the very risks that it is designed to reduce, an understanding of "health-health trade-offs" can be a valuable corrective.

These points have many implications for current problems. In the context of global warming, for example, regulation is indeed desirable, because the risk appears to be real. But we should attempt to use the cheapest possible tools (such as economic incentives), so that we do not drive up the price of energy or otherwise produce serious problems. At every point, our actions should be undertaken with close reference to the costs, economic and potentially even environmental, of our efforts to reduce global warming. Should fuel economy standards be heightened for new cars? Very possibly, in order to increase energy independence and especially because such standards can reduce the risk of global warming. But any fuel economy standards should be designed so as not to create smaller, less safe vehicles.

In the context of genetic modification of food, it is important to see that there is immense opportunity for producing nutritious, cheaper food, of special importance for poor people. Efforts to regulate genetic engineering should be undertaken with this point in mind. Indeed, organic foods are often less healthy than foods that contain preservatives; the natural should not be identified with the safe. If we are really concerned to reduce risks to life and health, we will increase the effort to reduce cigarette smoking, which continues to kill hundreds of thousands of people each year. We will also take steps to combat obesity and to ensure better diet and more exercise; these are areas where real health gains can be achieved. For example, trans-fatty acids in foods such as margarine, cookies, and french fries increase the risk of heart disease; steps should be taken to reduce their consumption. In the context of fears induced by terrorism, it is important not to overreact. Airplane travel remains extremely safe. As of this writing, people have been irrationally, and excessively, worried about the threat of anthrax contamination. Should every American receive smallpox vaccine? Everything depends on the consequences of widespread vaccination. It is certainly possible that vaccination would be too expensive to be worthwhile—and that the health risks of vaccination would outweigh the health benefits. I do not mean to take a stand on the particular issue, but to point to the questions that sensible officials should be asking.

More generally, I have urged that government should perform cost-benefit calculations for all major regulations and that agencies should be required to show that the benefits justify the costs. If an agency seeks to proceed even though the benefits do not justify the costs, it should explain itself, perhaps by showing that the risk at issue is faced disproportionately by children or is especially hard to avoid—or that the benefits of the regulation would be enjoyed mostly by the poor, and the costs imposed mostly on the wealthy. In the process of making these arguments, I have raised doubts about the internationally influential "precautionary principle." Some precautions simply are not worthwhile, and other precautions would actually increase risks, environmental and otherwise. Precautions against the risks created by pesticides, for example, might make the food supply less safe, by encouraging people to consume natural foods, which contain risks of their own. Often the precautionary principle is paralyzing, because risks are produced by action and inaction, and by everything in between. The real challenge is to put all of the consequences on the public viewscreen, so that informed choices can be made.

More particularly, I have attempted to identify and defend the cost-benefit default principles, designed to increase the rationality and sense of regulatory policy. Courts have been allowing agencies to exempt trivial risks, to consider substitute risks, and to take account of costs in deciding on the appropriate degree of regulation. I have attempted to explain the meaning of these principles and to give a sense of the questions that might be asked in the future, and also of some possible answers. I have urged that in attempting to clean the air, the Environmental Protection Agency should be as quantitative as possible. This is not because the numbers tell us nearly everything that we need to know, but because without the numbers we do not know nearly enough. Understood in a certain way, cost-benefit analysis deserves wide approval—not a bit less so than the deregulation of the 1970s and 1980s, and the 1990s shift to economic incentives as opposed to national command-and-control. More than that, cost-benefit analysis can be seen as the general framework for evaluating both deregulation and economic incentives—and for approving them in many contexts. Indeed, I believe that cost-benefit analysis should have the same relationship to the first decade of the twenty-first century as its predecessors had to the closing decades of the twentieth.

The best defense of cost-benefit analysis relies not on controversial claims from neoclassical economics, but on a simple appreciation of how we all make mistakes in thinking about risks—and on an understanding that when people err, governments will err too. This is not at all a claim that in the areas of health, safety, and the environment, American government suffers from a systematic problem of "overregulation." It is far more accurate to say that we have both overregulation and underregulation, or what has been called a system of simultaneous "paranoia and neglect."[1] The best starting point for assessing the situation involves a comprehensive understanding of the effects of regulation and, to the extent possible, an attempt to quantify those effects. This will allow us to attack the most serious problems and to ensure that we do not devote our limited resources to the least serious ones.

It is well past time to go beyond 1970s environmentalism, with its emphasis on the existence of serious problems and the need for prompt action. What is needed instead is an approach that attempts to assess the magnitude of problems and to ensure sensible priority setting. Properly understood, cost-benefit analysis should not be seen as a method of converting all human values to monetary terms, or even as a purely technocratic tool suited for an elite corps of government bureaucrats. On the contrary, cost-benefit analysis should be treated as an instrument for ensuring that government regulation will actually promote our purposes by guaranteeing that it will improve, rather than undermine, human well-being.

1. *See* John Graham, *Making Sense of Risk, in* RISKS, COSTS, AND LIVES SAVED 183, Robert Hahn ed. (Cambridge Univ. Press, 1996).

APPENDIX A

COST-BENEFIT NUMBERS FOR OZONE AND PARTICULATES

In order to give a more specific sense of how cost-benefit analysis works, I provide here a number of tables from the EPA's regulatory impact analysis of its ozone and particulates rules. Notice that it is often possible to give ranges of expected health gains, and also to convert those gains into monetary equivalents. The particular numbers might, of course, be argued. I offer them here simply to provide an illustration of how two pollutants, and several possible regulatory targets, have been evaluated.

Table A-1
Proposed PM$_{10}$ Standard (50/150 _g/m³)
99th Percentile
National Annual Health Incidence Reductions
Estimates are incremental to the current ozone and PM NAAQS
(year = 2010)

Endpoint		Partial Attainment Scenario
	Annual PM$_{2.5}$ (_g/m³) Daily PM$_{2.5}$ (_g/m³)	50 150
1. Mortality: short-term exposure long-term exposure		360 340
2. Chronic Bronchitis		6,800
Hospital Admissions: 3. All respiratory (all ages) All respiratory (ages 65 +) Pneumonia (ages 65 +) COPD (ages 65 +) 4. Congestive heart failure 5. Ischemic heart disease		190 470 170 140 130 140
6. Acute Bronchitis		1,100
7. Lower Respiratory Symptoms 8. Upper Respiratory Symptoms Shortness of breath Asthma attacks		10,400 5,300 18,300 8,800
9. Work Loss Days		106,000
10. Minor Restricted Activity Days (MRADs)		879,000

Table A-2
Ozone: National Annual Health Incidence Reductions
Estimates are incremental to the current ozone NAAQS (year = 2010)

Endpoint	Partial Attainment Scenario		
	0.08 5th Max High-end Estimate	0.08 4th Max Low- to High-end Estimate	0.08 3rd Max High-end Estimate
Ozone Health:			
1. Mortality	80	0 - 80	120
Hospital Admissions			
2. All respiratory (all ages)	280	300 - 300	420
All respiratory (ages 65 +)	2,300	2,330 - 2,330	1,570
Pneumonia (ages 65 +)	860	870 - 870	600
COPD (ages 65 +)	260	260-260	200
Emergency department visits for asthma	120	130 - 130	180
3. Acute Respiratory			
Symptoms (any of 19)	28,510	29,840 - 29,840	42,070
Asthma attacks	60	60 - 60	90
MRADs	620	650 - 650	920
4. Mortality from air toxics	1	1 - 1	2
Ancillary PM Health:			
1. Mortality: short-term exposure	60	0 - 80	110
Long-term exposure	180	0 - 250	340
2. Chronic Bronchitis	400	0 - 530	690
Hospital Admissions:			
3. All respiratory (all ages)	70	0 - 90	120
All respiratory (ages 65 +)	50	0 - 60	80
Pneumonia (ages 65 +)	20	0 - 20	30
COPD (ages 65 +)	10	0 - 20	20
4. Congestive heart failure	10	0 - 20	20
5. Ischemic heart disease	10	0 - 20	20

Table A-2
Ozone: National Annual Health Incidence Reductions
(continued)

Endpoint	Partial Attainment Scenario		
	0.08 5th Max High-end Estimate	0.08 4th Max Low- to High-end Estimate	0.08 3rd Max High-end Estimate
6. Acute Bronchitis	290	0 - 400	530
7. Lower Respiratory Symptoms	3,510	0 - 4,670	6,190
8. Upper Respiratory Symptoms	320	0 - 430	570
Shortness of breath	800	0 - 1,220	1,660
Asthma attacks	4,210	0 - 5,510	7,200
9. Work Loss Days	38,700	0 - 50,440	66,160
10. Minor Restricted Activity Days (MRADs)	322,460	0 - 420,300	551,300

Table A-3
Willingness-to-Pay Estimates (Mean Values)

Health Endpoint	Mean WTP Value per Incident (1990 $)
Mortality Life saved Life year extended	$4.8 million $120,000
Hospital Admissions:	
All Respiratory Illnesses, all ages	$12,700
Pneumonia, age < 65	$13,400
COPD, age > 65	$15,900
Ischemic Heart Disease, age < 65	$ 20,600
Congestive Heart Failure, age > 65	$ 16,600
Emergency Visits for Asthma	$9,000
Chronic Bronchitis	$260,000
Upper Respiratory Symptoms	$19
Lower Respiratory Symptoms	$12
Acute Bronchitis	$45
Acute Respiratory Symptoms (any of 19)	$18
Asthma	$32
Shortness of Breath	$5.30
Sinusitis and Hay Fever	Not monetized
Work Loss Days	$83
Restricted Activity Days (RAD) Minor RAD Respiratory RAD	$38 not monetized
Worker Productivity	$1 per worker per 10% change in ozone
Visibility: residential	$14 per unit decrease in deciview per household
Recreational	Range of $7.30 to $11 per unit decrease in deciview per household (see U.S. EPA, 1997a)
Household Soiling Damage	$2.50 per household per $?g/m^3$

Table A-4
Proposed PM$_{10}$ Standard (50/150 _g/m³) 99th Percentile

National Annual Monetized Health Benefits Incidence Reductions
Estimates are incremental to the current ozone (0.12 ppm, 1-hr.)
(billions of 1990 $; year = 2010)

Endpoint		Partial Attainment Scenario High-end Estimate
	Annual PM$_{2.5}$ (_g/m³)	50
	Daily PM$_{2.5}$ (_g/m³)	150
1. **Mortality: short-term exposure**		$1.7
Long-term exposure		$1.6
2. **Chronic Bronchitis**		$1.8
Hospital Admissions:		
3. All respiratory (all ages)		$0.002
All respiratory (ages 65 +)		$0.006
Pneumonia (ages 65 +)		$0.003
COPD (ages 65 +)		$0.002
4. Congestive heart failure		$0.002
5. Ischemic heart disease		$0.003
6. **Acute Bronchitis**		$0
7. **Lower Respiratory Symptoms**		$0
8. **Upper Respiratory Symptoms**		$0
Shortness of breath		$0
Asthma attacks		$0
9. **Work Loss Days**		$0.009
10. **Minor Restricted Activity Days (MRADs)**		$0.034
Total monetized benefits		
Using long-term mortality		$3.4
Using short-term mortality		$3.5

Table A-5
Ozone: National Annual Monetized Health Benefits Estimates
Estimates are incremental to the current ozone NAAQS (0.12 ppm, 1-hour)
(billions of 1990 $; year = 2010)

Endpoint	Partial Attainment Scenario		
	0.08 5th Max High-end Estimate	0.08 4th Max Low- to High-end Estimate	0.08 3rd Max High-end Estimate
Ozone Health:			
1. Mortality	$0.370	$0.000 - $0.380	$0.570
Hospital Admissions			
2. All respiratory (all ages)	$0.004	$0.004 - $0.004	$0.006
All respiratory (ages 65 +)	$0.029	$0.029 - $0.029	$0
Pneumonia (ages 65 +)	$0.014	$0.014 - $0.014	$0.010
COPD (ages 65 +)	$0.004	$0.004 - $0.004	$0.003
Emergency department visits for asthma	$0.001	$0.001 - $0.001	$0.002
3. Acute Respiratory Symptoms (any of 19)	$0.001	$0.001 - $0.001	$0.001
Asthma attacks	$0	$0 - $0	$0
MRADs	$0	$0 - $0	$0
4. Mortality from air toxics	$0.003	$0.006- $0.006	$0.011
Ancillary PM Health:			
1. Mortality: short-term exposure	$0.300	$0 - $0.400	$0.520
Long-term exposure	$0.870	$0 - $1.210	$1.640
2. Chronic Bronchitis	$0.110	$0 - $0.140	$0.180
Hospital Admissions:			
3. All respiratory (all ages)	$0.001	$0 - $0.001	$0.001
All respiratory (ages 65 +)	$0.001	$0 - $0.001	$0.001
Pneumonia (ages 65 +)	$0	$0 - $0	$0
COPD (ages 65 +)	$0	$0 - $0	$0

Table A-5
Ozone: National Annual Monetized Health Benefits Estimates
(continued)

Endpoint	Partial Attainment Scenario		
	0.08 5th Max High-end Estimate	0.08 4th Max Low- to High-end Estimate	0.08 3rd Max High-end Estimate
4. Congestive heart failure	$0	$0 - $0	$0
5. Ischemic heart disease	$0	$0 - $0	$0
6. **Acute Bronchitis**	$0	$0 - $0	$0
7. **Lower Respiratory Symptoms**	$0	$0 - $0	$0
8. **Upper Respiratory Symptoms**	$0	$0 - $0	$0
Shortness of breath	$0	$0 - $0	$0
Asthma attacks	$0	$0 - $0	$0
9. **Work Loss Days**	$0.003	$0 - $0.004	$0.005
10. **Minor Restricted Activity Days (MRADs)**	$0.012	$0 - $0.016	$0.020
Total monetized benefits Using short-term PM mortality	$0.790	$0.056	$1.300
Using long-term PM mortality	$1.400	$1.785	$2.400

Table A-6
Ozone: Summary of National Annual Monetized
Health and Welfare Benefits[a]
Estimates are incremental to the current ozone and PM NAAQS
(billions of 1990 $; year = 2010)

Endpoint	Partial Attainment Scenario		
	0.08 5th Max High-end Estimate	0.08 4th Max Low- to High-end Estimate	0.08 3rd Max High-end Estimate
Health Benefits	$1.4	$0.06 to $1.76	$2.4
Welfare Benefits	$0.25	$0.32 to $0.32	$0.5
Total monetized benefits	$1.6	$0.4 to $2.1	$2.9

Table A-7
Comparison of Annual Benefits and Costs of
PM Alternatives in 2010[a,b] (1990 $)

PM$_{2.5}$ Alternative (_g/m³)	Annual Benefits of Partial Attainment[c] (billion $) (A)	Annual Costs of Partial Attainment[c] (billion $) (B)	Net Benefit of Partial Attainment[c] (billion $) (A - B)	Number of Residual Nonattainment[c] Counties
16/65 (high-end estimate)	90	5.5	85	19
15/65 (low-end estimate) (high-end estimate)	19 - 104	8.6	10 - 95	30
15/50 (high-end estimate)	108	9.4	98	41

a. All estimates are measured incremental to partial attainment of the current PM$_{10}$ standard (PM$_{10}$ 50/150, 1 expected exceedance per year).

b. The results for 16/65 and 15/50 are only for the high-end assumptions range. The low-end estimates were not calculated for these alternatives.

c. Partial attainment benefits based upon post-control air quality as defined in the control cost analysis.

Table A-8
Comparison of Annual Benefits and Costs of
Ozone Table Alternatives in 2010[a,b] (1990 $)

Ozone (pp/m)	Annual Benefits Alternative Attainment (billion $) (A)	Annual Costs of Partial Attainment[c] (billion $)[c] (B)	Net Benefits of Partial Attainment[c] (billion $) (A - B)	Number of Residual or Partial Nonattainment[c] Areas
0.08 5th Max (high-end estimate)	1.6	0.9	0.7	12
0.08 4th Max (low-end estimate) (high-end estimate)	0.4 - 2.1	1.1	(0.7) - 1.0	17
0.08 3rd Max (high-end estimate)	2.9	1.4	1.5	27

a. All estimates are measured incremental to partial attainment of the baseline current ozone standard (0.12ppm, 1 expected exceedance per year).
b. The results for 0.08, 5th and 0.08, 3rd max. are only for the high-end assumptions. The low-end estimates were not calculated for these alternatives.
c. Partial attainment benefits based upon post-control air-quality estimates as defined in the control cost analysis.

APPENDIX B

DOSE-RESPONSE CURVES: WHAT LAWYERS, JUDGES, AND CITIZENS SHOULD KNOW

To evaluate risks associated with toxic substances, and to undertake cost-benefit analysis, it is often important to have a sense of the dose-response curve. The purpose of this appendix is to give a general overview of the possibilities. The general lesson is that a number of shapes are possible and that the benefits to be received from regulation depend largely on the shape in the particular case. If the dose-response curve shows a safe threshold, then the adverse effects, by definition, disappear at a certain point. If the dose-response curve shows a supralinear relationship, then serious adverse effects might be seen at low doses.

Often scientists are unable to specify the dose-response curve, because they lack sufficient information about the relationship between low doses and adverse effects. Here policymakers must engage in a degree of guesswork. Government agencies generally assume a linear relationship in the face of scientific uncertainty—an assumption that is based largely on a judgment that doubts should be resolved in favor of promoting public health. To understand many problems in regulatory policy and the nature of cost-benefit analysis, it is essential to have a general sense of the possibilities discussed here.

Linear Relationships

As noted, the dose-response curve can have a variety of shapes, including linear, where response increases proportionally with dose. Figure B-1 displays the linear relationship between a dietary dose of organophosphate insecticide dioxathion and inhibition of the enzyme cholinesterase in rats.

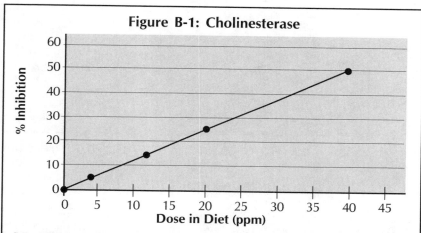

Figure B-1: Cholinesterase

S.D. Murphy & K.L. Cheever, *Effects of Feeding Insecticides: Inhibition of Carboxylesterase and Cholinesterase Activities in Rats,* 17 ARCH. ENVIRON. HEALTH, 749 (1968), reprinted in CASARETT AND DOULL'S TOXICOLOGY: THE BASIC SCIENCE OF POISONS 19, fig. 2-2 (Mary O. Amdur et al., eds., Pergamon Press 4th ed. 1991).

Figure B-2 demonstrates another linear relationship, this one between subcutaneous administration of the carcinogenic hydrocarbon dibenzanthracene and tumor incidence in mice.

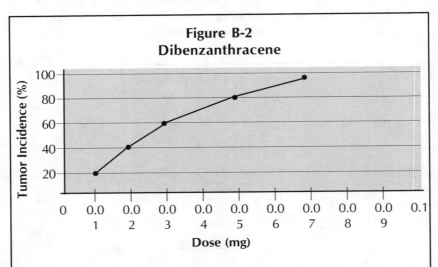

Figure B-2
Dibenzanthracene

CASARETT AND DOULL'S TOXICOLOGY: THE BASIC SCIENCE OF POISONS 23, fig. 2-5 (Mary O. Amdur et al., eds., Pergamon Press 4th ed. 1991), modified from W.R. Bryan & M.B. Shimkin, *Quantitative Analysis of Dose-Response Data Obtained with Three Carcinogenic Hydrocarbons in Strain C3H Male Mice*, 3 J. OF NATL. CANCER INST. 503 (1943).

Sublinear Relationships

Chemicals such as benzene, radon, and formaldehyde exhibit sublinear dose-response relationships, where elicited responses are less than proportional. Figure B-3 displays a sublinear relationship for primary pulmonary (lung) tumors in rats following exposure to plutonium dioxide.

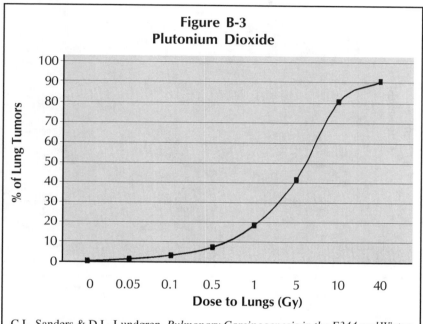

Figure B-3
Plutonium Dioxide

C.L. Sanders & D.L. Lundgren, *Pulmonary Carcinogenesis in the F344 and Wistar Rat after Inhalation of Plutonium Dioxide*, 144 RADIATION RES. 206, 212 (1995).

Figure B-4 exhibits a sublinear dose-response relationship between the number of female rat liver foci (a precursor to cancer) and the log dose of phenobarbital expressed as picomole per kilogram.

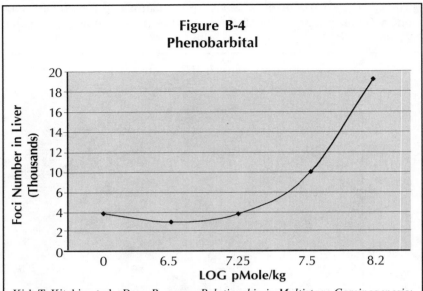

Figure B-4
Phenobarbital

Kirk T. Kitchin et al., *Dose-Response Relationship in Multistage Carcinogenesis: Promoters*, 102 (Suppl. 1) Env. Health Persp. 255, 257 (1994).

Threshold Relationships

Some chemicals produce no adverse effects below a certain level, resulting in a threshold curve. Threshold-model agents include dioxins and chrysotile asbestos; in addition, nongenotoxic carcinogens are generally assumed to have threshold doses. Figure B-5 demonstrates a threshold for the carcinogenic hydrocarbon benzpyrene causing sarcomas in mice.

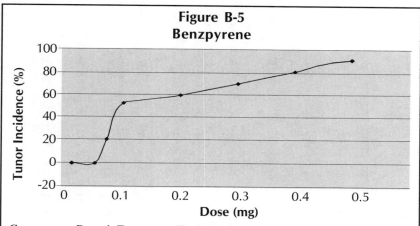

Figure B-5
Benzpyrene

CASARETT AND DOULL'S TOXICOLOGY: THE BASIC SCIENCE OF POISONS 23, fig. 2-5 (Mary O. Amdur et al., eds., Pergamon Press 4th ed. 1991), modified from W.R. Bryan & M.B. Shimkin, *Quantitative Analysis of Dose-Response Data Obtained with Three Carcinogenic Hydrocarbons in Strain C3H Male Mice*, 3 J. OF NATL. CANCER INST. 503 (1943).

Supralinear Relationships

Dose-response relationships exceeding proportionality, such as vinyl chloride, are supralinear. Figure B-6 demonstrates a supralinear curve for the inhibition of carboxylesterase enzyme activities in rats as a function of insecticide dioxathion dose.

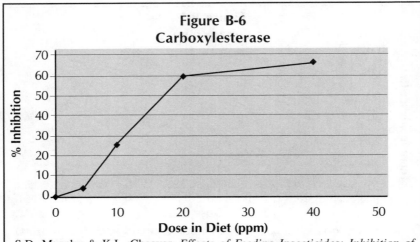

S.D. Murphy & K.L. Cheever, *Effects of Feeding Insecticides: Inhibition of Carboxylesterase and Cholinesterase Activities in Rats*, 17 ARCH. ENVIRON. HEALTH, 749 (1968), reprinted in CASARETT AND DOULL'S TOXICOLOGY: THE BASIC SCIENCE OF POISONS 19, fig. 2-2 (Mary O. Amdur et al., eds., Pergamon Press 4th ed. 1991).

The slight concave-upward pattern in Figure B-7 demonstrates a weaker supralinear relationship between exposure to radiation via an atomic bomb and cancer deaths per 10,000 people.

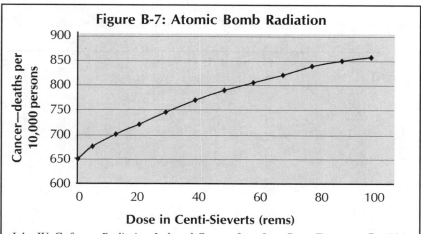

Figure B-7: Atomic Bomb Radiation

John W. Gofman, *Radiation-Induced Cancer from Low-Dose Exposure*, fig. 14A, 14F (1990), *available at* http://www.ratical.org/radation/CNR/RIC/chp14F.html#fig14e.

U-Shaped Relationships

Hermatic chemicals such as essential nutrients and vitamins exhibit beneficial effects at low doses and toxic effects at high doses, resulting in a u-shaped curve. The dose-response relationship of fluoride, which exerts positive effects at lower doses but is toxic at high doses, is outlined in Figure B-8.

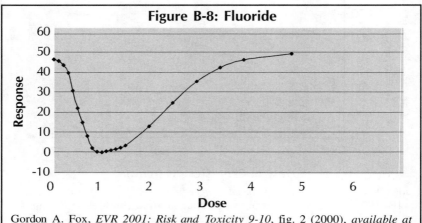

Figure B-8: Fluoride

Gordon A. Fox, *EVR 2001: Risk and Toxicity 9-10*, fig. 2 (2000), *available at* chuma.cas.usf.edu/~gfox/EVR2001/risk_and_toxicity.pdf.

APPENDIX C

COST-BENEFIT GUIDELINES FROM OMB

This appendix provides material from the official guidelines of the Office of Management and Budget. I do not believe that the guidelines are immune from criticism, but they are valuable because of their general good sense and because they provide relatively specific answers to many questions about how cost-benefit analysis operates in practice.

•   •   •

Excerpts from Office of Management and Budget, "Best Practices" Guidelines, Economic Analysis of Federal Regulations Under Executive Order 12866:

Introduction

In accordance with the regulatory philosophy and principles provided in Sections 1(a) and (b) and Section 6(a)(3)(C) of Executive Order 12866, an Economic Analysis (EA) of proposed or existing regulations should inform decisionmakers of the consequences of alternative actions. In particular, the EA should provide information allowing decisionmakers to determine that:

- There is adequate information indicating the need for and consequences of the proposed action;
- The potential benefits to society justify the potential costs, recognizing that not all benefits and costs can be described in monetary or even in quantitative terms, unless a statute requires another regulatory approach;
- The proposed action will maximize net benefits to society (including potential economic, environmental, public health and safety, and other advantages; distributional impacts; and equity), unless a statute requires another regulatory approach;
- Where a statute requires a specific regulatory approach, the proposed action will be the most cost-effective, including reliance on performance objectives to the extent feasible;
- Agency decisions are based on the best reasonably obtainable scientific, technical, economic, and other information. . . .

Analysis of the risks, benefits, and costs associated with regulation must be guided by the principles of full disclosure and transparency. Data, models, inferences, and assumptions should be identified and evaluated explicitly, together with adequate justifications of choices made, and assessments of the effects of these choices on the analysis. The existence of plausible alternative models or assumptions, and their implications, should be identified. In the absence of adequate valid data, properly identified assumptions are necessary for conducting an assessment. . . .

I. Statement of Need for the Proposed Action

In order to establish the need for the proposed action, the analysis should discuss whether the problem constitutes a significant market failure. If the problem does not constitute a market failure, the analysis should provide an alternative demonstration of compelling public need, such as improving governmental processes or addressing distributional concerns. If the proposed action is a result of a statutory or judicial directive, that should be so stated.

A. Market Failure

The analysis should determine whether there exists a market failure that is likely to be significant. In particular, the analysis should distinguish actual market failures from potential market failures that can be resolved at relatively low cost by market participants. Examples of the latter include spillover effects that affected parties can effectively internalize by negotiation, and problems resulting from information asymmetries that can be effectively resolved by the affected parties through vertical integration. Once a significant market failure has been identified, the analysis should show how adequately the regulatory alternatives to be considered address the specified market failure.

The major types of market failure include: externality, natural monopoly, market power, and inadequate or asymmetric information.

1. Externality

An externality occurs when one party's actions impose uncompensated benefits or costs on another. Environmental problems are a classic case of externality. Another example is the case of common property resources that may become congested or overused, such as fisheries or the broadcast spectrum. A third example is a "public good," such as defense or basic scientific research, which is distinguished by the fact that it is inefficient, or impossible, to exclude individuals from its benefits.

2. Natural Monopoly

A natural monopoly exists where a market can be served at lowest cost only if production is limited to a single producer. Local gas and electricity distribution services are examples.

3. Market Power

Firms exercise market power when they reduce output below what a competitive industry would sell. They may exercise market power collectively or unilaterally. Government action can be a source of market power—for example, if regulatory actions exclude low-cost imports, allowing domestic producers to raise prices by reducing output.

4. Inadequate or Asymmetric Information

Market failures may also result from inadequate or asymmetric information. The appropriate level of information is not necessarily perfect or full information because information, like other goods, is costly. The market may supply less than the appropriate level of information because it is often infeasible to exclude nonpayers from reaping benefits from the provision of information by others. In markets for goods and services, inadequate information can generate a variety of social costs, including inefficiently low innovation, market power, or inefficient resource allocation resulting from deception of consumers. Markets may also fail to allocate resources efficiently when some economic actors have more information than others.

On the other hand, the market may supply a reasonably adequate level of information. Sellers have an incentive to provide informative advertising to increase sales by highlighting distinctive characteristics of their products. There are also a variety of ways in which "reputation effects" may serve to provide adequate information. Buyers may obtain reasonably adequate information about product characteristics even when the seller does not provide that information—for example, if buyer search costs are low (as when the quality of a good can be determined by inspection at point of sale), if buyers have previously used the product, if sellers offer warranties, or if adequate information is provided by third parties. In addition, insurance markets are important sources of information about risks.

Government action may have unintentional harmful effects on the efficiency of market outcomes. For this reason there should be a presumption against the need for regulatory actions that, on conceptual grounds, are not expected to generate net benefits, except in special circumstances. In light of actual experience, a particularly demanding burden of proof is required to demonstrate the need for any of the following types of regulations:

- price controls in competitive markets; production or sales quotas in competitive markets;
- mandatory uniform quality standards for goods or services, unless they have hidden safety hazards or other defects or involve exter-

nalities and the problem cannot be adequately dealt with by voluntary standards or information disclosing the hazard to potential buyers or users; or controls on entry into employment or production, except (a) where indispensable to protect health and safety (e.g., FAA tests for commercial pilots) or (b) to manage the use of common property resources (e.g., fisheries, airwaves, federal lands, and offshore areas).

B. Appropriateness of Alternatives to Federal Regulation

Even where a market failure exists, there may be no need for federal regulatory intervention if other means of dealing with the market failure would resolve the problem adequately or better than the proposed federal regulation would. These alternatives may include the judicial system, antitrust enforcement, and workers' compensation systems. Other nonregulatory alternatives could include, for example, subsidizing actions to achieve a desired outcome; such subsidies may be more efficient than rigid mandates.

Similarly, a fee or charge, such as an effluent discharge fee, may be a preferable alternative to banning or restricting a product or action. Legislative measures that make use of economic incentives, such as changes in insurance provisions, should be considered where feasible. Modifications to existing regulations should be considered if those regulations have created or contributed to a problem that the new regulation is intended to correct, and if such changes can achieve the goal more efficiently or effectively.

Another important factor to consider in assessing the appropriateness of a federal regulation is regulation at the state or local level, if such an option is available. In some cases, the nature of the market failure may itself suggest the most appropriate governmental level of regulation. For example, problems that spill across state lines (such as acid rain whose precursors are transported widely in the atmosphere) are probably best controlled by federal regulation, while more localized problems may be more efficiently addressed locally. Where regulation at the federal level appears appropriate—for example, to address interstate commerce issues—the analysis should attempt to determine whether the burdens on interstate commerce arising from different state and local regulations, including the compliance costs imposed on national firms, are greater than the potential advantages of diversity, such as improved performance from competition among governmental units in serving taxpayers and citizens and local political choice.

II. An Examination of Alternative Approaches

The EA should show that the agency has considered the most important alternative approaches to the problem and provide the agency's reasoning for selecting the proposed regulatory action over such alternatives. Ordinarily, it will be possible to eliminate some alternatives by a preliminary analysis, leaving a manageable number of alternatives to be evaluated according to the principles of the Executive Order. The number and choice of alternatives to be selected for detailed benefit-cost analysis is a matter of judgment. There must be some balance between thoroughness of analysis and practical limits to the agency's capacity to carry out analysis. With this qualifier in mind, the agency should nevertheless explore modifications of some or all of a regulation's attributes or provisions to identify appropriate alternatives.

Alternative regulatory actions that should be explored are reviewed below.

1. More performance-oriented standards for health, safety, and environmental regulations

Performance standards are generally to be preferred to engineering or design standards because performance standards provide the regulated parties the flexibility to achieve the regulatory objective in a more cost-effective way. It is therefore misleading and inappropriate to characterize a standard as a performance standard if it is set so that there is only one feasible way to meet it; as a practical matter, such a standard is a design standard. In general, a performance standard should be preferred wherever that performance can be measured or reasonably imputed. Performance standards should be applied with a scope appropriate to the problem the regulation seeks to address. For example, to create the greatest opportunities for the regulated parties to achieve cost savings while meeting the regulatory objective, compliance with air emission standards can be allowed on a plant-wide, firm-wide, or region-wide basis rather than vent by vent, provided this does not produce unacceptable air quality outcomes (such as "hot spots" from local pollution concentration).

2. Different requirements for different segments of the regulated population

There might be different requirements established for large and small firms, for example. If such a differentiation is made, it should be based on perceptible differences in the costs of compliance or in the benefits to be expected from compliance. It is not efficient to place a heavier burden on one segment of the regulated population solely on the grounds that it is better able to afford the higher cost; this has the potential to load on the most productive sectors of the economy costs that are disproportionate to the damages they create.

3. Alternative levels of stringency

In general, both the benefits and costs associated with a regulation will increase with the level of stringency (although marginal costs generally increase with stringency, whereas marginal benefits decrease). It is important to consider alternative levels of stringency to better understand the relationship between stringency and the size and distribution of benefits and costs among different groups.

4.   Alternative effective dates of compliance

The timing of a regulation may also have an important effect on its net benefits. For example, costs of a regulation may vary substantially with different compliance dates for an industry that requires a year or more to plan its production runs efficiently. In this instance, a regulation that provides sufficient lead time is likely to achieve its goals at a much lower overall cost than a regulation that is effective immediately, although the benefits also could be lower.

5.   Alternative methods of ensuring compliance

Compliance alternatives for federal, state, or local enforcement include on-site inspection, periodic reporting, and compliance penalties structured to provide the most appropriate incentives. When alternative monitoring and reporting methods vary in their costs and benefits, promising alternatives should be considered in identifying the regulatory alternative that maximizes net benefits. For example, in some circumstances random monitoring will be less expensive and nearly as effective as continuous monitoring in achieving compliance.

6.   Informational measures

Measures to improve the availability of information include government establishment of a standardized testing and rating system (the use of which could be made mandatory or left voluntary), mandatory disclosure requirements (e.g., by advertising, labeling, or enclosures), and government provision of information (e.g., by government publications, telephone hotlines, or public interest broadcast announcements). If intervention is necessary to address a market failure arising from inadequate or asymmetric information, informational remedies will often be the preferred approaches. As an alternative to a mandatory product standard or ban, a regulatory measure to improve the availability of information (particularly about the concealed characteristics of products) gives consumers a greater choice. Incentives for information dissemination also are provided by features of product liability law that reduce liability or damages for firms that have provided consumers with notice.

   Except for prohibiting indisputably false statements (whose banning can be presumed beneficial), specific informational measures should be evaluated in terms of their benefits and costs. The key to analyzing informational measures is a comparison of the actions of the affected parties with the information provided in the baseline (including any information displaced by mandated disclosures) and the actions of affected parties with the information requirements being imposed. Some effects of informational measures can easily be overlooked. For example, the costs of a mandatory disclosure requirement for a consumer product include not only the cost of gathering and communicating the required information, but also the loss of net benefits of any information displaced by the mandated information, the effect of providing too much information that is ignored or information that is misinterpreted, and inefficiencies arising from the incentive that mandatory disclosure may give to overinvest in a particular characteristic of a product or service.

Where information on the benefits and costs of alternative informational measures is insufficient to provide a clear choice between them, as will often be the case, the least intrusive informational alternative, sufficient to accomplish the regulatory objective, should be considered. For example, to correct an informational market failure it may be sufficient for government to establish a standardized testing and rating system without mandating its use, because competing firms that score well according to the system will have ample incentive to publicize the fact.

7. More market-oriented approaches

In general, alternatives that provide for more market-oriented approaches, with the use of economic incentives replacing command-and-control requirements, are more cost-effective and should be explored. Market-oriented alternatives that may be considered include fees, subsidies, penalties, marketable permits or offsets, changes in liabilities or property rights (including policies that alter the incentive of insurers and insured parties), and required bonds, insurance or warranties. (In many instances, implementing these alternatives will require legislation.)

8. Considering specific statutory requirements

When a statute establishes a specific regulatory requirement and the agency has discretion to adopt a more stringent standard, the agency should examine the benefits and costs of the specific statutory requirement as well as the more stringent alternative and present information that justifies the more stringent alternative if that is what the agency proposes.

III. Analysis of Benefits and Costs

The preliminary analysis described in Sections I and II will lead to the identification of a workable number of alternatives for consideration.

1. Baseline

The benefits and costs of each alternative must be measured against a baseline. The baseline should be the best assessment of the way the world would look absent the proposed regulation. That assessment may consider a wide range of factors, including the likely evolution of the market, likely changes in exogenous factors affecting benefits and costs, likely changes in regulations promulgated by the agency or other government entities, and the likely degree of compliance by regulated entities with other regulations. Often it may be reasonable for the agency to forecast that the world absent the regulation will resemble the present. For the review of an existing regulation, the baseline should be no change in existing regulation; this baseline can then be compared against reasonable alternatives.

When more than one baseline appears reasonable or the baseline is very uncertain, and when the estimated benefits and costs of proposed rules are likely to vary significantly with the baseline selected, the agency may choose to measure benefits and costs against multiple alternative baselines as a form of sensitivity analysis. For example, the agency may choose to conduct a sensitivity analysis involving the consequences for benefits and costs of different assumptions about likely regulation by other governmental entities, or the degree of compliance with the agency's own existing rules. In every case, an agency must measure both benefits and costs against the identical baseline. The agency should also provide an explanation of the plausibility of the alternative baselines used in the sensitivity analysis.

2. Evaluation of Alternatives

Agencies should identify (with an appropriate level of analysis) alternatives that meet the criteria of the Executive Order as summarized at the beginning of this document, as well as identifying statutory requirements that affect the selection of a regulatory approach. If legal constraints prevent the selection of a regulatory action that best satisfies the philosophy and principles of the Order, these constraints should be identified and explained, and their opportunity cost should be estimated. To the fullest extent possible, benefits and costs should be expressed in discounted constant dollars. Appropriate discounting procedures are discussed in the following section.

Information on distributional impacts related to the alternatives should accompany the analysis of aggregate benefits and costs. Where relevant and feasible, agencies can also indicate how aggregate benefits and costs depend on the incidence of benefits and costs. Agencies should present a reasoned explanation or analysis to justify their choice among alternatives....

Where monetization is not possible for certain elements of the benefits or costs that are essential to consider, other quantitative and qualitative characterizations of these elements should be provided (see Sections 7 and 8 below). Cost-effectiveness analysis also should be used where possible to evaluate alternatives. Costs should be calculated net of monetized benefits. Where some benefits are monetizable and others are not, a cost-effectiveness analysis will generally not yield an unambiguous choice; nevertheless, such an analysis is helpful for calculating a "breakeven" value for the unmonetized benefits (i.e., a value that would result in the action having positive net benefits). Such a value can be evaluated for its reasonableness in the discussion of the justification of the proposed action. Cost-effectiveness analysis should also be used to compare regulatory alternatives in cases where the level of benefits is specified by statute.

If the proposed regulation is composed of a number of distinct provisions, it is important to evaluate the benefits and costs of the different provisions separately. The interaction effects between separate provisions (such that the existence of one provision affects the benefits or costs arising from another provision) may complicate the analysis but does not eliminate the need to examine provisions separately. In such a case, the desirability of a specific provision may be appraised by determining the net benefits of the proposed regulation with and without the provision in question. Where the number of provisions is large and interaction effects are pervasive, it is obviously impractical to analyze all possible combinations of provisions in this way. Some judgment must be used to select the most significant or suspect provisions for such analysis.

3. Discounting

One of the problems that arises in developing a benefit-cost analysis is that the benefits and costs often occur in different time periods. When this occurs, it is not appropriate, when comparing benefits and costs, to simply add up the benefits and costs accruing over time. Discounting takes account of the fact that resources (goods or services) that are available in a given year are worth more than the identical resources available in a later year. One reason for this is that resources can be invested so as to return more resources later. In addition, people tend to be impatient and to prefer earlier consumption over later consumption.

a.   Basic considerations

Constant-dollar benefits and costs must be discounted to present values before benefits and costs in different years can be added together to determine overall net benefits. To obtain constant dollar estimates, benefit and cost streams in nominal dollars should be adjusted to correct for inflation. . . . The discount rate specified in that guidance is intended to be an approximation of the opportunity cost of capital, which is the before-tax rate of return to incremental private investment. The [suggested] rate, which was revised in 1992 based on an extensive review and public comment, reflects the rates of return on low-yielding forms of capital, such as housing, as well as the higher rates of returns yielded by corporate capital. This average rate currently is estimated to be 7 percent in real terms (i.e., after adjusting for inflation). . . . [A]gencies may also present sensitivity analyses using other discount rates, along with a justification for the consideration of these alternative rates. The economic analysis also should contain a schedule indicating when all benefits and costs are expected to occur.

In general, the discount rate should not be adjusted to account for the uncertainty of future benefits and costs. Risk and uncertainty should be dealt with according to the principles presented in Section 4 below and not by changing the discount rate.

Even those benefits and costs that are hard to quantify in monetary terms should be discounted. The schedule of benefits and costs over time therefore should include benefits that are hard to monetize. In many instances where it is difficult to monetize benefits, agencies conduct regulatory "cost-effectiveness" analyses instead of "net benefits" analyses. When the effects of alternative options are measured in units that accrue at the same time that the costs are incurred, annualizing costs is sufficient and further discounting of non-monetized benefits is unnecessary; for instance, the annualized cost per ton of reducing certain polluting emissions can be an appropriate measure of cost-effectiveness. However, when effects are measured in units that accrue later than when the costs are incurred, such as the reduction of adverse health effects that occur only after a long period of exposure, the annualized cost per unit should be calculated after discounting for the delay between accrual of the costs and the effects.

In assessing the present value of benefits and costs from a regulation, it may be necessary to consider implications of changing relative prices over time. For example, increasing scarcity of certain environmental resources could increase their value over time relative to conventional consumer goods. In such a situation, it is inappropriate to use current relative values for assessing regulatory impacts. However, while taking into account that changes over time in relative values may have an effect similar to discounting environmental impacts at a lower rate, it is important to separate the effects of discounting from the effects of relative price changes in the economic analysis. In particular, the discount rate should not be adjusted for expected changes in the relative prices of goods over time. Instead, any changes in relative prices that are anticipated should be incorporated directly in the calculations of benefit and cost streams.

b.   Additional considerations
Modern research in economic theory has established a preferred model for discounting, sometimes referred to as the shadow price approach. The basic concept is that economic welfare is ultimately determined by consumption; investment affects welfare only to the extent that it affects current and future consumption. Thus, any effect that a government program has on public or private investment must be converted to an associated stream of effects on consumption before being discounted.

Converting investment-related benefits and costs to their consumption-equivalents as required by this approach involves calculating the "shadow price of capital." This shadow price reflects the present value of the future changes in consumption arising from a marginal change in investment, using the consumption rate of interest (also termed the rate of time preference) as the discount rate. The calculation of the shadow price of capital requires assumptions about the extent to which government actions—including regulations—crowd out private investment, the social (i.e., before-tax) returns to this investment, and the rate of reinvestment of future yields from current investment.

Estimates of the shadow price are quite sensitive to these assumptions. For example, in some applications it may be appropriate to assume that access to global capital markets implies no crowding out of private investment by government actions or that monetary and fiscal authorities determine aggregate levels of investment so that the impact of the contemplated regulation on total private investment can be ignored. Alternatively, there is evidence that domestic saving affects domestic investment and that regulatory costs may also reduce investment. In these cases, more substantial crowding out would be an appropriate assumption.

The rate of time preference is also a complex issue. Generally, it is viewed as being approximated by the real return to a safe asset, such as government debt. However, a substantial fraction of the population does little or no saving and may borrow at relatively high interest rates.

While the shadow price approach is theoretically preferred, there are several practical challenges to its use. Agencies wishing to use this methodology should consult with OMB prior to doing so, and should clearly explain their solutions to the methodological and empirical challenges noted above.

c. Intergenerational analysis

Comparisons of benefits and costs across generations raise special questions about equity, in addition to conventional concerns about efficiency. One approach to these questions is to follow the discounting procedures described above and to address equity issues explicitly rather than through modification of the discount rate.

An alternative approach is to use a special social rate of time preference when conducting intergenerational analyses in order to properly value changes in consumption in different generations. For example, one philosophical perspective is that the social marginal rate of substitution between the well-being of members of successive generations may be less than the individual rate of time preference, and that future generations should not have their expected welfare discounted just because they come later in time. Instead, this view suggests that discounting should reflect only the growth of per capita consumption and the corresponding decrease in marginal utility over time. As this approach uses a consumption-based rate of interest, costs and benefits must also be adjusted to reflect the shadow price of capital. As in other cases when agencies seek to use the shadow price of capital approach, they should consult with OMB prior to conducting special analyses of regulations having substantial intergenerational effects.

4. Treatment of Risk and Uncertainty

The effects of regulatory actions frequently are not known with certainty but can be predicted in terms of their probability of occurrence. The term "risk" in this document refers generally to a probability distribution over a set of outcomes. When the outcomes in question are hazards or injuries, risk can be understood to refer to the probabilities of different potential severities of hazard or injury. For example, the risk of cancer from exposure to a chemical means a change in the probability of contracting cancer caused by that exposure. There also are risks associated with economic benefits and costs—e.g., the risk of a financial loss of $X means the probability of losing $X.

Often risks, benefits, and costs are measured imperfectly because key parameters are not known precisely; instead, the economic analysis must rely upon statistical probability distributions for the values of parameters. Both the inherent lack of certainty about the consequences of a potential hazard (for example, the odds of contracting cancer) and the lack of complete knowledge about parameter values that define risk relationships (for example, the relationship between presence of a carcinogen in the food supply and the rate of absorption of the carcinogen) should be considered.

The term "uncertainty" often is used in economic assessments as a synonym for risk. However, in this document uncertainty refers more specifically to the fact that knowledge of the probabilities and sets of possible outcomes that characterize a probability distribution of risks, based on experimentation, statistical sampling, and other scientific tools, is itself incomplete. Thus, for example, a cancer risk might be described as a one-in-one-thousand chance of contracting cancer after 70 years of exposure. However, this estimate may be uncertain because individuals vary in their levels of exposure and their sensitivity to such exposures; the science underlying the quantification of the hazard is uncertain; or there are plausible competitors to the model for converting scientific knowledge and empirical measures of exposures into risk units. Estimates of regulatory benefits entail additional uncertainties, such as the appropriate measures for converting from units of risk to units of value. Cost estimates also will be uncertain when there are uncertainties in opportunity costs or the compliance strategies of regulated entities.

Estimating the benefits and costs of risk-reducing regulations includes two components: a risk assessment that, in part, characterizes the probabilities of occurrence of outcomes of interest; and a valuation of the levels and changes in risk experienced by affected populations as a result of the regulation. It is essential that both parts of such evaluations be conceptually consistent. In particular, risk assessments should be conducted in a way that permits their use in a more general benefit-cost framework, just as the benefit-cost analysis should attempt to capture the results of the risk assessment and not oversimplify the results (e.g., the analysis should address the benefit and cost implications of probability distributions).

Risk management is an activity conceptually distinct from risk assessment or valuation, involving a policy of whether and how to respond to risks to health, safety, and the environment. The appropriate level of protection is a policy choice rather than a scientific one. The risk assessment should generate a credible, objective, realistic, and scientifically balanced analysis; present information on hazard, dose-response, and exposure (or analogous material for non-health assessments); and explain the confidence in each assessment by clearly delineating strengths, uncertainties, and assumptions, along with the impacts of these factors on the overall assessment. The data, assumptions, models, and inferences used in the risk assessment to construct quantitative characterizations of the probabilities of occurrence of health, safety, or ecological effects should not reflect unstated or unsupported preferences for protecting public health and the environment, or unstated safety factors to account for uncertainty and unmeasured variability. Such procedures may introduce levels of conservatism that cumulate across assumptions and make it difficult for decisionmakers to evaluate the magnitude of the risks involved.

a. Risk assessment
The assessment of outcomes associated with regulatory action to address risks to health, safety, and the environment raises a number of scientific difficulties. Key issues involve the quality and reliability of the data, models, assumptions, scientific inferences, and other information used in risk analyses. Analysts rarely, if ever, have complete information. It may be difficult to identify the full range of impacts. Little definitive may be known about the structure of key relationships and therefore about appropriate model specification. Data relating to effects that can be identified may be sketchy, incomplete, or subject to measurement error or statistical bias. Exposures and sensitivities to risks may vary considerably across the affected population. These difficulties can lead, for example, to a range of quantitative estimates of risk in health and ecological risk assessments that can span several orders of magnitude. Uncertainties in cost estimates also can be significant, in particular because of lack of experience with the adjustments that markets can make to reduce regulatory burdens, the difficulty of identifying and quantifying opportunity cost, and the potential for enhanced or retarded technical innovation. All of these concerns should be reflected in the uncertainties about outcomes that should be incorporated in the analysis.

The treatment of uncertainty in developing risk, benefit, and cost information also must be guided by the principles of full disclosure and transparency, as with other elements of an EA. Data, models, and their implications for risk assessment should be identified in the risk characterization. Inferences and assumptions should be identified and evaluated explicitly, together with adequate justifications of choices made, and assessments of the effects of these choices on the analysis.

Informed judgment is necessary to evaluate conflicting scientific theories. In some cases it may be possible to weigh conflicting evidence in developing the overall risk assessment. In other cases, the level of scientific uncertainty may be so large that a risk assessment can only present discrete alternative scenarios without a quantitative assessment of their relative likelihood. For example, in assessing the potential outcomes of an environmental effect, there may be a limited number of scientific studies with strongly divergent results. In such cases, the assessment should present results representing a range of plausible scenarios, together with any information that can help in providing a qualitative judgment of which scenarios are more scientifically plausible.

In the absence of adequate valid data, properly identified assumptions are necessary for conducting an assessment. The existence of plausible alternative models and their implications should be carried through as part of each risk characterization product. Alternative models and assumptions should be used in the risk assessment as needed to provide decisionmakers with information on the robustness of risk estimates and estimates of regulatory impacts. As with other elements of an EA, there should be balance between thoroughness of analysis in the treatment of risk and uncertainty and practical limits on the capacity to carry out analysis. The range of models, assumptions, or scenarios presented in the risk assessment need not be exhaustive, nor is it necessary that each alternative be evaluated at every step of the assessment. The assessment should provide sufficient information for decisionmakers to understand the degree of scientific uncertainty and the robustness of estimated risks, benefits, and costs. The choice of models or scenarios used in the risk assessment should be explained.

Where feasible, data and assumptions should be presented in a manner that permits quantitative evaluation of their incremental effects. The cumulative effects of assumptions and inferences should also be evaluated. A full characterization of risks should include findings for the entire affected population and relevant subpopulations. Assumptions should be consistent with reasonably obtainable scientific information. Thus, for example, low-dose toxicity extrapolations should be consistent with physiological knowledge; assumptions about environmental fate and transport of contaminants should be consistent with principles of environmental chemistry.

The material provided should permit the reader to replicate the analysis and quantify the effects of key assumptions. Such analyses are becoming increasingly easy to perform because of advances in computing power and new methodological developments. Thus, the level and scope of disclosure and transparency should increase over time.

In order for the EA to evaluate outcomes involving risks, risk assessments must provide some estimates of the probability distribution of risks with and without the regulation. Whenever it is possible to quantitatively characterize the probability distributions, some estimates of central tendency (e.g., mean and median) must be provided in addition to ranges, variances, specified low-end and high-end percentile estimates, and other characteristics of the distribution.

Overall risk estimates cannot be more precise than their most uncertain component. Thus, risk estimates should be reported in a way that reflects the degree of uncertainty present in order to prevent creating a false sense of precision. The accuracy with which quantitative estimates are reported must be supported by the quality of the data and models used. In all cases, the level of precision should be stated explicitly.

Overall uncertainty is typically a consequence of uncertainties about many different factors. Appropriate statistical techniques should be used to combine uncertainties about separate factors into an overall probability distribution for a risk. When such techniques cannot be used, other methods may be useful for providing more complete information:

> Monte Carlo analysis and other simulation methods can be used to estimate probability distributions of the net benefits of alternative policy choices. It requires explicit quantitative characterization of variability to derive an overall probability distribution of net benefits. Parameter or model probability distributions may be derived empirically (for example, directly from population data or indirectly from regression or other statistical models) or by assumption. This approach has the advantage of weighing explicitly the likelihood of alternative outcomes, permitting evaluation of their relative importance. However, care must be taken to consider the entire output of the analysis rather than placing undue reliance on any one statistic. Because of the sensitivity of such simulations to assumptions about correlations between parameters, the likelihood that a particular specification is correct, omitted factors, and assumptions about the distribution of parameters, etc., special care should be taken to address these potential pitfalls. The quality of the overall analysis is only as good as the quality of its components; faulty assumptions or model specifications will yield faulty results.

Sensitivity analysis is carried out by conducting analyses over the full range of plausible values of key parameters and plausible model specifications. Sensitivity analysis is particularly attractive when there are several easily identifiable critical assumptions in the analysis, when information is inadequate to carry out a more formal probabilistic simulation, or when the nature and scope of the regulation do not warrant more extensive analysis. One important form of sensitivity analysis involves estimating "switch points," that is, critical parameter values at which estimated net benefits change sign. Sensitivity analysis is useful for evaluating the robustness of conclusions about net benefits with respect to changes in model parameters. Sensitivity analysis should convey as much information as possible about the likely plausibility or frequency of occurrence of different scenarios (sets of parameter values) considered. . . .

Meta-analysis involves combining data or results from a number of different studies. For example, one could re-estimate key model parameters using combined data from a number of different sources, thereby improving confidence in the parameter estimates. Alternatively, one could use parameter estimates (elasticities of supply and demand, implicit values of mortality risk reduction) from a number of different studies as data points, and analyze variations in those results as functions of potential causal factors. Care must be taken to ensure that the data used are comparable, that appropriate statistical methods are used, and that spurious correlation problems are considered. One significant pitfall in the use of meta-analysis arises from combining results from several studies that do not measure comparable independent or dependent variables. . . .

Uncertainty may arise from a variety of fundamentally different sources, including lack of data, variability in populations or natural conditions, limitations in fundamental scientific knowledge (both social and natural) resulting in lack of knowledge about key relationships, or fundamental unpredictability of various phenomena. The nature of these different sources may suggest different approaches. For example, when uncertainty is due to lack of information, one policy alternative may be to defer action pending further study. One factor that may help determine whether further study is justifiable as a policy alternative is an evaluation of the potential benefits of the information relative to the resources needed to acquire it and the potential costs of delaying action. When uncertainty is due largely to observable variability in populations or natural conditions, one policy alternative may be to refine targeting, that is, to differentiate policies across key subgroups. Analysis of such policies should consider the incremental benefits of improved efficiency from targeting, any incremental costs of monitoring and enforcement, and changes in the distribution of benefits and costs.

b. Valuing risk levels and changes

To value changes in risk arising from variability in expected outcomes as a consequence of regulation, agencies should consider the expected net benefits of the risk change, taking into account the probability distribution of potential outcomes with and without the regulation. The more familiar examples deal with valuing risks associated with incurring possible future costs. When costs are subject to risk, they are generally appraised by risk-averse individuals at more than the expected value. For example, riskier financial instruments must generally earn a higher average rate of return in order to attract investors. Similarly, the owner of a facility may be willing to pay more to reduce the probability of fire than the reduction in expected loss, because of aversion to the risk of the loss. This also explains why property owners are willing to buy fire insurance at a price that exceeds expected losses. To accurately value the net benefits of a regulation, regulation-induced changes in expenditures on self-protection, mitigation, or other risk-reduction measures should be included.

Under the standard assumption in economic theory that individuals make choices among outcomes subject to risks to maximize expected utility, risk aversion is incorporated into net benefits estimates by expressing benefits and costs in terms of their certainty equivalents. Certainty equivalents are defined as net benefits occurring with certainty that would have the same value to individuals as the expected value of an alternative whose net benefits are subject to risk. For risk-averse individuals, the certainty equivalent of such a net benefit stream would be smaller than the expected value of those net benefits, because risk intrinsically has a negative value. The difference between the expected value of net benefits subject to risk and the certainty equivalent is called the risk premium. Similarly, regulations that reduce the overall variability of net benefits will have a certainty equivalent value that is larger than the expected value of the net benefits by an amount that reflects the value of the variability of outcomes.

Typically total expected net benefits and risk premia are calculated on the basis of a representative set of individual preferences. Agencies should also present available information on the incidence of benefits, costs, and risks where necessary for judging distributional consequences. Where information is available on differences in valuation across income levels or other identifiable criteria, agencies can use this information and information on the incidence of regulatory effects in calculating total net benefits estimates.

The importance of including estimates of individuals' willingness to pay for risk reduction varies. Willingness to pay for reduced risks is likely to be more significant if risks are difficult to diversify because of incomplete risk and insurance markets, or if the net benefits of the regulation are correlated with overall market returns to investment. When the effects of regulation fall primarily on private parties, it is sufficient to incorporate measures of individual risk aversion. For regulatory benefits or costs that accrue to the federal government (for example, income from oil production), the federal government should be treated as risk-neutral because of its high degree of diversification.

As noted in the previous section, the discount rate generally should not be adjusted as a device to account for the uncertainty of future benefits or costs. Any allowance for uncertainty should be made by adjusting the monetary values of changes in benefits or costs (for the year in which they occur) so that they are expressed in terms of their certainty equivalents. The adjustment for uncertainty may well vary over time because the degree of uncertainty may change. For example, price forecasts are typically characterized by increasing uncertainty (forecast error) over time, because of an increasing likelihood of unforeseen (and unforeseeable) changes in market conditions as time passes. In such cases, the certainty equivalents of net benefits will tend to change systematically over time; these changes should be taken into account in analyzing regulations that have substantial effects over a long time period. Uncertainty that increases systematically over time will result in certainty equivalents that fall systematically over time; however, these decreases in certainty equivalents will mimic the effects of an increase in the discount rate only under special circumstances.

5. Assumptions

Where benefit or cost estimates are heavily dependent on certain assumptions, it is essential to make those assumptions explicit and, where alternative assumptions are plausible, to carry out sensitivity analyses based on the alternative assumptions. If the value of net benefits changes sign with alternative plausible assumptions, further analysis may be necessary to develop more evidence on which of the alternative assumptions is more appropriate. Because the adoption of a particular estimation methodology sometimes implies major hidden assumptions, it is important to analyze estimation methodologies carefully to make hidden assumptions explicit. . . .

The effectiveness of proposed rules may depend in part upon agency enforcement strategies, which may vary over time as agency priorities and budgetary constraints change. Because an agency usually cannot commit to an enforcement strategy at the time the rule is promulgated, the analysis of a rule's benefits and costs should generally assume that compliance with the rule is complete, although there may be circumstances when other assumptions should be considered as well. The analysis of a new or revised rule should differentiate between its benefits and costs, given an assumed level of compliance, and the implications of changes in compliance with an existing rule.

6. International Trade Effects

In calculating the benefits and costs of a proposed regulatory action, generally no explicit distinction needs to be made between domestic and foreign resources. If, for example, compliance with a proposed regulation requires the purchase of specific equipment, the opportunity cost of that equipment is ordinarily best represented by its domestic cost in dollars, regardless of whether the equipment is produced domestically or imported. The relative value of domestic and foreign resources is correctly represented by their respective dollar values, as long as the foreign exchange value of the dollar is determined by the exchange market. Nonetheless, an awareness of the role of international trade may be quite useful for assessing the benefits and costs of a proposed regulatory action. For example, the existence of foreign competition may make the demand curve facing a domestic industry more elastic than it would be otherwise. Elasticities of demand and supply frequently can significantly affect the magnitude of the benefits or costs of a regulation. . . .

7. Nonmonetized Benefits and Costs

Presentation of monetized benefits and costs is preferred where acceptable estimates are possible. However, monetization of some of the effects of regulations is often difficult if not impossible, and even the quantification of some effects may not be easy. Effects that cannot be fully monetized or otherwise quantified should be described. Those effects that can be quantified should be presented along with qualitative information to characterize effects that are not quantified.

Irrespective of the presentation of monetized benefits and costs, the EA should present available physical or other quantitative measures of the effects of the alternative actions to help decisionmakers understand the full effects of alternative actions. These include the magnitude, timing, and likelihood of impacts, plus other relevant dimensions (e.g., irreversibility and uniqueness). For instance, assume the effects of a water quality regulation include increases in fish populations and habitat over the affected stream segments and that it is not possible to monetize such effects. It would then be appropriate to describe the benefits in terms of stream miles of habitat improvement and increases in fish population by species (as well as to describe the timing and likelihood of such effects, etc.). Care should be taken, however, when estimates of monetized and physical effects are mixed in the same analysis so as to avoid double-counting of benefits. Finally, the EA should distinguish between effects unquantified because they were judged to be relatively unimportant and effects that could not be quantified for other reasons.

8. Distributional Effects and Equity

Those who bear the costs of a regulation and those who enjoy its benefits often are not the same people. The term "distributional effects" refers to the description of the net effects of a regulatory alternative across the population and economy, divided up in various ways (e.g., income groups, race, sex, industrial sector). Benefits and costs of a regulation may be distributed unevenly over time, perhaps spanning several generations. Distributional effects may also arise through "transfer payments" arising from a regulatory action. For example, the revenue collected through a fee, surcharge, or tax (in excess of the cost of any service provided) is a transfer payments.

Where distributive effects are thought to be important, the effects of various regulatory alternatives should be described quantitatively to the extent possible, including their magnitude, likelihood, and incidence of effects on particular groups. Agencies should be alert for situations in which regulatory alternatives result in significant changes in treatment or outcomes for different groups. Effects on the distribution of income that are transmitted through changes in market prices can be important, albeit sometimes difficult to assess. The EA should also present information on the streams of benefits and costs over time in order to provide a basis for judging intertemporal distributional consequences, particularly where intergenerational effects are concerned.

There are no generally accepted principles for determining when one distribution of net benefits is more equitable than another. Thus, the EA should be careful to describe distributional effects without judging their fairness. These descriptions should be broad, focusing on large groups with small effects per capita as well as on small groups experiencing large effects per capita. Equity issues not related to the distribution of policy effects should be noted when important and described quantitatively to the extent feasible.

B. Benefit Estimates

The EA should state the beneficial effects of the proposed regulatory change and its principal alternatives. In each case, there should be an explanation of the mechanism by which the proposed action is expected to yield the anticipated benefits. An attempt should be made to quantify all potential real incremental benefits to society in monetary terms to the maximum extent possible. A schedule of monetized benefits should be included that would show the type of benefit and when it would accrue; the numbers in this table should be expressed in constant, undiscounted dollars. Any benefits that cannot be monetized, such as an increase in the rate of introducing more productive new technology or a decrease in the risk of extinction of endangered species, should also be presented and explained.

The EA should identify and explain the data or studies on which benefit estimates are based with enough detail to permit independent assessment and verification of the results. Where benefit estimates are derived from a statistical study, the EA should provide sufficient information so that an independent observer can determine the representativeness of the sample, the reliability of extrapolations used to develop aggregate estimates, and the statistical significance of the results.

The calculation of benefits (including benefits of risk reductions) should reflect the full probability distribution of potential consequences. For example, extreme safety or health results should be weighted, along with other possible outcomes, by estimates of their probability of occurrence based on the available evidence to estimate the expected result of a proposed regulation. To the extent possible, the probability distributions of benefits should be presented. Extreme estimates should be presented as complements to central tendency and other estimates. If fundamental scientific disagreement or lack of knowledge precludes construction of a scientifically defensible probability distribution, benefits should be described under plausible alternative assumptions, along with a characterization of the evidence underlying each alternative view. This will allow for a reasoned determination by decisionmakers of the appropriate level of regulatory action.

It is important to guard against double-counting of benefits. For example, if a regulation improves the quality of the environment in a community, the value of real estate in the community might rise, reflecting the greater attractiveness of living in the improved environment Inferring benefits from changes in property values is complex. On the one hand, the rise in property values may reflect the capitalized value of these improvements. On the other hand, benefit estimates that do not incorporate the consequences of land use changes will not capture the full effects of regulation. For regulations with significant effects on land uses, these effects must be separated from the capitalization of direct regulatory impacts into property values.

1. General Considerations

The concept of "opportunity cost" is the appropriate construct for valuing both benefits and costs. The principle of "willingness-to-pay" captures the notion of opportunity cost by providing an aggregate measure of what individuals are willing to forgo to enjoy a particular benefit. Market transactions provide the richest data base for estimating benefits based on willingness-to-pay, as long as the goods and services affected by a potential regulation are traded in markets. It is more difficult to estimate benefits where market transactions are difficult to monitor or markets do not exist. Regulatory analysts in these cases need to develop appropriate proxies that simulate market exchange. Indeed, the analytical process of deriving benefit estimates by simulating markets may suggest alternative regulatory strategies that create such markets.

Either willingness-to-pay (WTP) or willingness-to-accept (WTA) can provide an appropriate measure of benefits, depending on the allocation of property rights. The common preference for WTP over WTA measures is based on the empirical difficulties in estimating the latter.

Estimates of willingness-to-pay based on observable and replicable behavior deserve the greatest level of confidence. Greater uncertainty attends benefit estimates that are neither derived from market transactions nor based on behavior that is observable or replicable. While innovative benefit estimation methodologies will be necessary or desirable in some cases, use of such methods intensifies the need for quality control to ensure that estimates are reliable and conform as closely as possible to what would be observed if markets existed.

2. Principles for Valuing Benefits Directly Traded in Markets

Ordinarily, goods and services are to be valued at their market prices. However, in some instances, the market value of a good or service may not reflect its true value to society.

If a regulatory alternative involves changes in such a good or service, its monetary value for purposes of benefit-cost analysis should be derived using an estimate of its true value to society (often called its "shadow price"). For example, suppose a particular air pollutant damages crops. One of the benefits of controlling that pollutant will be the value of the crop saved as a result of the controls. That value would typically be determined by reference to the price of the crop. If, however, the price of that crop is held above the unregulated market equilibrium price by a government price-support program, an estimate based on the support price would overstate the value of the benefit of controlling the pollutant. Therefore, the social value of the benefit should be calculated using a shadow price for crops subject to price supports. The estimated shadow price is intended to reflect the value to society of marginal uses of the crop (e.g., the world price if the marginal use is for exports). If the marginal use is to add to very large surplus stockpiles, the shadow price would be the value of the last units released from storage minus storage cost. Therefore, where stockpiles are large and growing, the shadow price is likely to be low and could well be negative.

In other cases, market prices could understate social values, for example where production of a particular good also provides opportunities for improving basic knowledge.

3. Principles for Valuing Benefits That Are Indirectly Traded in Markets

In some important instances, a benefit corresponds to a good or service that is indirectly traded in the marketplace. Examples include reductions in health-and-safety risks, the use-values of environmental amenities and scenic vistas. To estimate the monetary value of such an indirectly traded good, the willingness-to-pay valuation methodology is considered the conceptually superior approach. As noted in Sections 4 and 5 immediately following, alternative methods may be used where there are practical obstacles to the accurate application of direct willingness-to-pay methodologies.

A variety of methods have been developed for estimating indirectly traded benefits. Generally, these methods apply statistical techniques to distill from observable market transactions the portion of willingness-to-pay that can be attributed to the benefit in question. Examples include estimates of the value of environmental amenities derived from travel-cost studies, hedonic price models that measure differences or changes in the value of land, and statistical studies of occupational-risk premiums in wage rates. For all these methods, care is needed in designing protocols for reliably estimating benefits or in adapting the results of previous studies to new applications. The use of occupational-risk premiums can be a source of bias because the risks, when recognized, may be voluntarily rather than involuntarily assumed, and the sample of individuals upon which premium estimates are based may be skewed toward more risk-tolerant people.

Contingent-valuation methods have become increasingly common for estimating indirectly traded benefits, but the reliance of these methods on hypothetical scenarios and the complexities of the goods being valued by this technique raise issues about its accuracy in estimating willingness to pay compared to methods based on (indirect) revealed preferences. Accordingly, value estimates derived from contingent-valuation studies require greater analytical care than studies based on observable behavior. For example, the contingent valuation instrument must portray a realistic choice situation for respondents—where the hypothetical choice situation corresponds closely with the policy context to which the estimates will be applied. The practice of contingent valuation is rapidly evolving, and agencies relying upon this tool for valuation should judge the reliability of their benefit estimates using this technique in light of advances in the state of the art.

4. Principles and Methods for Valuing Goods That Are Not Traded Directly or Indirectly in Markets

Some types of goods, such as preserving environmental or cultural amenities apart from their use and direct enjoyment by people, are not traded directly or indirectly in markets. The practical obstacles to accurate measurement are similar to (but generally more severe than) those arising with respect to indirect benefits, principally because there are few or no related market transactions to provide data for willingness-to-pay estimates.

For many of these goods, particularly goods providing "nonuse" values, contingent-valuation methods may provide the only analytical approaches currently available for estimating values. The absence of observable and replicable behavior with respect to the good in question, combined with the complex and often unfamiliar nature of the goods being valued, argues for great care in the design and execution of surveys, rigorous analysis of the results, and a full characterization of the uncertainties in the estimates to meet best practices in the use of this method.

5. Methods for Valuing Health and Safety Benefits

Regulations that address health and safety concerns often yield a variety of benefits traded directly in markets, benefits indirectly traded in markets, and benefits not traded in markets. A major component of many such regulations is a reduction is the risk of illness, injury or premature death. There are differences of opinion about the various approaches for monetizing such risk reductions. In assessing health and safety benefits, the analysis should present estimates of both the risks of nonfatal illness or injury and fatality risks, and may include any particular strengths or weakness of such analyses the agencies think appropriate, in order to accurately assess the benefits of government action.

a. Nonfatal illness and injury

Although the willingness-to-pay approach is conceptually superior, measurement difficulties may cause the agency to prefer valuations of reductions in risks of nonfatal illness or injury based on the expected direct costs avoided by such risk reductions. For example, an injury-value estimate from a willingness-to-pay study may be an average over a specific combination of injuries of varying severity. If the average injury severity in such a study differs greatly from the injury severity addressed by the regulatory action, then the study's estimated injury value may not be appropriate for evaluating that action. More generally, willingness-to-pay estimates may be unavailable or too tentative to provide a solid base for the evaluation. The agency should use whatever approach it can justify as most appropriate for the decision at hand, keeping in mind that direct cost measures can be expected to understate the true cost. As discussed above (Section III.A.3), costs and benefits should be appropriately discounted to reflect the latency period between exposure and illness.

The primary components of the direct-cost approach are medical and other costs of offsetting illness or injury; costs for averting illness or injury (e.g., expenses for goods such as bottled water or job safety equipment that would not be incurred in the absence of the health or safety risk); and the value of lost production. Possibly important costs that might be omitted by the use of the direct-cost approach are the costs of pain, suffering and time lost (due to illness, injury, or averting behavior) from leisure and other activities that are not directly valued in the market. The present value of the expected stream of costs should be included. For long-term chronic illness or incapacitation the direct-cost approach may be particularly problematic compared to a willingness-to-pay estimate analogous to the valuation of mortality risks (discussed below).

Valuing lost production and other time-related costs gives rise to a number of methodological concerns. For occupational illness or injury, lost production can be measured by losses in workers' value of marginal product. In valuing the effects of broader environmental hazards, however, attention must be given to the composition of the exposed population. For example, some portion of the working-age population may be unemployed, while others will be retired. Still others may have chosen to be homemakers or home caregivers. Valuation of nonfatal illness or injury to these parts of the population presents a greater challenge than valuing the loss of employee services using wage rates. Finally, the valuation of health impacts on children or retirees through the direct-cost approach is especially problematic since their zero opportunity cost in the labor market is not a good proxy for the social cost of illness. The agency should use whatever approach it can justify but should provide a clear explanation of the assumptions and reasoning used in the valuation.

b. Fatality risks

Values of fatality risk reduction often figure prominently in assessments of government action. Estimates of these values that are as accurate as possible, given the circumstances being assessed and the state of knowledge, will reduce the prospects for inadequate or excessive action.

Reductions in fatality risks as a result of government action are best monetized according to the willingness-to-pay approach. The value of changes in fatality risk is sometimes expressed in terms of the "value of statistical life" (VSL) or the "value of a life." These terms are confusing at best and should be carefully described when used. It should be made clear that these terms refer to the willingness to pay for reductions in risks of premature death (scaled by the reduction in risk being valued). That is, such estimates refer only to the value of relatively small changes in the risk of death. They have no application to an identifiable individual.

There is also confusion about the term "statistical life." This terms refers to the sum of risk reductions expected in a population. For example, if the annual risk of death is reduced by one in a million for each of two million people, that represents two "statistical lives" saved per year (two million x one millionth = two). If the annual risk of death is reduced by one in 10 million for each of 20 million people, that also represents two statistical lives saved.

Another way of expressing reductions in fatality risks is in terms of the "value of statistical life-years extended" (VSLY). For example, if a regulation protected individuals whose average remaining life expectancy was 40 years, then a risk reduction of one fatality would be expressed as 40 life-years extended. This approach allows distinctions in risk-reduction measures based on their effects on longevity. However, this does not automatically mean that regulations with greater numbers of life-years extended will be favored over regulations with fewer numbers of life-years extended. VSL and VSLY ultimately depend on the willingness to pay for various forms of mortality risk reduction, not just longevity considerations.

As described below, there are several ways that the benefits of mortality risk reduction can be estimated. In considering these alternatives, however, it is important to keep in mind the larger objective of consistency—subject to statutory limitations—in the estimates of benefits applied across regulations and agencies for comparable risks. Failure to maintain such consistency prevents achievement of the most risk reduction from a given level of resources spent on risk reduction. The valuation of mortality risk reduction is an evolving area in terms of results and methodology. Agencies generally should utilize valuation estimates, either explicitly or implicitly calculated, that are consistent with the current state of knowledge at the time that the analysis is being performed, and should show that their approach to valuation reflects the current state of knowledge. Significant deviations from the prevailing state of knowledge should be explained.

c.   Alternative methodological frameworks for estimating benefits from reduced fatality risks

Several alternative ways of incorporating the value of reducing fatality risks into the framework of benefit-cost analysis may be appropriate. These may involve either explicit or implicit valuation of fatality risks, and generally involve the use of estimates of the VSL from studies on wage compensation for occupational hazards (which generally are in the range of 10-4 annually), on consumer product purchase and use decisions, or from a limited literature using contingent-valuation approaches. Because these estimates may not be entirely appropriate for the risk being evaluated in some cases (e.g., the use of occupational risk premia for environmental hazards), agencies should provide an explanation for their selection of estimates and for any adjustments of the estimates to reflect the nature of the risk being evaluated.

One acceptable explicit valuation approach would be for the agency to select a single estimate of the value of reductions in fatality risk at ordinarily encountered risk levels, or a distribution of such values, and use these values consistently for evaluating all its programs that affect ordinary fatality risks. Where the analysis uses a range of alternative values for reductions in fatality risk, it may be useful to calculate break-even values, as in other sensitivity analyses. This requires calculating the borderline value of reductions in fatality risk at which the net benefit decision criterion would switch over from favoring one alternative to favoring another (i.e., the value of fatality risk at which the net benefits of the two alternatives are equal). This method will frequently be infeasible because of its computational demands but, where feasible, it may be a useful addition to the sensitivity analysis.

An implicit valuation approach that could be used entails calculations of the net incremental cost per unit of reduction in fatality risk (cost per "statistical life saved") of alternative measures, with net incremental costs defined as costs minus monetized benefits. Alternatives can be arrayed in order of increasing reductions in expected fatalities. Generally this will also correspond to increasing incremental cost. (It is possible that there will be some initial economies of scale, with declining incremental costs. If incremental costs are declining over a broad range of alternative measures, it is likely that there are flaws in the definition of the measures or the estimation of their effects.) The incremental cost per life saved then can be calculated for each adjacent pair of alternatives. With this construction, the choice to undertake a certain set of measures while eschewing others implies a lower and upper bound for the value per life saved; it would be at least as large as the incremental cost of the most expensive measure undertaken, but not as large as the cheapest measure not undertaken. In contrast to explicit valuation approaches, this avoids the necessity of specifying in advance a value for reductions in fatality risks. However, the range of values should be consistent with estimated values of reductions in fatality risks calculated according to the willingness-to-pay methodology, and the method should be consistently applied across regulatory decisions (within statutory limitations), in order to assure that regulation achieves the greatest risk reduction possible from the level of resources committed to risk reduction.

While there are theoretical advantages to using a value of statistical life-year-extended approach, current research does not provide a definitive way of developing estimates of VSLY that are sensitive to such factors as current age, latency of effect, life years remaining, and social valuation of different risk reductions. In lieu of such information, there are several options for deriving the value of a life-year saved from an estimate of the value of life, but each of these methods has drawbacks. One approach is to use results from the wage compensation literature (which focus on the effect of age on WTP to avoid risk of occupational fatality). However, these results may not be appropriate for other types of risks. Another approach is to annualize the VSL using an appropriate rate of discount and the average life years remaining. This approach does not provide an independent estimate of VSLY; it simply rescales the VSL estimate. Agencies should consider providing estimates of both VSL and VSLY, while recognizing the developing state of knowledge in this area.

Whether the VSLs (or VSLYs) are chosen explicitly or are an implicit outcome of a cost-effectiveness approach, the choice of estimates ideally should be based on a comparison of the context of the regulation affecting risks and the context of the study or studies being relied on for value estimates. The literature identifies certain attributes of risk that affect value. These attributes include the baseline risk, the extent to which the risk is voluntarily or involuntarily assumed, and features (such as age) of the population exposed to risk. For regulations affecting some segments of the population (e.g., infants) more than those groups which have served as the basis for most of the information used to estimates VSLs (e.g., working-age adults), the use of VSLs from the literature may not be appropriate. At a minimum, differences in regulatory and study contexts should be acknowledged and a rationale for the choice of the value estimate should be provided.

Based on the literature, both the scale of baseline risks and their degree of voluntariness appear to affect VSLs. However, the risk from an involuntary hazard typically is too small to represent a significant portion of baseline risk. (For example, average annual mortality risks for men aged 55-64 are about two per hundred, while occupational fatality risk reductions typically achieved by regulations are between two per 10,000 and two per million annually.) In such cases, it may be legitimate to assume that the valuation of risks can be treated as independent of baseline risk.

To value reductions in more voluntarily incurred risks (e.g., those related to motorcycling without a helmet) that are "high," agencies should consider using lower values than those applied to reductions in involuntary risk. When a higher-risk option is chosen voluntarily, those who assume the risk may be more risk-tolerant, i.e., they may place a relatively lower value on avoiding risks. Empirical studies of risk premiums in higher-risk occupations suggest that reductions in risks for voluntarily assumed high-risk jobs (e.g., above 10-4 annually) are valued less than equal risk reductions for lower-risk jobs. However, when occupational choices are limited, the occupational risks incurred may be more involuntary in nature.

C. Cost Estimates

1. General Considerations

The preferred measure of cost is the "opportunity cost" of the resources used or the benefits forgone as a result of the regulatory action. Opportunity costs include, but are not limited to, private-sector compliance costs and government administrative costs. Opportunity costs also include losses in consumers' or producers' surpluses, discomfort or inconvenience, and loss of time. These effects should be incorporated in the analysis and given a monetary value wherever possible. (Producers' surplus is the difference between the amount a producer is paid for a unit of a good and the minimum amount the producer would accept to supply that unit. It is measured by the area between the price and the supply curve for that unit. Consumers' surplus is the difference between what a consumer pays for a unit of a good and the maximum amount the consumer would be willing to pay for that unit. It is measured by the distance between the price and the demand curve for that unit.)

The opportunity cost of an alternative also incorporates the value of the benefits forgone as a consequence of that alternative. For example, the opportunity cost of banning a product (e.g., a drug, food additive, or hazardous chemical) is the forgone net benefit of that product, taking into account the mitigating effects of potential substitutes. As another example, even if a resource required by regulation does not have to be paid for because it is already owned by the regulated firm, the use of that resource to meet the regulatory requirement has an opportunity cost equal to the net benefit it would have provided in the absence of the requirement. Any such forgone benefits should be monetized wherever possible and either added to the costs or subtracted from the benefits of that alternative. Any costs that are averted as a result of an alternative should be monetized wherever possible and either added to the benefits or subtracted from the costs of that alternative.

All costs calculated should be incremental, that is, they should represent changes in costs that would occur if the regulatory option is chosen compared to costs in the base case (ordinarily no regulation or the existing regulation) or under a less stringent alternative. Future costs that would be incurred even if the regulation is not promulgated, as well as costs that have already been incurred (sunk costs), are not part of incremental costs. If marginal cost is not constant for any component of costs, incremental costs should be calculated as the area under the marginal cost curve over the relevant range. A schedule of monetized costs should be included that would show the type of cost and when it would occur; the numbers in this table should be expressed in constant, undiscounted dollars.

The EA should identify and explain the data or studies on which cost estimates are based with enough detail to permit independent assessment and verification of the results. Where cost estimates are derived from a statistical study, the EA should provide sufficient information so that an independent observer can determine the representativeness of the sample, the reliability of extrapolations used to develop aggregate estimates, and the statistical significance of the results.

As with benefit estimates, the calculation of costs should reflect the full probability distribution of potential consequences. Extreme values should be weighted, along with other possible outcomes, by estimates of their probability of occurrence based on the available evidence to estimate the expected result of a proposed regulation. If fundamental scientific disagreement or lack of knowledge precludes construction of a scientifically defensible probability distribution, costs should be described under plausible alternative assumptions, along with a characterization of the evidence underlying each alternative view. This will allow for a reasoned determination by decisionmakers of the appropriate level of regulatory action. That level of action should derive from the decisionmaking process, not from adjusting cost estimates upward or downward at the information-gathering or analytical stages of the process.

Estimates of costs should be based on credible changes in technology over time. For example, a slowing in the rate of innovation or of adoption of new technology because of delays in the regulatory approval process or the setting of more stringent standards for new facilities than existing ones may entail significant costs. On the other hand, a shift to regulatory performance standards and incentive-based policies may lead to cost-saving innovations that should be taken into account. In some cases agencies are limited under statute to considering only technologies that have been demonstrated to be feasible. In these situations, it may also be useful to estimate costs and cost savings assuming a wider range of technical possibilities.

As in the calculation of benefits, costs should not be double counted. Two accounting cost concepts that should not be counted as costs in benefit-cost analysis are interest and depreciation. The time value of money is already accounted for by the discounting of benefits and costs. Generally, depreciation is already taken into account by the time distribution of benefits and costs. One legitimate use for depreciation calculations in benefit-cost analysis is to estimate the salvage value of a capital investment.

2. Real Costs Versus Transfer Payments

An important, but sometimes difficult, problem in cost estimation is to distinguish between real costs and transfer payments. Transfer payments are not social costs but rather are payments that reflect a redistribution of wealth. While transfers should not be included in the EA's estimates of the benefits and costs of a regulation, they may be important for describing the distributional effects of a regulation. Scarcity rents and monopoly profits, insurance payments, government subsidies and taxes, and distribution expenses are four potential problem areas that may affect both social benefits and costs as well as involve significant transfer payments.

a. Scarcity rents and monopoly profits

If, for example, sales of a competitively produced product were restricted by a government regulation so as to raise prices to consumers, the resulting profit increases for sellers are not a net social benefit of the rule, nor is their payment by consumers generally a net social cost, though there may be important distributional consequences. The social benefit-cost effects of the regulation would be represented by changes in producers' and consumers' surpluses, including the net surplus reduction from reduced availability of the product. The same conclusion applies if the government restriction provides an opportunity for the exercise of market power by sellers, in which case the net cost of the regulation would include the cost of reduced product provision due both to the government mandate and the induced change in market structure.

b. Insurance payments

Potential pitfalls in benefit-cost analysis may also arise in the case of insurance payments, which are transfers. Suppose, for example, a worker safety regulation, by decreasing employee injuries, led to reductions in firms' insurance premium payments. It would be incorrect to count the amount of the reduction in insurance premiums as a benefit of the rule. The proper measure of benefits for the EA is the value of the reduction in worker injuries, monetized as described previously, plus any reduction in real costs of administering insurance (such as the time insurance company employees needed to process claims) due to the reduction in worker insurance claims. Reductions in insurance premiums that are matched by reductions in insurance claim payments are changes in transfer payments, not benefits.

c. Indirect taxes and subsidies

A third instance where special treatment may be needed to deal with transfer payments is the case of indirect taxes (tariffs or excise taxes) or subsidies on specific goods or services. Suppose a regulation requires firms to purchase a $10,000 piece of imported equipment, on which there is a $1,000 customs duty. For purposes of benefit-cost analysis, the cost of the regulation for each firm ordinarily would be $10,000, not $11,000, since the $1,000 customs duty is a transfer payment from the firm to the Treasury, not a real resource cost.

This approach, which implicitly assumes that the equipment is supplied at constant costs, should be used except in special circumstances. Where the taxed equipment is not supplied at constant cost, the technically correct treatment is to calculate how many of the units purchased as a result of the regulation are supplied from increased production and how many from decreased purchases by other buyers. The former units would be valued at the price without the tax and the latter units would be valued at the price including tax. This calculation is usually difficult and imprecise because it requires estimates of supply and demand elasticities, which are often difficult to obtain and inexact. Therefore, this treatment should only be used where the benefit-cost conclusions are likely to be sensitive to the treatment of the indirect tax. While costs ordinarily should be adjusted to remove indirect taxes on specific goods or services as described here, similar treatment is not warranted for other taxes, such as general sales taxes applying equally to most goods and services or income taxes.

d. Distribution expenses

The treatment of distribution expenses is also a source of potential error. For example, suppose a particular regulation raises the cost of a product by $100 and that wholesale and retail distribution expenses are on average 50 percent of the factory-level cost. It would ordinarily be incorrect to add a $50 distribution markup to the $100 cost increase to derive a $150 incremental cost per product for benefit-cost analysis. Most real resource costs of distribution do not increase with the price of the product being distributed. In that case, either distribution expenses would be unchanged or, if they increased, the increase would represent distributor monopoly profits. Since the latter are transfer payments, not real resource costs, in neither case should additional distribution expenses be included in the benefit-cost analysis. However, increased distribution expenses should be counted as costs to the extent that they correspond to increased real resource costs of the distribution sector as a result of the change in the price or characteristics of the product, or if regulation directly affects distribution costs.

ABOUT THE AUTHOR

Cass R. Sunstein is the Karl N. Llewellyn Distinguished Service Professor at the University of Chicago Law School and Department of Political Science. Professor Sunstein has testified before the U.S. Congress on issues of law and regulatory policy on several occasions, and he has acted as an informal adviser for law reform efforts in many other countries.

Winner of the Goldsmith Book Prize from Harvard's Kennedy School, Professor Sunstein is the author of numerous books. His most recent publications include *Republic.com* (2001, Princeton University Press) and *Designing Democracy: What Constitutions Do* (2001, Oxford University Press). Professor Sunstein has appeared frequently as a guest on "Nightline" and other national television programs.

ACKNOWLEDGMENTS

I am grateful to many people for their help with this book. Thanks go first to officers of the administrative law section of the American Bar Association—Boyden Gray, Ronald Levin, and Randolph May—for their helpful comments and their interest in the project. I am especially grateful to Gray and Levin for detailed and very valuable suggestions on an earlier draft. Of those who read all or parts of the manuscript, I single out, for particular thanks, Robert Hahn, Lisa Heinzerling, Martha Nussbaum, Eric Posner, and Richard Posner. Laura Warren provided excellent research assistance. Special thanks to Robert Hahn for organizing several panel discussions at the AEI-Brookings Joint Center on Regulatory Studies, and to Carol Browner, Lisa Heinzerling, Christopher DeMuth, Edward Warren, and Jonathan Weiner for their comments on those occasions. I am also grateful to public officials at the Office of Information and Regulatory Affairs, including John Graham and John Morrall, for helpful discussions.

Parts of this book draw heavily on three previously published essays: *Is the Clean Air Act Unconstitutional?*, 98 Mich. L. Rev. 303 (1999); *Cost-Benefit Default Principles,* 99 Mich. L. Rev. 1651 (2001); *Is Cost-Benefit Analysis for Everyone?*, 53 Admin. L. Rev. 299 (2001). I am grateful, for permission to reprint those parts here, to the MICHIGAN LAW REVIEW and the ADMINISTRATIVE LAW REVIEW. This book is a close sibling to my forthcoming, much longer book, RISK AND REASON: SAFETY, LAW, AND THE ENVIRONMENT (Cambridge University Press, forthcoming 2001). Some of the material in this book is presented in condensed, less technical form there, and readers interested in linking the arguments here to broader claims about risk regulation might consult that volume.

INDEX